WALL
STREET
JOURNAL
BOOKS

THE WALL STREET JOURNAL

ESSENTIAL GUIDE TO BUSINESS STYLE AND USAGE

PAUL R. MARTIN
Style Editor

A WALL STREET JOURNAL BOOK

Published by Free Press
New York London Toronto Sydney Singapore

A WALL STREET JOURNAL BOOK

Published by Free Press
Rockefeller Center
1230 Avenue of the Americas
New York, NY 10020

This Wall Street Journal Book edition 2003

DESIGNED BY LISA CHOVNICK

For information about special discounts for bulk purchases,
please contact Simon & Schuster Special Sales:
1-800-456-6798 or business@simonandschuster.com

Manufactured in the United States of America

1 3 5 7 9 10 8 6 4 2

The Library of Congress has cataloged the hardcover edition as follows:

The Wall Street journal guide to business style and usage / Paul R. Martin, style editor.
p. cm—(A Wall Street journal book)
1. Journalism—Style manuals. I. Martin, Paul R. II. Wall Street journal. III. Series.
PN4783.W26 2002
808'.06665—dc21

2001040376

ISBN 0-7432-1295-9
ISBN 0-7432-2724-7 (Pbk)

INTRODUCTION

For anyone who writes—a journalist, an author, a public-relations specialist or just someone who is writing a formal letter—a style guide is a valuable beacon. For anyone who wants to write in an authoritative business style, The Wall Street Journal's stylebook sheds even more light. This guide, an updated and expanded version of the one long used by Journal reporters and editors, provides answers to everyday questions the computer's spelling checker won't resolve: Are the accepted forms *businessman, businesswoman* and *businesspeople?* Or is it *businesspersons?* Or is a hyphen involved? What about a person running a small business? Is he or she a *small-businessperson* or what?

With more than 3,875 alphabetized entries, this guide not only explains such broad concepts as the difference between the *New Economy* and the *Old* but also defines everything from *blue-chip stocks* to *junk bonds.* Confused about *intraday* and *interday* highs and lows in the market? Wondering about business and financial terms from *Ebitda* and *Ebita earnings* to *zero-coupon bonds?* It provides the answers.

The Web world's explosion of tech terms also is given due diligence, from *Alpha testing* to *twisted pair* and *vortal.* But perhaps the primary asset is the book's basic guidance to proper usage of the language in general. Do you confuse *fortuitous* and *fortunate? Flounder* and *founder?* Have you used *enervate* when you meant *energize?* Help is at hand.

Stylebooks, a relatively recent journalistic phenomenon, have become invaluable tools for maintaining standards and promoting consistency of usage. The Wall Street Journal, founded in 1889 by Charlie Dow, Eddie Jones and

Charles Bergstresser, somehow survived its first 60 years without a stylebook. In fact, the Journal long prided itself on the stylistic freedom of expression it provided its writers and editors without onerous constraints: "Our newsmen are not bound by formulas or patterns," a top editor wrote in 1967, a time when indeed there were very few newswomen at the Journal. "They are encouraged to be imaginative, flexible and different. The Wall Street Journal has no stylebook." The lack of a stylebook encouraged imagination, perhaps. Without doubt, it encouraged difference—and inconsistency.

Newspaper stylebooks in general were extremely rudimentary for the most part until about 1977, when the Associated Press issued the forerunner of many of today's comprehensive stylebooks. The Journal's earliest attempt at codifying rules for writers and editors was a 1952 guide on spelling, capitalization and use of figures and abbreviations that ran 14 small pages. An entry opposing the use of *all-time record* noted, without apologies to Gertrude Stein, that "a record is a record is a record."

The 1952 guide had this apologetic introduction: "The suggestions outlined here are not intended as a complete style manual for the Journal. They originated as an attempt to compile pointers which a newcomer to any one of our copy desks might find useful. Actually, as we attempted to set down our editing practices in a logical way, some appeared to be rather illogical—so our veteran editors will note that certain changes in past style are contained herein. . . . When the time seems ripe, a fresh edition of the style guide will be run off."

The time apparently didn't ripen quickly, but in 1961, a new 10-page guide for Journal staff members covered little more than capitalization and punctuation rules and then declared sweepingly that "common sense is the best guide in matters not covered by the guide." Common sense is indeed often a good guide to style decisions. The problem is that common sense is quite uncommon, and what one editor may postulate as common sense another may consider to be common rubbish. Meanwhile, with everyone employing a different common sense, arcane and archaic usages creep in, and inconsistencies storm in.

Some quirky Journal customs were passed along orally (as distinct from *verbally*) for years from copy editor to copy editor, and few even remembered their origins. A 16-page booklet for the news staff in 1970 provided a list of banned words, for example, that included *buck, shift, shut* and *shot.* Why? "The reasons should be obvious," the guide said, cryptically. In fact, the ban reflected editors' fears that inept or capricious typesetters would turn these innocent words into embarrassing ones. Thus, for many years, a factory had three *work turns* rather than three *shifts,* until word-processing systems replaced human typesetters.

As the Journal expanded through the 1970s, the need for a more comprehensive guide became apparent, especially to help train new reporters and copy editors. The prototype for this book was published in 1981, then as now using the latest Webster's New World College Dictionary as its reference. Updated editions of the stylebook appeared in 1987, 1992 and 1995, with the guidance and encouragement of Managing Editor Paul E. Steiger. Subsequently, with no one questioning the need for consistent style rules any longer, the Dow Jones Newswires, under the leadership of Richard J. Levine, also published style-guide editions in 1996 and 1999, and we gratefully acknowledge those editions' contributions to this volume.

Like the earlier Wall Street Journal Stylebook editions, this one reflects the collective wisdom of scores of Journal editors and writers, whose contributions are also gratefully acknowledged.

Aa

AAA The initials have become the formal name of the former *American Automobile Association.* Second reference may be to *the automobile association.* It is based in Heathrow, Fla.

a, an

Use *a* before consonant sounds: *a historic event* (the aspirated *h* is a consonant sound), *a university* (it sounds as if it begins with a *yew*), *a one-year term* (it sounds as if it begins with a *w*).

Use the article *an* before vowel sounds: *an engagement, an hour* (the *h* is silent), *an M.B.A.* (it sounds as if it begins with an *e*). Illogical though it may seem, make it *an herb,* but *a herbal tea* and *a herbicide* because the *h* in *herb* is silent, but the *h* in *herbal* and *herbicide* is sounded.

AARP Use this in all references to the group that changed its name in 1998 from *the American Association of Retired Persons.*

abbreviations and acronyms Widely recognized short forms are acceptable in second references, depending on the context. In general, for agencies such as the Bureau of Alcohol, Tobacco and Firearms, for example, try to use *the bureau* or *the agency* rather than *BATF* or the like after the first mention, to prevent a cluttered-looking text.

For proper-name acronyms of more than four letters, arbitrarily capitalize only the first letter: *Ascap, Awacs, Swapo, Unicef.* But unpronounceable abbreviations are uppercase: *NAACP.*

See **organizations and institutions.**

Guidance on particular abbreviations and acronyms is provided in individual entries. BEFORE A NAME: Abbreviate certain titles when they are used before a name: *Col., Gen., Gov., Lt. Gov., Rep., the Rev., Sen.* But *Mr., Mrs., Ms.* and *Dr.* (see entries) normally are used with the surname, only after the use of the full name in an article. Form plurals by adding *s* to the abbreviation: *Sens. Max Baucus and Bob Kerrey.* See individual listings for commonly used names.

See also **cabinet titles; legislative titles; military titles; religious titles.**

AFTER A COMPANY NAME: Abbreviate *Co., Corp., Inc.* and *Ltd.* after the name of a corporation.

See entries under these words. Also see **foreign companies.**

WITH DATES OR NUMERALS: Abbreviate *A.D., B.C., a.m., p.m., No.* and also certain months when they are used with the day of the month: *In 45 B.C.; at 8:10 p.m.; bus No.10; Nov. 17.*

See **months** and individual listings.

IN ADDRESSES: Abbreviate *Avenue, Boulevard, Road* and *Street* in addresses with numbers: *They live on Sunset Avenue—at 64 Sunset Ave., to be exact.*

See **addresses.**

STATES AND NATIONS: State names of more than five letters are abbreviated when used after cities, except for Alaska and Hawaii. (See state names and individual entries of nations, as some are abbreviated in certain circumstances). *U.S.*, *U.K.* and *U.N.* take periods, even in headlines. The *U.S.* abbreviation is used in most references, including company names.

COMPANIES AND ORGANIZATIONS: Abbreviated second references and acronyms don't take periods: *GM, GE, CIA, DAR, FBI, HUD, GOP, UCLA, MIT.*

Use the article *the* before abbreviated agencies, organizations and unions: *the DAR, the FCC, the UAW;* but don't use the article before acronyms: *HUD, NATO.* And don't use the article before company names.

AVOID the overuse of abbreviations and acronyms, and don't follow an organization's full name with an abbreviation or acronym in parentheses.

ABC The subsidiary of *Walt Disney Co.* no longer uses the name *American Broadcasting Co. ABC* and *ABC Television Network* may be used in the first reference.

ABCs

able-bodied

ABM, ABMs The abbreviations are acceptable in all references to *antiballistic missiles,* but the term should be defined in the story. Avoid the redundancy *ABM missiles.*

A-bomb Use *atomic bomb* unless a direct quotation is involved.

abortion rights (n.) **abortion-rights** (adj.) This is the preferred term to apply to the movement sometimes referred to as *pro-choice.*

See **antiabortion.**

about-face

aboveboard

absent-minded

absent without leave *AWOL* is acceptable in second references.

academic degrees If mention of degrees is necessary to establish someone's credentials, the preferred form is to avoid an abbreviation and use instead a phrase such as: *One has a doctorate and the other a master's in psychology.* Abbreviations such as *B.A., M.A., M.B.A., J.D.* and *Ph.D.* should be used only in stories where the need to identify many individuals by degree on first reference would make the preferred form cumbersome. Use these abbreviations only after a full name—never after just a last name. When in doubt about the proper abbreviation for a degree, follow the first listing in Webster's New World Dictionary. IN HEADLINES: Use the same form, with the periods.

See **doctor.**

academic departments Use lowercase except for words that are proper nouns or adjectives: *the department of history, the history department, the department of English, the English department.*

academic titles Capitalize and spell out such formal titles as dean, president, chancellor and chairman when they precede a name. Lowercase elsewhere. But for professor: *John Smith, a professor of history; the professor, Prof. Smith, Mr. Smith.* See titles.

academy *See* **military academies.**

Academy Awards The awards, also known as *the Oscars,* are presented annually by the Academy of Motion Picture Arts and Sciences. Lowercase the academy and the awards when they stand alone.

Accenture It became the new name for Andersen Consulting after its split from Arthur Andersen, the accounting firm.

accept, except
Accept means to receive.
Except means to exclude.

access As a verb, confine it to the technological sense: *He accessed the files in a database. You may access your cash at an ATM.*

accommodate

accounting firms The *Big Four* are PricewaterhouseCoopers; Ernst & Young; KPMG LLP and Deloitte & Touche LLP. (Deloitte & Touche is the U.S. affiliate of Deloitte Touche Tohmatsu. Both the umbrella organization and the affiliate are based in New York.)

accounts payable They are the current liabilities or debts of a business that must be paid soon, usually within a year.

accounts receivable They are the amounts due to a company for merchandise or services sold on credit. These are considered short-term assets.

accused To avoid implying the guilt of someone merely charged with a crime, don't use constructions such as *accused arsonist.*

An individual is accused *of,* not with, a crime.

See **allege.**

Achilles' heel The unusual possessive style applies to classical names.

acknowledgment

acoustics It usually takes plural verbs and pronouns: *The acoustics were not at their best.*

Use singular verbs and pronouns when referring to the study: *Acoustics is an exact science.*

acre Equal to 43,560 square feet, or 4,840 square yards. The metric equivalent is 0.4 (two-fifths) hectare, or 4,047 square meters.

To convert to hectares, multiply by 0.4 (5 acres x 0.4 equals 2 hectares).

acronyms
See **abbreviations and acronyms.**

act Capitalize when part of the name for pending or implemented legislation: *the Taft-Hartley Act.*

acting Always lowercase, but capitalize any formal title that may follow before a name: *acting Mayor Peter Barry.*

See **titles.**

actor, actress

Actors' Equity Association The apostrophe is in the union's formal name.

A.D. The abbreviation is acceptable in all references for *anno Domini:* in the year of the Lord. Place A.D. before the year: *The town was founded in A.D. 96.*

Don't write: *The fourth century A.D. The fourth century* is sufficient. If A.D. is not specified with a year, the year is presumed to be A.D.

See **B.C.**

addresses Use *Ave., Blvd., Rd.* and *St.* only with a numbered address: *64 Sunset Ave.* Spell them out and capitalize them when they are of a street name without a number: *Sunset Avenue.* Lowercase and spell out when they are used alone or with more than one street name: *Sunset and Sunrise avenues.*

Similar words (*alley, square, terrace*) are spelled out, even with numbers. Capitalize them when they are part of a name without a number; lowercase when used alone or with two or more names.

Always use figures for an address number: *7 Vine St.*

Spell out and capitalize *First* through *Ninth* when used as street names; use figures with two letters for streets *10th* and above: *6 Seventh Ave., 66 32nd St.*

adjusted gross income It consists of an individual's gross income from taxable sources, minus certain items such as payments to a deductible individual retirement account. Adjusted gross income minus deductions and personal exemptions equals *taxable income.*

adjusted gross receipts In the gambling industry, this is a casino's measure of revenue. Adjusted gross receipts divided by total admissions are considered a casino's *win per person.*

ad lib

administration Lowercase: *the administration, the president's administration, the governor's administration, the Bush administration.*

administrative law judge This is the federal title for the position formerly known as hearing examiner. Capitalize it when used as a formal title before a name.

To avoid the long title, seek a construction that sets the title off by commas: *The administrative law judge, John Williams, disagreed.* On subsequent references, *Mr. Williams*—not *Judge Williams.*

Hearing officer (not *judge*) is a short form for headlines and other references.

administrator Never abbreviate. Capitalize when used as a formal title before a name.

admiral

See **military titles.**

admissible

admit, admitted These words may in some contexts give the erroneous connotation of wrongdoing. A person who announces he is a homosexual, for example, may be proclaiming it to the world, not admitting it. *Said* is usually sufficient. In other contexts: *He conceded he was wrong.*

adopt, approve, enact, pass

Amendments, ordinances, resolutions and rules are *adopted* or *approved.*

Bills are *passed.*

Laws are *enacted.*

adoption The adoptive status of a child or his or her parents should be mentioned only when its relevance is made clear. Use the term *biological parents* to refer to the nonadoptive parents.

Adrenalin It is a trademark for the synthetic or chemically extracted forms of epinephrine, a substance produced by the adrenal glands. The nonproprietary terms are *epinephrine hydrochloride* or *adrenaline.* Also: *His adrenaline was flowing.*

adverse (adj.), **averse** (adv.) *Adverse* means unfavorable, and *averse* means unwilling or reluctant. *They were* averse *to making the trip because they expected* adverse *weather.*

adviser, advisory

Aer Lingus The Irish national airline.

Aeroflot The airline's headquarters is Moscow.

AeroMexico The short form for Aerovias de Mexico is acceptable in all references.

aesthetic Not *esthetic.*

affect, effect

Affect normally is a verb. It means to have an influence on something: *The game will affect the standings.*

Effect is used most often as a noun meaning result or influence: *The effect was overwhelming. The death had a great effect on him. He miscalculated the effect of his actions.*

When used as a verb, *effect* means to bring something about: *She effected many changes in the company.*

affiliate It normally is a company whose

voting stock is less than 50% owned by another company. In general usage, affiliation can be applied to any intercompany relationship short of a parent-subsidiary relationship. Don't call an affiliate a *unit.*

afloat In international trade, prices are often quoted and trades completed for commodities that are said to be *afloat* between origin country and destination port.

AFL-CIO Preferred in all references for *the American Federation of Labor and Congress of Industrial Organizations.*

A-frame

African Pertaining to Africa and its people. Do not use it as a synonym for *black.* In some parts of Africa, the word *colored* is applied to those of mixed white and black ancestry. Elsewhere, the term is considered derogatory, so avoid the usage or put the term in quotation marks and explain it.

African-American (n. and adj.) It is an acceptable alternative term applying to U.S. blacks. Always hyphenated: *an African-American; an African-American teenager.*

African, Caribbean and Pacific The so-called *ACP* regions receive special dispensation from import duties on certain products entering the European Union.

Afrikaans, Afrikaner

Afrikaans is an official language of South Africa.

An *Afrikaner* is a South African of certain European ancestry, especially Dutch.

AFTA This is the second-reference term for Asean Free Trade Area. Asean stands for the Association of Southeast Asian Nations. No hyphen in either of the full names.

See **Association of Southeast Asian Nations.**

after- No hyphen after this prefix when it is used to form a noun: *aftereffect, afterthought.* Follow *after* with a hyphen when it is used to form compound modifiers: *after-dinner drink, after-theater snack.*

after-hours trading The rise of electronic communications networks, or ECNs, has changed the market once called the *third market,* to distinguish it from the major exchanges and the regional exchanges. Nasdaq now incorporates ECNs in its linkage to the other markets, calling the system the Nasdaq InterMarket. Late-day trades are also made on the Instinet and the Chicago Stock Exchange, for example, so all transactions after the 4 p.m. listings for New York Stock Exchange composite trading are referred to as *after-hours trading.*

The Journal's statistics department issues an *after-hours snapshot* on our intranet after 6:30 p.m. Until that hour, when an after-hours stock quote is needed for an article, get it from Instinet, and cite Instinet as the source. But update this for later editions with our intranet quote, without the need to mention the source. For example: *Intel rose to $132.68 in after-hours trading.*

See **stock prices.**

afterward Not *afterwards.*

Aftra It is acceptable on second reference for the *American Federation of Television and Radio Artists.*

AG The designation follows many German, Austrian and Swiss company names. It indicates the company has shareholders.

against actuals In the London markets for cocoa and coffee futures, *against actuals* represent straightforward trades of futures positions against physical positions. They have no impact on prices.

Agana The capital of Guam has been renamed Hagatna.

Agency for International Development AID is acceptable on second reference.

agency shop
See **closed shop.**

agenda A list. It takes singular verbs and pronouns: *The agenda has run its course.* The plural is *agendas.*

agent Usually not a formal title: *FBI agent William Smith.*
See **titles.**

ages Use figures for ages of people, and normally use *years old* only with the first age provided in each story: *Eric Martin, 29 years old; Graham Goble, 4, and Tess Langan, 9 months.* Also: *The 4-year-old James Goble; 35-year-old Eric Martin appears to be in his 20s* (no apostrophe). *The defendant is a 25-year-old.* But: *a two-year-old law.* Ages should be included in stories of executive changes but aren't necessary in Who's News column briefs that involve directors or executives below the level of chief executive, chairman or president.

aggravate It means *make worse.* Don't use it to mean irritate.

A-head The term is used in-house at The Wall Street Journal to refer to the page-one, column-four article or articles inside the paper with the same type of headline.

ahold Avoid the word, which is a regionalism at best. One may, however, *get a hold on* something or *get hold of* someone.

aid, aide
Aid is assistance.
An *aide* is a person who serves as an assistant.

aide-de-camp, aides-de-camp A military officer who serves as assistant and confidential secretary to a superior.

AIDS The acronym is acceptable in all references to the disease *acquired immune deficiency syndrome.*

AIDS is the end stage of *HIV (human immune deficiency virus)* infections that compromise immune systems and leave infected people vulnerable to infectious diseases and certain cancers.

AIDS is distinguished from "congenital" or "combined" immune deficiency syndrome, which is present at birth.

HIV is spread by sexual contact, transfusions of contaminated blood, contaminated hypodermic needles or syringes, and by women passing the virus to their offspring. Distinction should be made between *AIDS,* the disease, and *HIV,* the virus. People infected with HIV, described as being *HIV-positive,* can remain healthy for years. Only after they develop serious symptoms should they be described as having *AIDS.*

See **HIV.**

ain't Use the substandard contraction only in quoted matter or for special effect.

air It means to ventilate a space or to voice grievances.

As it is used in broadcasting, it is jargon and best avoided, though the passive voice is less jarring: *The show will be aired soon.* But better: *The show will be shown soon.*

air bag

air base Two words. Follow the practice of the U.S. Air Force, which uses Air Force Base as part of the proper name for its bases in the U.S. and Air Base for its installations abroad. On second reference: *the Air Force base, the air base,* or *the base.*

Airbus The aircraft maker no longer uses *Industrie* as part of its name, since the former consortium converted to a corporation. It is based in Toulouse, France.

Air Canada

air-condition, air-conditioned (v. and adj.), **air conditioner, air conditioning** (n.)

aircraft names Use a hyphen, generally, when changing from letters to figures and no hyphen when adding a letter after figures.

Some examples: *B-1, BAC-111, C-5A, DC-10, FH-227, F-15 Eagle, F111, L-1011, MiG-21, 727-100C, 747, 747B, VC-10.* Airbus models are an exception: *Airbus A300* and *A320.* Some jet planes in commercial use: *the BAC-111; Boeing 727, 737, 747, 777; the Convair 880; the DC-8, DC-9* and *DC-10,* and *the L-1011.*

Do not use quotation marks for aircraft with names: *Air Force One, the Concorde, the Enola Gay, the F-22 Raptor.*

For plurals: *DC-10s, 727s, 747B's.* (The apostrophe is used to denote the plurals of single letters.)

See **plurals.**

Use Arabic figures, without hyphens, for numbered spacecraft and missiles: *Apollo 10.*

airfield

air force Capitalize it when referring to U.S. forces: *the U.S. Air Force, the Air Force, Air Force regulations.* Do not use the abbreviation *USAF.*

Use lowercase for the forces of other nations: *the Israeli air force.*

See **military academies; military titles.**

air force base

See **air base.**

Air Force One The name applies to any Air Force aircraft the president uses. The vice president uses *Air Force Two.*

Air France

airlines, air lines, airways Capitalize *airlines, air lines* and *airways* when they are used as part of a proper airline name. Major airlines are listed separately by name.

Companies that use *airlines* include *Alaska, American, America West, Continental, Hawaiian, Japan* (it uses the abbreviation *JAL* nevertheless), *Northwest, Saudi Arabian, Southwest, Trans World* and *United.*

Companies that use *air lines* include *Delta.*

Companies that use *airways* include *All Nippon, British, Cathay Pacific, Qantas, Thai International, US Airways* and *Virgin Atlantic.*

Companies that use none of these include *Aer Lingus, AeroMexico, Air Canada, Air France, Air India, Alitalia, Iberia, KLM, Korean Air, Lufthansa, Swissair and Scandinavian Airlines System.*

On second reference for any of these, use *the airline, the carrier* or such short forms as *SAS, TWA* or *JAL.* For US Airways, the second reference is *US Air.*

Never use *Inc., Co.* or *Corp.* with airline names.

airmail

airman *See* **military titles.**

Air National Guard

airport Capitalize as part of a proper name: *La Guardia Airport, Newark International Airport.* The first name of an individual and the word *international* may be deleted from a formal airport name while the rest is capitalized: *John F. Kennedy International Airport, Kennedy International Airport* or *Kennedy Airport.*

Don't make up names, however. There is no *Boston Airport,* for example. *The Boston airport* would be acceptable if for some reason the proper name, Logan International Airport, was not used.

airtight

airways *See* **airlines, air lines, airways**

Alabama Abbreviate as *Ala.* after city

names. Residents are *Alabamans.*
See **state names.**

a la carte

a la king, a la mode

Alaska Don't abbreviate it. The state has the largest land area of the 50 states. Residents are *Alaskans.*
See **state names.**

Alaska Standard Time, Alaska Daylight Time It applies in most of Alaska. The western Aleutians and St. Lawrence Island are on *Hawaii-Aleutian Standard Time.*
See **time zones.**

Alberta A province of western Canada. Don't abbreviate.
See **datelines.**

albino, albinos

Alcan Aluminium Ltd. The Canadian company uses the British spelling, *aluminium.* Its U.S. subsidiary is *Alcan Aluminum Corp.*

Alcoa Inc. It formerly was *Aluminum Co. of America.*

alcoholic Use *recovering,* not *reformed,* in referring to those who have been afflicted with the disease of alcoholism.

Al Fatah A Palestinian guerrilla organization. Drop the article *Al* if preceded by an English article: *the Fatah leader.*

alibi A legal term used in a claim that an accused was not at the scene of a crime. Do not use it to mean an excuse.

alien Use the word carefully to apply to an immigrant or foreigner. For those entering illegally, the term *illegal immigrant* is preferred.

alkylate This high-quality gasoline component is made by combining isobutane and propylene or butylene.

all- *All-clear, all-out, all-star.*

All-America, All-American *An All-American,* but *an All-America player.*

allege, alleged Use the words with care, and consider alternatives such as *apparent, suggested, reputed* and *ostensible.*
—Specify where an *allegation* comes from. In a criminal case, it should be an arrest record, an indictment or the statement of a public official connected with the case. In a civil case, it should come from court records or lawyers connected with the case.
—If you use *alleged conspiracy* or the like to make clear that an unproven action isn't being considered as fact, be sure that the source of the charge is specified in the story.
—Avoid unnecessary use of *alleged,* as in: *The police chief accused him of participating in an alleged conspiracy.*
—Don't refer to an *alleged* event when it is someone's participation in the event that is at issue. *He allegedly attended the meeting.* Not: *He attended the alleged meeting.*

Alleghany Corp. The financial-services company is based in New York.

Allegheny Technologies Inc. It is based in Pittsburgh. Its Allegheny Ludlum Corp. subsidiary makes stainless steel.

Allegheny Mountains Or simply: *the Alleghenies.*

allies, allied Capitalize *allies* or *allied* only when referring to the combination of the U.S. and its allies during World War I or World War II: *The Allies defeated Germany. He was in the Allied invasion of France. The allies won the Persian Gulf War.*

allot, allotted, allotting

allowable Avoid word in favor of *permissible* in such constructions as *permissible oil production.*

alloy steel This steel, formed by combining iron with one or more elements in addition to carbon, is harder and more malleable.

all right (adv.) Don't use *alright.* Hyphenate only if used colloquially as an adjective: *He is an all-right guy.*

all-round Not *all-around: He was an all-round athlete, with varsity letters in three sports.*

all-time Avoid this in constructions such as *all-time record.* It is superfluous—and transitory. In stock-market columns, when it is necessary to distinguish a record level from a 52-week high for an issue, use phraseology such as *highest level ever* or *highest closing on record.*

allude, refer

To *allude* to something is to speak of it without direct mention.

To *refer* is to mention it directly.

allusion, illusion

Allusion means an indirect reference: *The allusion was to his opponent's war record.*

Illusion means an unreal or false impression: *The scenic director created the illusion of choppy seas.*

alpha testing It refers to the testing of the *alpha version* of new software products. This first stage of testing is carried out by the manufacturer.

See **beta testing** and **gamma testing.**

alma mater

almost never Use *seldom* or *hardly ever* instead.

also-ran (n.)

altar (n.), **alter** (v.)

An *altar* is a church platform.

To *alter* is to change.

alternate, alternative Because *alternate* can mean every second one (*The club meets on alternate Tuesdays*), generally use *alternative* to mean substitute: *Mutual funds are an alternative to stocks.* The noun *alternative* once meant a choice between two but now can mean a choice among more than two.

aluminum The metal obtained from bauxite is used in construction, heavy industry and consumer products, such as beverage cans. After copper, it is the most actively traded metal on the London Metal Exchange. Don't use the British spelling *aluminium* except in a proper name.

alumnus, alumna, alumni, alumnae An *alumnus* is a male graduate. The plural is *alumni.* An *alumna* is a female graduate. The plural is *alumnae.*

Use *alumni* when referring to a group of men and women graduates.

AM Acceptable in all references for *amplitude modulation.*

a.m. Use only with a numeral: *10 a.m.* Avoid redundant phrases such as *10 a.m. that morning.* Lowercase in headlines.

Amazon.com Inc. The online retailer is based in Seattle.

ambassador Use for both men and women. Capitalize only as a formal title before a name.

See **titles.**

ambassador-at-large, ambassador extraordinary, ambassador plenipotentiary

amendments to the Constitution Use *First Amendment, 10th Amendment,* etc. Lowercase generic descriptions such as *women's-rights amendment.* Define what the amendment provides.

(-)American Hyphenate references to foreign heritage, both as nouns and adjectives: *She is an Asian-American; she is of Asian-American heritage.* Also: *Italian-American, Irish-American, German-American, African-American.*

American The term is commonly used in reference to a resident of the U.S. It may also be applied to residents elsewhere in North and South America. Adjectivally, it is usually preferable to use *U.S.: U.S. foreign policy; U.S. citizens.*

American Baptist Churches in the U.S.A.
See **Baptist churches.**

American Civil Liberties Union *ACLU* is acceptable on second reference.

American depositary receipt It is a receipt for a security that physically remains in a foreign country, usually in the custody of a bank there. *ADR* (plural: *ADRs*) on second reference.

American Express Co. *AmEx* is acceptable for second references in articles. Use it sparingly in headlines to avoid confusion with *Amex,* for the American Stock Exchange.

Based in New York, *American Express* provides travel-related, financial-advisory and international-banking services.

American Federation of Labor and *Congress* of Industrial Organizations *AFL-CIO* is preferred in all references.

American Federation of Television and Radio Artists *AFTRA* is acceptable on second reference.

American Indian Or use *Indian* alone if the context avoids confusion with residents of India. If possible in reference to American Indians, use the tribe's name: *an Iroquois man, a Sioux reservation.*

Native American is acceptable in quotations and names of organizations.

Words such as *wampum, warpath, powwow, tepee, brave* and *squaw* can be offensive. Avoid them if any disparagement may be inferred.

Americanisms Many words peculiar to the English spoken in the U.S. are marked with a star in Webster's New World Dictionary. Most of these words are generally acceptable, but the context should be the guide as to when their use is appropriate.

American League (baseball)

American Legion Capitalize also *the Legion* in second reference. Members are *Legionnaires. Legion* and *Legionnaires* are capitalized because they aren't being used in their common-noun sense. A *legion,* lowercase, is a large group of soldiers or any large number: *His friends are legion.*

See **fraternal organizations and service clubs.**

American Medical Association *AMA* is acceptable on second reference. Also: *the medical association, the association.*

American Petroleum Institute It is the U.S. oil industry's main lobbying group, which publishes oil inventory data every Tuesday.

API also denotes a system to measure the weight of crude oils. A lower API number means a heavier grade of crude.

See also **gravity.**

American Society of Composers, Authors and Publishers *ASCAP* is acceptable in second reference.

American Stock Exchange In second reference, *the American Exchange, the Amex, the* *exchange.* In combination with others: *The New York and American stock exchanges,* or *the New York and American exchanges.*

American Telephone & Telegraph Co. *AT&T Corp.* now is the formal name.

American Veterans of World War II, Korea and Vietnam *Amvets* is acceptable in all references.

Americas Cup (golf), **America's Cup** (yachting)

Amex
See **American Stock Exchange.** Avoid *Amex* as a reference to American Express Co., though *AirEx* is sometimes used.

amid Not *amidst.*

amidships

Amish (n. and adj.) The evangelical Christian group split from the Mennonites in the 17th century. The members favor plain dress and shun technology. Their congregational leaders are called *bishops.*

ammunition
See **weapons.**

amnesty
See **pardon, parole, probation.**

Amoco Corp.
See **BP PLC.**

amok Not *amuck.*

among Not *amongst.*

amortization It is the allocating of the value of intangible assets (such as patents, royalty agreements and goodwill) over the period of their existence. *See* **depreciation.**

ampersand (&) Always use the ampersand in names of companies, partnerships, businesses and stores, even if they prefer *and.* Also use the ampersand for such foreign forms as German *und* and French *et.* An exception: If a company uses the abbreviation to differentiate between a parent and subsidiary: *X&Y Co.* (parent); *X and Y Co.* (subsidiary). But use *and* in names of unions, government agencies and other organizations.

The ampersand shouldn't otherwise be used in place of *and* except for special effect in feature headlines.

amplitude modulation *AM* is acceptable in all references.

a.m., p.m. Avoid redundancies such as *10 a.m. this morning.* Lowercase *a.m.* and *p.m.* in headlines too.

Amsterdam The Dutch city stands alone in datelines.

Amsterdam Stock Exchange
See **Euronext.**

Amtrak This acronym, drawn from the words American travel by track, may be used in all references to *National Railroad Passenger Corp.*

The corporation was established by Congress in 1970 to take over intercity passenger operations from those railroads that wanted to drop passenger service. *Amtrak* contracts with railroads for the use of their track and of certain other operating equipment and crews on routes where it offers passenger service. *Amtrak* is subsidized in part by federal funds appropriated by Congress and administered through the Department of Transportation. *Amtrak* is required to operate without federal subsidies by 2003 or face possible restructuring or liquidation. But it will continue to need government capital funds.

anemia, anemic

anesthetic A drug or gas used to create *anesthesia.*

A

Anglican Communion In this association of 22 national Anglican churches, each national church is autonomous. But a special position of honor is accorded to the archbishop of Canterbury as head of the original Anglican body, the Church of England. The main division between Roman Catholics and Anglicans (or *Episcopalians* in the U.S.) is the dispute that led to the formation of the Church of England—the refusal to acknowledge the authority of the pope over the bishops.

Members of the *Anglican Communion* include the Church of England, the Scottish Episcopal Church, the Anglican Church of Canada and, in the U.S., the Protestant Episcopal Church.

See **Episcopal Church.**

Anglo It may be used as a counterpart of Latino, particularly in the context of the Southwest, but *white* is generally preferable.

Anglo- It is always capitalized. Don't use a hyphen if what follows is in lowercase:

Anglomania	Anglophobe
Anglophile	

Use a hyphen if a following word is capitalized:

Anglo-American	Anglo-Indian
Anglo-Catholic	Anglo-Saxon

angry One can be *angry at* someone or *with* someone.

angst Lowercase the noun meaning anxiety, although it is capitalized in German.

an herb, a herbal tea Illogical though it may seem, the *h* in *herb* is silent, but the *h* in *herbal* is sounded.

animals Apply a personal pronoun to an animal only if its sex has been established or it has a name: *The dog was frightened; it barked. Spot was frightened; he barked. The cat, which was frightened, ran away. Lady the cat, who was frightened, ran away. The bull lowers his head.*

Capitalize the name of a specific animal, and use Roman numerals to show sequence: *Rover, Secretariat II.*

For breed names, follow the spelling and capitalization in Webster's New World Dictionary. For breeds not listed in the dictionary, capitalize words adopted or derived from proper nouns; use lowercase elsewhere: *basset hound, Boston terrier.*

Annapolis An acceptable alternative reference for the *U.S. Naval Academy* at Annapolis, Md.

See **military academies.**

anno Domini *See* **A.D.**

annual meeting Lowercase it in all uses.

annuity A contract sold by life insurance companies guaranteeing a future payment to the investor, usually starting at retirement. With a *fixed annuity,* the payments are in regular installments. With a *variable annuity,* the payments depend on the value of the underlying investments.

anoint

anonymous sources

See **sources.**

another *Another* is not a synonym for *an additional.* If you are going to have *another* five complaints, you must have had the same number of complaints already: *Ten women passed, another 10 failed.* But: *Ten women passed, six others failed.*

antarctic, Antarctica

ante- Solid: *antebellum, antedate.*

anthems

See **composition titles.** Lowercase the term *national anthem.*

anti- The rules in **prefixes** apply. Words are unhyphenated *(antibias, antiballistic missile)* except for those in which the i is doubled *(anti-intellectual)* and those in which the base word itself is capitalized *(anti-American, anti-Semitic).*

antiabortion This is the preferred term to apply to the movement sometimes referred to as *pro-life.*

See **abortion rights.**

anticipate It means to expect something and prepare for it, not simply expect something.

antimony The minor metal is used in the manufacture of the fire retardants, plastics and to harden lead.

antitrust It is applied to any law or policy designed to encourage competition by curtailing monopolistic power and unfair business practices.

anxious, eager

Anxious means worried.

Eager means enthusiastic.

anybody, any body, anyone, any one Use the one-word version for an indefinite reference; two words to stress individual elements: *Anyone can do it. Any one of them can do it.*

anyplace, any place

Anyplace is substandard.

Any place means any location; it shouldn't be used in place of the adverb *anywhere.*

anytime

AOL Time Warner Inc. The media and Internet company is based in New York.

AP The initials are used in logotypes and are acceptable in second references for *the Associated Press.*

APEC

See **Asia-Pacific Economic Cooperation.**

API *See* **American Petroleum Institute.**

apostrophe (')

Use apostrophes for omitted numerals: *class of '62, the '20s.* But *1974–76.* For plurals of a single letter: *A's* and *B's, Oakland A's.*

Don't use apostrophes in these contexts: *in his 70s; in the 1970s.*

See **possessives.**

Apple Computer Inc. It is based in Cupertino, Calif.

appraise, apprise One *appraises* a diamond, but one *apprises* another of his appraisal.

approbation, opprobrium

Approbation means praise.

Opprobrium means disapproval.

Arabic terms in place names They include: Ain (spring), Bab (gate), Bahr (sea, lake and sometimes river), Bir (well), Birket (pond), Burj (tower), Dahr (mountaintop), Dar (abode of), Deir (monastery), Jebel (mountain), Jisr (bridge), Kafr (hamlet), Khan (caravansary), Marj (meadow), Nahr (river), Naqb (pass), Qasr or Kasr (castle), Ras (promontory, cape), Suq (market), Tell (hill), Wadi (dry riverbed, ravine).

Arab names In general, use an established English spelling or one preferred by the individual. Many Arabs incorporate the article *al-* or *el-* in English when their full names are used: *Osama el-Baz.* But drop the article on subsequent references: Mr. *Baz.* Many others drop the article from their names in English: *Moammar Gadhafi, Col. Gadhafi.*

Ibn, ben or *bin,* meaning "son of," is

sometimes part of a name: *Osama bin Laden.* He is *Mr. bin Laden* in subsequent references, but some drop the "son of" equivalent: *Abdullah bin Hamad al-Attiyah; Mr. Attiyah.*

The titles *king, emir, sheik* and *imam* are used, but *prince* usually replaces *emir.* Some Arabs are known only by the title and a given name on first reference: *King Abdullah of Jordan.* Others use a complete name on first reference: *Sheik Zayed bin Sultan al-Nahayan,* with the later references *Sheik Zayed.*

arabica This type of coffee bean, grown at a higher altitude than *robusta,* mostly in Colombia and other South American countries, is used in specialty coffees.

See **robusta.**

arbitrage, arbitrager Arbitrage is a technique of buying and selling securities to take advantage of small differences in price—e.g., buying a stock at $50 on one exchange and simultaneously selling it or an equivalent at $51 on another. One who uses this technique is an *arbitrager.* The short form *arb* is acceptable after the first reference.

Takeover-stock speculators also are commonly called *arbitragers* or *arbs.* They buy stocks in companies that are rumored or reported to be takeover targets, hoping to reap profits when the transactions are completed. This meaning has largely supplanted the earlier meaning. These arbitragers formerly were called *risk arbitragers.*

arbitrate, mediate Both terms are used in reports about labor negotiations, but they should not be interchanged.

An *arbitrator* hears evidence from all persons concerned, then hands down a binding decision on the issues raised. Thus *binding arbitration* is redundant.

A *mediator* listens to arguments of both parties and tries by the exercise of reason or persuasion to bring them to an agreement.

arch- The rules in **prefixes** apply. No hyphen after this prefix unless it precedes a capitalized word:

archbishop	arch-Republican
archenemy	archrival

archaeology Not *archeology.*

archbishop

See **Episcopal Church; Roman Catholic Church;** and **religious titles.**

archbishop of Canterbury Lowercase *archbishop* unless used before the name of the individual who holds the office.

archdiocese Capitalize it as part of a proper name: *the Archdiocese of Chicago, the Chicago Archdiocese.* Lowercase it whenever it stands alone.

archetype

arctic, Arctic Circle, arctic fox, Arctic Ocean

are (n.) The *are* is a unit of surface measure in the metric system, equal to 100 square meters. It is equal to about 1,076.4 square feet, or 119.6 square yards.

See **hectare** and **metric system.**

area codes *See* **telephone numbers.**

Argentine Use this rather than *Argentinian* to refer to the people of Argentina.

Arizona Abbreviate as *Ariz.* after city names. Residents are *Arizonans.*

See **state names.**

Arkansas Abbreviate as *Ark.* after city names. Residents are *Arkansans.*

See **state names.**

Armenia *See* **Commonwealth of Independent States.**

Armenian Church of America It includes the Eastern Diocese and, in California alone, the Western Diocese.

See **Eastern Orthodox churches.**

Armistice Day It is now *Veterans Day.*

army Capitalize it when it refers to U.S. forces: *the U.S. Army, the Army, Army regulations.* Do not use the abbreviation *USA.* Use lowercase for the forces of other nations: *the French army.*

See **military academies** and **military titles.**

aromatics This high-octane class of petrochemicals, including benzene, toluene and xylene, is used in making petrochemicals and premium grades of gasoline.

arrive Do not omit a preposition, as airline dispatchers often do: *The flight will arrive (at) Newark.*

arsenic The minor metal is used in chemicals, lead-based alloys, electronics, semiconductors and poisons.

Art Deco Capitalize references to the art and architecture style of the 1920s and 1930s.

article This term is preferred to apply to pieces appearing in the newspaper. To the layman, a *story* is more appropriately a work of fiction.

artifact

artillery *See* **weapons.**

Art Nouveau Capitalize references to the decorative style of the early 20th century.

artworks *See* **composition titles.**

as *See* **like, as.**

ashcan, ashtray

Ascap The formal name of the union is *the American Society of Composers, Authors and Publishers.* The full name should be included in articles that focus on the union.

Asean *See* **Association of Southeast Asian Nations.**

Asia-Pacific Economic Cooperation The Pacific Rim trade forum's 21 members meet annually. They are Australia, Brunei, Canada, Chile, China, Hong Kong, Indonesia, Japan, Malaysia, Mexico, Papua New Guinea, New Zealand, Peru, the Philippines, Russia, Singapore, South Korea, Taiwan, Thailand, the U.S. and Vietnam.

APEC is acceptable in second reference. Note that the name is *Asia-Pacific,* although *Asian-Pacific* is the preferred adjectival form in contexts that don't involve proper names.

Asian-American

Asian, Asiatic Use *Asian* or *Asians* when referring to people. Some Asians regard *Asiatic* as offensive when applied to people.

Asian Development Bank Based in Manila, it provides loans and grants to promote economic and social programs of its developing member nations. Its capital stock is the property of 57 members, including 16 from outside the region. Japan and the U.S. are its biggest shareholders.

Asian flu

Asian geographic terms

—*East Asia* is preferable to Far East, which is less precise. *East Asia* refers to the countries along Asia's eastern seaboard.

—*Asia Minor* refers to the peninsula in western Asia between the Black Sea and the Mediterranean, including the Asian portion of Turkey.

—*Australasia* is a region variously defined but always including Australia and New Zealand and sometimes Melanesia and the island of New Guinea.

—*Indochina* refers to Vietnam, Laos and Cambodia.

—*South Asia* refers to India, Pakistan, Sri Lanka, Bangladesh, Afghanistan and the Maldives.

—*Southeast Asia* refers to Brunei, Cambodia, Indonesia, Laos, Malaysia, Myanmar, the Philippines, Singapore, Thailand and Vietnam.

—*Pacific Basin* and *Pacific Rim* are synonyms, referring to countries and islands bordering the Pacific Ocean in Asia, Australia and the Americas and Russia.

Asian subcontinent It encompasses Bangladesh, Bhutan, India, Nepal, Pakistan, Sikkim and Sri Lanka.

See **Far East; Middle East; Southeast Asia.**

Asian Wall Street Journal, The Capitalize *The* in the name.

as if Use *as if* (or *as though*), rather than *like*, when introducing a clause: *The company spent money as if there were no tomorrow.*

asphalt Use *asphalt* rather than *bitumen* to describe the bottom-of-barrel refined petroleum product used for paving road surfaces.

assassination, date of A public figure is shot one day and dies the next. Which day was he assassinated? The day he was attacked.

assassin, killer, murderer

An *assassin* is a politically motivated killer or the killer of a prominent person.

A *killer* is anyone who kills.

A *murderer* is one who is convicted of murder in a court of law.

See **execute** and **homicide, murder, manslaughter.**

assault, battery In legal terms, an *assault* is an unlawful threat or unsuccessful attempt to harm someone physically.

Assault and battery is the term when the threat is carried out.

assembly Capitalize it when it is part of the proper name for the lower house of a legislature: *the California Assembly.* Retain capitalization if the state name is dropped but the reference is specific: *SACRAMENTO, Calif.—The state Assembly . . .*

And later in the story: *The Assembly . . .*

If a legislature is known as a general assembly, use: *the Missouri General Assembly, the General Assembly, the assembly. Legislature* may also be used as the proper name, however.

See **legislature.**

Lowercase all plural uses: *the California and New York assemblies.*

assemblyman, assemblywoman

See **legislative titles.**

asset-backed securities The securities are backed by collateral such as credit-card receivables or auto loans.

assets Everything a company or individual owns or is owed.

Assets may be categorized further as:

—*Current assets:* cash, investments, money due to a corporation, unused raw materials and inventories of finished but unsold products.

—*Fixed assets:* buildings, machinery and land.

—*Intangible assets:* patents and goodwill.

See **goodwill.**

assistant Don't abbreviate. Capitalize only when part of a formal title before a name: *Assistant Secretary of State George Ball.* Wherever practical, however, an appositional construction should be used: *George Ball, assistant secretary of state.*

See **titles.**

associate Never abbreviate. Apply the same capitalization norms listed under assistant.

Associated Press *AP* may be used in second references.

The address is 50 Rockefeller Plaza, New York, NY 10020.

association Don't abbreviate. Capitalize as part of a proper name: *American Medical Association.*

Association of Coffee Producing Countries The London-based organization of producing countries sets export quotas.

Association of Southeast Asian Nations *Asean* is acceptable in second reference. It is based in Jakarta. Its members are Brunei, Cambodia, Indonesia, Laos, Malaysia, Myanmar, the Philippines, Singapore, Thailand and Vietnam.

assure *See* **ensure, insure, assure.**

astronaut It isn't a formal title. Don't capitalize when used before a name: *astronaut John Glenn.*

AstroTurf A trademark for a type of artificial grass.

AT&T Corp. The company, based in New York, no longer uses the longer name.

athlete's foot, athlete's heart

athletic teams Capitalize teams, associations and recognized nicknames: *the Red Sox, the Big Ten, the A's, the Colts.*

Atlanta The city in Georgia stands alone in datelines.

Atlantic Ocean *See* **oceans.**

Atlantic Richfield Co. It was merged into BP PLC, of Britain.

Atlantic Standard Time, Atlantic Daylight Time Used in the Maritime Provinces of Canada and in Puerto Rico.

See **time zones.**

at-large Hyphenate combinations such as *ambassador-at-large, delegate-at-large.*

ATM It stands for automated teller machine. Avoid the redundancy *ATM machine.*

Atomic Age It began Dec. 2, 1942, with the creation of the first self-sustaining nuclear chain reaction.

Atomic Energy Commission It no longer exists.

See **Nuclear Regulatory Commission.**

attache It is not a formal title. Always lowercase.

attorney general, attorneys general Never abbreviate. Capitalize only when used as a title before a name: *Attorney General John Ashcroft.*

attorney, lawyer In common usage the words are interchangeable, but *lawyer* is the more appropriate term for referring to an attorney at law.

Technically, an *attorney* is someone (usually, but not necessarily, a lawyer) empowered to act for another. Such an individual occasionally is called an *attorney in fact.* A *lawyer* is a person admitted to practice in a court system. Such an individual occasionally is called an *attorney at law.*

Do not abbreviate. Do not capitalize unless it is an officeholder's title before a name: *defense attorney Julia Martin, attorney Julia Martin, District Attorney Greg Langan, U.S. Attorney Bruce Ohr.*

See **lawyer.**

auger, augur

An *auger* is a boring tool.

Augur is usually used as a verb meaning to foreshadow, but it is also a noun for a fortuneteller.

A

August
See **months.**

author It is a noun, used for both men and women. Don't use it as a verb.

auto maker, auto makers

automatic
See **pistol** and **weapons.**

automobiles Capitalize brand names: *Buick, Ford, Mustang, MG, Impala.* Lowercase generic terms: a *Volkswagen van,* a *Mack truck.*

auto worker, auto workers Many are members of *the United Auto Workers union.*

autumn
See **seasons.**

avant-garde (n. and adj.), **avant-gardism, avant-gardist**

avenue
See **addresses.**

average, mean, median, mode, norm
Average may be used to refer to *mean,* but for clarity, don't use it as a synonym for median, mode or norm.

Mean is calculated by adding up the observations involved and then dividing by the number of observations. The mean of 1, 3, 3 and 9 would be 4. The mean, also called the *arithmetic average,* can be the *median* and *mode* as well, as in this example: 2, 4, 6, 8 and 10.

Median is found by arranging the numbers from highest to lowest and then taking the middle one. The median of 1, 3, 3, 4 and 9 would be 3). *Median* is especially useful when a set of numbers is skewed by a few numbers that range much higher than the rest. For instance, thanks to a small number of very rich people, the *mean* wealth in the U.S. is much higher than the *median.*

Mode is the number that occurs most often in a grouping of numbers. In the set of numbers 1, 1, 3, 3, 3 and 9, 3 is the *mode.* You might use this method to calculate the numbers who retire at a given age, with the largest groupings probably occurring at age 65.

Norm implies a standard of average performance for a given group: The child was below the *norm* for her age in reading comprehension.

average of The phrase takes a plural verb in constructions such as: *An average of 100 new jobs are created daily.*

averse See **adverse, averse.**

Avianca It is the Colombian national airline.

aviator Use for both men and women.

Awacs It stands for *airborne warning and control system.*

awards and decorations Capitalize them: *Bronze Star, Medal of Honor.*
See **Nobel Prize** and **Pulitzer Prize.**

awe-struck

awhile, a while
He plans to stay awhile.
He plans to stay for a while.

AWOL Acceptable in all references for absent without leave.

ax Not *axe.*

Axis The alliance of Germany, Italy and Japan during World War II.

Bb

baby boom The bulge in population growth that appeared after World War II is considered by demographers to be the 18 years from 1946 through 1964. Those born in these years are *baby boomers.*

See **Generation X** and **Generation Y** entries.

baby-sit, baby-sitting (v.), **baby sitting** (n.), **baby sitter**

baccalaureate

bachelor Confine its use to men who have never been married, even though some dictionaries say it may applied to any man who isn't married.

bachelor of arts, bachelor of science Bachelor's degree is acceptable in all references.

See **academic degrees** for guidelines on when the abbreviations *B.A.* or *B.S.* are acceptable.

back to back In the world of commerce, it refers to a virtually risk-free financial transaction, in which a company buys a cargo at a given price, knowing in advance it can sell the cargo at a profit. In sports writing, usually as a modifier with hyphens, it is a tired and illogical cliché meaning consecutive.

back up (v.), **backup** (n. and adj.)

backward Not *backwards.*

backyard

bacterium (sing.), **bacteria** (pl.)

bad, badly I feel bad is correct because "feel" is a copulative verb, followed by the adjective form.

Bahamas Do not precede by *the* in datelines. But in stories, use *the Bahamas.*

bail *Bail* is money or property deposited to ensure an accused person's appearance. It is forfeited if the accused individual fails to appear for a hearing or a trial. The accused person or his agent may deposit the amount set by the court, or its equivalent in collateral. Bail bondsmen charge a percentage of the total figure and guarantee to pay the full amount in the event the individual fails to appear. In these cases, it is correct to say that the accused person *posted bail* or *posted a bail bond,* as the money held by the court is a form of a *bond.*

bailout (n. and adj.)

baker's dozen It means 13.

balance of payments A country's *balance of payments* is its accounting of its transactions with the rest of the world, representing all the international business done by individuals,

B

businesses and government agencies during a given period of time. Transactions that cause money to flow into a country are credits, and transactions that cause money to leave are debits.

—The *current account* of a balance-of-payments statement includes the *balance of trade,* which involves *merchandise trade* and *services* such as tourist spending and fees from patents and copyrights. The current account also includes *income receipts* such as dividends on stockholdings and interest on debt securities, as well as *unilateral transfers* such as workers' remittances from abroad and direct foreign aid.

—The *capital account* includes *direct foreign investment* such as establishing of a business abroad or purchasing of corporate assets abroad; *portfolio investment* records involving transfers of securities; *bank-related flows* between financial institutions; and *official reserve transactions* by central banks transferring assets.

balance sheet It is a listing of assets, liabilities and net worth, showing the financial position of a company at a specific time. A bank's *balance sheet* is often referred to as a *statement of condition.*

ball carrier, ball club, ballgame, ballpark, ballplayer, ballroom

balloon loan It is a loan or mortgage whose amortization schedule leaves a large *balloon payment* to be made at the end of the loan period.

ballpoint pen

baloney Use this spelling for foolish or exaggerated talk. The luncheon meat is *bologna.*

Baltimore The city in Maryland stands alone in datelines.

Band-Aid It is a trademark for a type of adhesive bandage.

Bangladesh Its citizens are *Bangladeshi(s).* But *Bengali(s)* applies to an ethnic group in Bangladesh and India.

Bank of America Corp. Based in Charlotte, N.C., it is a national leader in retail branch banking.

bankers' acceptances They are negotiable interest-bearing documents that allow a seller of merchandise to be paid before the buyer is ready to pay. The seller receives the buyer's promise to pay the amount involved on a specified date. The buyer's bank stamps the draft "accepted," guaranteeing the payment. Accepted drafts are sold to banks and others.

Bankers Trust Corp. The New York company is a unit of Deutsche Bank.

Bank for International Settlements *BIS* is acceptable on second reference. Based in Basel, Switzerland, it was founded in 1930 to promote cooperation among national central banks and to provide additional facilities for international financial operations. Its chief members are *G10* nations.

See **G10.**

bankruptcy Avoid calling a debtor *bankrupt* unless he, she or it has been legally adjudged as bankrupt.

The legal sense of the word applies only if a court has told an individual or organization to liquidate assets and distribute the proceeds to creditors.

The action may be involuntary, as the result of a suit by creditors, or it may be a voluntary effort to deal with bills that can't be paid.

Bankruptcy Code People or corporations involved in proceedings under the code are *debtors.* Any person or corporation obtaining relief under the code should be referred to as being *in bankruptcy proceedings.* A story announcing a bankruptcy filing should provide the chapter under which the reorganization is sought and describe the basic provisions, specifying whether the debtor will continue to operate the business.

The *Bankruptcy Code* is divided into chapters that provide different types of relief:

CHAPTER 7. This chapter governs liquidation (rather than reorganization) under the code. A case under Chapter 7 may be begun by the voluntary filing of a petition by the debtor. The case may also be begun by the filing of an involuntary petition against the debtor, a procedure by which the requisite number of creditors may be allowed to force the debtor into bankruptcy proceedings. After the case is commenced, the debtor is required to file a list of creditors and a schedule of assets and liabilities. Shortly after the filing of a petition, the creditors must meet and elect a trustee, and, if they wish, a creditors' committee that functions in an advisory capacity.

CHAPTER 9. This chapter provides for municipal debt adjustments. In order to obtain relief under Chapter 9, the municipality must be insolvent or unable to meet its debts as they mature, and it ordinarily must show some prior efforts to negotiate a settlement with its various creditors. A municipality may not liquidate under Chapter 7; it must attempt to formulate a plan under Chapter 9 and then, only if the state involved allows, resort to federal bankruptcy law. Chapter 9 of the code was designed to forestall widespread resort to bankruptcy proceedings by municipalities.

Chapters 11, 12 and 13 of the Bankruptcy Code constitute the reorganization and repayment provisions applicable to troubled businesses and individuals. Only individuals with limited debts may obtain relief under Chapter 13. Chapter 12 is for farmers or closely held farming corporations having debt of no more than $1.5 million.

CHAPTER 11. This is the provision under which most corporate reorganizations occur. As with a liquidation under Chapter 7, a case under Chapter 11 of the code is initiated by the filing of a voluntary or involuntary petition and, after the commencement of the case, the debtor is required to file a list of creditors and a schedule of assets and liabilities. The court (or the U.S. trustee, in most areas of the U.S.) appoints a committee of unsecured creditors to consult with the debtor and generally represent the creditors during the proceedings. Ordinarily, the debtor will continue to operate its business as a "debtor in possession," but in some cases a disinterested trustee may be appointed. The filing of the petition automatically stays unilateral action by any creditor to enforce or secure a lien on the debtor's property. The stay protects a debtor from the time and expense involved defending lawsuits. The stay is not permanent and can be lifted by the court. The proceeding culminates in a plan of reorganization that classifies the claims against the debtor and provides for satisfaction of those claims, insofar as possible. A plan of reorganization must be approved by the court. A technique commonly referred to as "prepackaged" bankruptcy has become increasingly common, particularly for companies such as those that were targets of leveraged buyouts that need to restructure the debt side of their balance sheets. A prepackaged plan of reorganization is one in which the solicitation of votes on the plan occurs before the company enters bankruptcy proceedings—an approach that has generally permitted companies to emerge from bankruptcy much more quickly than if terms and solicitation of votes on the plan had taken place after the company filed for bankruptcy. As is the case with the traditional process, the plan of reorganization in a prepackaged case requires court approval for confirmation.

CHAPTER 13. This chapter of the code, under attack in Congress in recent times as too lenient, provides for so-called individual debt adjustments and is intended as an alternative to liquidation under Chapter 7. Chapter 13 may be utilized voluntarily only by an individual with a regular source of income whose unsecured debts are less than $350,000. A Chapter 13 debtor retains all his or her assets and proposes a plan for the repayment of his or her debts over a period of three years or less (unless the court extends the time up to a maximum of five years). The plan must be accepted by all the debtor's secured creditors, but unsecured creditors have no right to vote on the Chapter 13 plan. Instead, the court must find that unsecured creditors will receive more under the proposed plan than they would have received had the debtor liquidated under Chapter 7. If the plan is rejected by secured creditors, or if the court finds that Chapter 7 would be more beneficial to unsecured creditors, the case may be converted to Chapter 7 by the court.

baptist, Baptist A person who baptizes is a *baptist* (lowercase). A *Baptist* (uppercase) is a person who is a member of a Protestant Baptist denomination.

Baptist churches The Southern Baptist Convention is the largest of the more than 20 Baptist bodies in the U.S. Its members are mostly in the South. The American Baptist Churches in the U.S.A. is the largest Northern body.

Members of the Baptist clergy may be referred to as *ministers. Pastor* is appropriate if the individual leads a congregation. On first reference, use *the Rev.* before an individual's name. On later references, use *Mr., Mrs., Miss* or *Ms.* with the last name.

See **religious titles.**

Barbados The people are *Barbadians* or, informally, *Bajans.*

barbecue (n. and v.)

Barclays PLC Based in the U.K., it is the parent of Barclays Bank.

barmaid

bar mitzvah The similar rite for girls is the *bas mitzvah.* The term applies both to the Jewish ceremony and the young person marking the 13th birthday.

baroque Capitalize references to the artistic style in Europe in the 17th century and into the 18th. Lowercase otherwise in reference to the elaborate detail that was characteristic of that period's art and music.

barrel A barrel of oil is equal to 42 gallons. One ton of crude oil equals about 7.33 barrels.

barrio It is any Hispanic neighborhood.

barrister

See **lawyer.**

Barron's The national business and financial weekly is published by Dow Jones & Co.

barroom

baseball

See **major leagues, major leaguer.**

base metal

See **aluminum; copper; lead; nickel; tin; zinc.**

basis, basis point

In securities trading, *basis* is the difference between the spot or cash price and the futures price of the same or related security or commodity.

In bond-market jargon, one *basis point* equals one-hundredth of a percentage point. Except in quotations, generally use percentage points instead, describing *50 basis points* as *0.5 percentage point.* But in bond-market commentary, the term *basis point* is permissible.

basket case Use the term advisedly, as some find it an offensive allusion to the disabled.

bated breath

Batswana (sing. and pl.) It is the term for the people of *Botswana.*

battalion Capitalize it when used with a figure to form a name: the *Third Battalion, the 10th Battalion.*

battlefield, battlefront, battleground, battleship But *battle station.*

baud rate The original data-processing term for the speed, in seconds, at which a digital-message unit may be transmitted over a communications channel has largely been replaced by *bits per second.*

See **bits per second.**

bay Capitalize as an integral part of a proper name: *Hudson Bay, San Francisco Bay.* Capitalize also *San Francisco Bay area* and *the Bay area* when they refer to the nine-county area that has San Francisco as its focal point.

bazaar It is a fair. *Bizarre* means very odd.

BBC Generally spell out *British Broadcasting Corp.* on first reference.

B.C. As an abbreviation for *before Christ,* it follows the year: *The town was founded in 43 B.C.*

But A.D., for anno Domini, precedes the year.

See **A.D.**

bearer bond The owner's name isn't registered on the books of the company issuing a *bearer bond.* Interest and principal are thus payable to the bondholder.

bearer stock Stock certificates that aren't registered in any name are *bearer stock.* The shares are negotiable without endorsement and transferable by delivery.

bear hug The jargon term applies to a friendly approach made to a takeover target, carrying an implicit threat that events could turn hostile. Explain the term if you use it.

Bear Stearns Co. The broker-dealer unit of the New York company is *Bear, Stearns & Co.* with a comma on first reference. Second reference for the parent or unit is *Bear Stearns,* without the comma.

Beaux-Arts

Capitalize the reference to the art and architecture style.

Lowercase, it means simply *fine arts.*

because, since Use *because* to denote a specific cause-effect relationship: *He went because he was told.*

Use *since* in a causal sense only to indicate that the first event in a sequence led logically to the second but was not its direct cause: *He went to the game, since he had been given the tickets.*

before Christ

See **B.C.**

beg the question Generally use *raise the question* or *evade the issue* instead, if that is the intended meaning. *Begging the question* refers to the use of an argument that assumes the truth of what you are trying to prove. A better-understood term for this is *circular logic.*

behalf *In behalf of* means for the benefit of or as a benefactor: *We raised money in behalf of the March of Dimes.* But *on behalf of* means as the agent of or in place of: *The chairman acted on behalf of the board.*

"beige book" The Federal Reserve Board's periodic reports on regional economies in the U.S. are informally called the "beige book" reports because of the color of the covers. Refer to them simply as *Fed studies of regional economies,* but add *known as the "beige book" reports* or refer to them as the *so-called beige book reports.* The formal name is *Summary of Commentary On Current Economic Conditions by Federal Reserve District.* The summaries of economic conditions in the 12 Federal Reserve districts are used as guides by policy makers at Federal Open Market Committee meetings.

See **Federal Open Market Committee.**

Beijing The Chinese capital stands alone in datelines.

Belarus The adjective is *Belarussian.*

See **Commonwealth of Independent States.**

Belize The former British Honduras has Belmopan as its capital.

BellSouth Corp. It is based in Atlanta.

bellwether It is one who takes the lead, as a sheep wearing a bell leads the flock. In the business world, it is any acknowledged indicator of trends.

bemused It means *stupefied* or *deep in thought.* It does *not* mean *amused.*

benefit, benefited, benefiting

Benelux countries They are Belgium, the Netherlands and Luxembourg.

Ben-Gurion International Airport Located at Lod, Israel, near Tel Aviv.

See **airport.**

Benzedrine A trademark for amphetamine.

Berlin The German capital stands alone in datelines.

Bermuda collar, Bermuda grass, Bermuda onion, Bermuda shorts

Bermuda Triangle It is the area in the Atlantic Ocean bounded by Bermuda, Puerto Rico and Florida, in which many ships are said to have disappeared.

beside, besides

Beside means at the side of.

Besides means in addition to.

besiege

bestseller (n.), **best-selling** (adj.)

beta testing The second-stage testing, of the *beta version* of a new software product, is conducted by knowledgeable users for feedback on how to improve the product for its commercial release.

See **alpha testing** and **gamma testing.**

bettor A person who bets.

Bhutan Its citizens are *Bhutanese.*

bi- Words with the prefix are solid: *biaxial, bifocal, bilingual, bilateral, bipartisan.*

biannual, biennial *Biannual,* like *semiannual,* means twice a year. *Biennial* means every two years. Avoid *biannual* in favor of *semiannual* whenever possible to prevent confusion. Or, even better, say *twice a year.*

Bible

Capitalize it, without quotation marks, when referring to the Scriptures of the Old Testament or the New Testament. Capitalize also related terms such as *the Book, the Good Book, the Word of God, the Gospels, Gospel of St. Mark, the Scriptures, the Holy Scriptures.*

Lowercase *biblical* in all uses.

Lowercase *bible* as a nonreligious term: *The stylebook is our bible.*

Do not abbreviate individual books of the Bible.

Citations listing the number of chapter and verse(s) use this form: *Matthew 3:16, Luke 21:1–13, 1 Peter 2:1.*

Bible Belt Generally the Southern states of the U.S., where evangelical fervor prevails. Use the term with care to avoid disparaging Southerners in general.

bicycle

bid and asked In the securities business, the *bid* price is what the prospective buyer is willing to pay, and the *asked* price or *offer* price is what a prospective seller is willing to accept. In real estate, the prospective buyer similarly makes a *bid* at a given price, and a prospective seller sets an *asking* price.

big-bang theory It holds that the universe began with the explosion of a superdense primeval atom and has been expanding ever since.

Big Board It is acceptable in second reference for *the New York Stock Exchange. NYSE* is also acceptable.

Big Brother Capitalized, it refers to the watchful eye of big government, from George Orwell's "1984." It also can refer to members of *Big Brothers and Sisters of America Inc.,* based in Philadelphia.

Big Three auto makers General Motors, Ford, Chrysler.

Big Four accounting firms The *Big Four* are PricewaterhouseCoopers, Ernst & Young, KPMG LLP and Deloitte & Touche LLP.

bigwig

biological parents Use this term to differentiate from *adoptive parents.*

billings In the advertising business, they represent the cost to clients of placing ads. Agencies' fees typically are 15% of billings.

billion A thousand million. For forms, see **millions, billions, trillions.**

Bill of Rights It comprises the first 10 Amendments to the Constitution.

bimonthly It means every other month. *Semimonthly* means twice a month.

bipolar disorder In psychiatry, the term now is preferred over *manic-depressive illness.*

birthday Capitalize it as part of the name for a holiday: *Washington's Birthday.* Lowercase in other uses.

birthrate

BIS

See **Bank for International Settlements.**

bishop

See **religious titles** and the entry for the denomination in question.

bismuth The minor metal, mostly a byproduct of lead production, can be used as a nontoxic substitute for lead, especially in gunshot, brass fittings and pharmaceuticals.

bit It is a computer acronym for *binary digit,* the smallest units of information. Eight bits form a *byte.*

See **byte.**

bits per second This is the principal measure of the amount of data being sent over a communications line. An earlier term, *baud rate,* represented the number of frequency changes in sending data over a line.

B

bitumen
See **asphalt.**

biweekly It means every other week. *Semiweekly* means twice a week.

bizarre It means very odd. A *bazaar* is a fair.

black Lowercase *black, white* and other references to skin color. *African-American* is an alternative designation for American blacks.

Black Death The disease that devastated Europe and Asia in the 14th century is thought to have been bubonic plague.

blackout, brownout
A *blackout* is a total power failure over a large area or the concealing of lights that might be visible to enemy raiders.
A *brownout* is a small voltage reduction to conserve power, usually 2% to 8%.

blast furnace In the steel industry, a blast furnace creates combustion by forcing a current of air under pressure and obtains iron by the reduction of iron ore with suitable fuel and fluxes at high temperatures.

blast off (v.), **blastoff** (n. and adj.)

bleached hardwood kraft This key grade of pulp is produced mainly in the tropics, especially Southeast Asia and Brazil, from trees such as acacia and eucalyptus. It tends to have shorter fibers, which make it well-suited for making the white paper used for stationery or for use in photocopiers.

Blessed Sacrament, Blessed Virgin

blizzard *See* **weather terms.**

bloc, block
A *bloc* is a coalition of persons or groups with a common purpose or goal.
A *block* is any group of people or things treated as a unit.

blockade, blockade runner, blockbuster, blockhead, blockhouse

blond, blonde; brunet, brunette
Use *blond* and *brunet* as nouns for males and as adjectives for both sexes.
Use *blonde* and *brunette* as nouns for females.

bloodhound

Bloody Mary The drink is made principally of vodka and tomato juice. The name is derived from the nickname for Mary I of England.

Bloomingdale's It is a subsidiary of Federated Department Stores Inc., Cincinnati.

blue blood (n.), **blue-blooded** (adj.)

blue-chip stocks They are stocks of companies known for their long-established record of earning profits and paying dividends, including the stocks in the Dow Jones Industrial Average.

blue law A law prohibiting business or certain other activities on Sundays.

board of directors Use *board* instead of board of directors provided it is unambiguous in context. In corporations, the board members are elected by shareholders, usually at an annual meeting, to exercise such corporate oversight functions as naming senior management, issuing or repurchasing shares and issuing dividends.
The board usually includes both *inside directors,* or senior corporate executives, and

outside directors, who come from other companies or the community at large. Directors don't exercise day-to-day oversight, but meet several times a year. They are usually paid for their services.

boardroom

boats, ships A *ship* is a large, seagoing vessel, and a *boat* is usually a smaller vessel. *Boat,* however, is used in some terms applied to large craft: *ferryboat, PT boat, gunboat.*

Do not put the names in quotation marks: *the Delta Queen, the USS Arizona, the Queen Elizabeth 2.*

Vessels may be referred to by the pronoun *it* or *she* (or the corresponding possessive pronouns). Let the context determine which to use.

bodybuilder, bodybuilding

Boeing Co. The aircraft maker in 2001 planned to move its headquarters from Seattle to Chicago.

bogey, bogeys, bogeyed The golf terms mean one stroke over par, or the making of that score.

bologna This is the sausage. *Baloney* is foolish or exaggerated talk.

Bolshevik

bona fide

bonbon

bondholder

Bond Market Association It is a trade association for bond traders.

bond ratings The leading rating companies are Moody's Investors Service Inc. and Standard & Poor's Corp. They rate corporate, municipal and foreign bonds as well as other types of debt. *Triple-A* (as we write it, rather than AAA, as the agencies do) has been the top bond rating at both companies.

The ratings designations are changed periodically, but as a guide, *Moody's* has used these ratings, beginning with the highest investment-quality designation: *triple-A, double-A, single-A, Baa, Ba, B, Caa, Ca* and C. The first four of these ratings, including Baa, refer to bonds that are considered *investment grade.* The others are termed *junk bonds,* or, as securities firms prefer, *high-yield bonds.*

Standard & Poor's uses these basic grades, from highest to lowest: *triple-A, double-A, single-A, triple-B, double-B, single-B, triple-C, double-C, single-C, CI* (reserved for income bonds on which no interest is paid) and D (for debt on which interest payments are in default). Occasionally, S&P adds a *-plus* or *-minus* to double-A through triple-C. The so-called *junk* rating starts with double-B, on down.

bonds

See **loan terminology.**

book-building In this way of conducting an *initial public offering* of shares, the offer price is based on actual demand for shares among institutional investors. Underwriters build a "book" by accepting orders from fund managers that indicate the number of shares they want to buy and the price they are willing to pay.

See **initial public offering.**

book titles *See* **composition titles.**

book value In corporations, it is *cost minus accumulated depreciation.* Book value is the value at which assets are carried on the balance sheet. Office equipment, for example, would be put on the books at its cost when purchased, and the value would be reduced

each year as depreciation of the equipment is charged to income. Because the main function of depreciation accounting for the equipment is to allow the company to recover its cost, book value may bear little resemblance to market value.
See **depreciation.**

boost As a synonym for *increase,* it is overused in business writing.

born, borne A cost or burden is *borne.* Before a child is *born,* it is *borne* by its mother.

Bosnia and Herzegovina It was split from Yugoslavia in 1992. On second reference, *Bosnia* and *Bosnian* are acceptable. Also *Bosnian Croat* or *Bosnian Serb.*

Bosporus, the Not *the Bosporus Strait.*

Boston The city in Massachusetts stands alone in datelines.

Boston brown bread, Boston cream pie, Boston ivy, Boston terrier

Botswana (n. and adj.) The people are *Batswana,* singular and plural.

botulism A food poisoning, but not all food poisoning is *botulism.*

boulevard
See **addresses.**

boundary

bourgeoisie

bowlegged

bowl games Capitalize them: *Cotton Bowl, Orange Bowl, Rose Bowl.*

box office (n.), **box-office** (adj.)

boy Use *boy* in reference only to the very young.

boycott It is an organized refusal to buy a particular product or service, or to deal with a particular merchant or group of merchants.
See **embargo.**

boyfriend, girlfriend

BP PLC The oil company is based in London. It formerly was *British Petroleum Co.* and then briefly *BP Amoco PLC.*

brackets In news stories, bracketed and indented paragraphs are used for material from a news-gathering source other than that used in the rest of the story—an AP insert in a DJ story or vice versa, for example. These paragraphs should give the source and the city of origin: [In Paris yesterday, the Associated Press said . . .]

Avoid having such paragraphs as the final paragraphs of the story.

Brackets are also used within quotations to indicate material not specifically provided by the person quoted. But because brackets tend to impede the flow of a sentence they should be used sparingly. Paraphrasing is often the better path.

Brady bonds They are bonds issued by developing countries in exchange for previously rescheduled commercial-bank loans. The principal is guaranteed by zero-coupon U.S. Treasury bonds, and near-term interest payments are collateralized as well. They are named for then-Treasury Secretary Nicholas Brady, who offered government and multilateral support to debtor countries in obtaining debt-service relief from foreign commercial bank creditors. Mexico was the first issuer, in 1990.

Brahmin(s) This applies to the priestly

Hindu caste and to aristocracy in general: *a Boston Brahmin.*

brand names Capitalized brand names may be used if they are germane or if their use lends color or authenticity in an article. Manufacturers usually register brand names or designs as trademarks to prevent competitors from using them.

See **trademark.**

brand-new

Brasilia The capital of Brazil stands alone in datelines.

breach, breech

A *breach* refers to a break or violation.

Breech refers to the lower or back part, or *breech birth,* meaning feet-first.

Breeches or *britches* are trousers extending below the knee.

break bulk

See **bunker, bunker market.**

break down (v.), **breakdown** (n. and adj.)

break even (v.), **break-even** (n. and adj.)

break in (v.), **break-in** (n. and adj.)

break off (v.), **breakoff** (n. and adj.)

breakout (n.), **break through** (v.) The terms apply to a security's move through a support or resistance level. In technical analysis, a *breakout* presages a major move for the security.

See **resistance level; support level; technical analysis.**

break up (v.), **breakup** (n. and adj.)

Brent It is the formal name for the North Sea benchmark crude oil from the Brent field.

Breton It applies to a resident of Brittany, a province of France.

bridal, bridle

Bridal refers to weddings.

Bridle refers to a horse's head harness or, by extension, any restraints.

brigadier

See **military titles.**

Bright's disease Named for Richard Bright, the London physician who first diagnosed it, it is a form of kidney disease.

Brill's disease Named for N. E. Brill, a U.S. physician, it is a form of epidemic typhus fever in which the disease recurs years after the original infection.

bring, take *Bring* denotes movement toward the speaker or toward the dateline or toward the U.S. *Take* denotes movement that is not toward the speaker. In a datelined article, *bring* means conveyance toward the dateline city. In headlines, *bring* normally refers to movement toward the U.S. from abroad.

Bristol-Myers Squibb Co. The pharmaceutical company is based in New York.

Britain Confine *Great Britain* to quotations. *Britain* comprises England, Scotland and Wales. The United Kingdom comprises Britain and Northern Ireland.

See **United Kingdom.**

British Airways

British, Briton(s) They are the people of Britain: *the English, the Scots and the Welsh.* Generally avoid *Brit,* as it is sometimes considered pejorative.

British Broadcasting Corp. *BBC* is acceptable in second references.

British Columbia The Canadian province bounded on the west by the Pacific Ocean. Don't abbreviate.

See **datelines.**

British Commonwealth

See **Commonwealth, the.**

British thermal unit It is the amount of heat required to increase the temperature of a pound of water one degree Fahrenheit. *BTU* or *BTUs* is acceptable on second reference.

British ton

See **ton.**

British Virgin Islands In datelines, the city name is used in all caps, followed by British Virgin Islands. Don't abbreviate. Specify an individual island, if needed, in the text.

broadband It describes cable or other devices that carry a wide range of frequencies or channels and large amounts of information.

See **open access.**

broadcast Use *broadcast* also for the past tense, not *broadcasted.*

broccoli

brokerage Brokerage is the business of the *brokerage firm.* Don't use it as a synonym for brokerage firm.

brokerage firms Give the corporate names of their owners, unless the reference is offhand, as to a firm's analyst who is simply providing market commentary in an article. They are still called firms, idiomatically, although few of them remain partnerships.

Among the major U.S. stock-brokerage firms and banks with large Wall Street business lines:

Merrill Lynch & Co.

Morgan Stanley & Co. It was Morgan Stanley Dean Witter & Co.

Salomon Smith Barney. It is owned by Citigroup Inc.

UBS Paine Webber Inc. It is part of UBS AG's UBS Warburg unit.

Fidelity Investments. It is officially FMR Corp. But FMR does business as *Fidelity Investments,* and that name is generally sufficient in reference to the big mutual-fund and trading company. Fidelity Management & Research is FMR's money-management unit. FMR also has some nonfinancial entities, such as telephone companies.

Prudential Securities. It is a unit of Prudential Insurance Co. of America.

Bear Stearns & Co. The securities firm is owned by Bear Stearns Cos. Each is Bear Stearns in second reference. Because the names are so similar, *Bear Stearns Cos.* is acceptable in first reference for the securities firm.

Lehman Brothers Holdings Inc.

Goldman Sachs Group Inc.

Credit Suisse First Boston. It is owned by Credit Suisse Group of Zurich, and it incorporates the former Donaldson, Lufkin & Jenrette. Its *CSFBdirect* unit, the successor to DLJdirect, is publicly traded as a separate entity.

J.P. Morgan Chase & Co.

Deutsche Banc Alex. Brown. It is part of Germany's Deutsche Bank AG.

Robertson Stephens. It is a unit of FleetBoston Financial.

Chase H&Q, formerly Hambrecht & Quist. It is a unit of Chase Manhattan Corp.

Chase Manhattan Bank. It is owned by Chase Manhattan Corp.

Banc of America Securities. Owned by Bank of America Corp., it incorporates the former Montgomery Securities.

U.S. Bancorp Piper Jaffray Inc. It is owned by U.S. Bancorp.

Jefferies Group Inc. Note the spelling.

E*Trade Group Inc.

CIBC World Markets Corp. It is a unit of Canadian Imperial Bank of Commerce.

Friedman, Billings, Ramsey & Co.

A.G. Edwards Inc. It owns A.G. Edwards & Sons.

Legg Mason Inc. It owns Legg Mason Wood Walker Inc.

brokers and dealers *Brokers* bring buyers and sellers together for a commission. In the cash, forward and swap markets for securities, brokers don't take market positions on their own, as *dealers* do. A *futures broker* traditionally fills orders from traders for commission, adding value through research and other means.

Bronze Age The age characterized by the development of bronze tools and weapons, from 3500 to 1000 B.C. Usually regarded as coming between the Stone Age and the Iron Age.

Brookings Institution

brother *See* **Roman Catholic Church.**

Brothers In formal company names, abbreviate as *Bros.* only if the company does. But the abbreviation is allowed in names in headlines.

brownout
See **blackout, brownout.**

browser It refers to software that enables personal computer users to find sites on the World Wide Web and to perform various operations once they are linked with sites. Major browsers include *Netscape Navigator* and *Microsoft Internet Explorer.*

brunet, brunette
Use *brunet* as a noun for males and as an adjective for both sexes.

Use *brunette* as a noun for females.

Brussels The Belgian city stands alone in datalines.

Brussels carpet, Brussels lace, Brussels sprouts

Brussels Stock Exchange
See **Euronext.**

b-to-b, b-to-c Use these constructions rather than *B2B* and *B2C* for second references to business-to-business and business-to-consumer commerce on the Internet.

BTU, BTUs
See **British thermal unit.**

Bucharest The capital of Romania stands alone in datelines.

Budapest The capital of Hungary stands alone in datelines.

Buddha, Buddhism

Buenos Aires The capital of Argentina stands alone in datelines.

Bufferin It is trademark for a buffered aspirin compound.

bug, tap
Bug is a concealed listening device designed to pick up sounds, or the act of using such a device.

Tap is a device attached to a telephone circuit to pick up conversations on the line, or the act of using such a device.

building Capitalize the proper names of buildings: *the Empire State Building.*

B

build up (v.), **buildup** (n. and adj.)

built-in (adj.)

bull's-eye

bullet *See* **weapons.**

bullet payment It is a payment method in which the principal and interest accumulate in an account until the end of the accumulation period. Funds in the account are reinvested in securities consistent with the rating on the transaction.

See also **asset-backed securities.**

bullfight, bullfighter, bullfighting

bullion, bullion coin

Bullion refers to unminted precious metals of standards suitable for coining.

A *bullion coin* is one with its market value determined by its inherent precious-metal content. The coins are bought and sold mainly for investment purposes.

bullpen It refers to a place where baseball pitchers warm up as well as to a pen for cattle.

bully pulpit A position of influence used to promote one's own causes.

Bundesbank Use *Deutsche Bundesbank* on first reference to the German central bank. Or simply call it *the German central bank.*

bundle For computers, two or more retail products sold together, usually as part of a sales promotion or operating package. Bundles often involve computer hardware-software combinations, or software combinations between two different companies.

In commodities, a *bundle* is a stack of copper cathodes strapped together for shipping.

bunker (n., adj. v.), **bunker market**

Bunker fuel describes a range of high-sulfur fuel oil grades, or marine diesel or marine gasoil, used to power ocean-going vessels. To *bunker* an ocean-going vessel means to supply fuel to the vessel.

The *bunker market* is a subset of the larger fuel-oil and gasoil cargo markets. Traders break bulk, buying large fuel oil, diesel and gasoil cargoes and selling smaller quantities of the fuel to the marine market. Fujairah, Saudi Arabia, Singapore and Rotterdam are the world's biggest bunker-market centers.

See also **cargo market.**

bureau Capitalize only when part of the formal name for an organization or agency: *the Bureau of Labor Statistics, the Newspaper Advertising Bureau.*

Bureau of Alcohol, Tobacco and Firearms *BATF* is acceptable in headlines. In second reference in articles, try to use *the bureau* or *the agency* instead of the abbreviation.

burglary, larceny, robbery, theft

Legal definitions of *burglary* vary, but in general it involves entering a building (not necessarily by breaking in) and remaining unlawfully with the intention of committing a crime.

Larceny is the legal term for the wrongful taking of property. Its nonlegal equivalents are *stealing* or *theft.*

Robbery in the legal sense implies the use of violence or threat in committing larceny.

Theft implies a larceny that did not involve threat, violence or plundering.

burgundy, Burgundy *See* **wine.**

Burkina Faso It formerly was Upper Volta.

Burlington *Burlington Coat Factory Warehouse Corp.*, Burlington, N.J., isn't related to *Burlington Industries Inc.*, the Greensboro, N.C., textile company. A caveat is normally included in articles about the retailer.

Burlington Northern Santa Fe Corp. The railroad operator is based in Fort Worth, Texas.

Burma It now is called *Myanmar.*
See **Myanmar.**

burns In medicine, there are three degrees of burns:
A *first-degree burn* is a reddening of the skin. Most sunburns fall in this category.
A *second-degree burn* is a blistering.
A *third-degree burn* involves destruction of the skin and the tissues under it.
The size of the burn is crucial. *Second-degree burns* covering 90% of the body are likely to be more dangerous than *third-degree burns* on 5% of the body.

burro, burrow
A *burro* is an ass.
A *burrow* is a hole in the ground.

burst The past tense is also *burst.*

bus, buses Transportation vehicles.
See **buss.**

bushel It is the unit of account for agricultural products such as wheat, corn and soybeans. One bushel equals 35.2383 liters. To ensure a common reference unit in stories that also refer to metric tons, use the following conversion rates:

Bushels per metric ton:

wheat	36.743333
soybeans	36.743333
corn	39.367857
grain sorghum	39.367857
barley	45.929166
oats	68.893750
rice	22.046

businessman, businesswoman, businesspeople But *small-business man, small-business woman, small-business people.* Or, if applicable, *small-business owners.*

Business Roundtable A group of leading businesspeople, involved in policy issues.

business-to-business, business-to-customer Use *b-to-b* instead of B2B for the second-reference short versions referring to *business-to-business* commerce and use *b-to-c* in second references to business-to-customer commerce on the Internet.

buss, busses The words refer to kisses. *See* **bus.**

butane A light hydrocarbon, usually a gas, it is an important component of liquefied petroleum gas; occasionally, it is used as a component of gasoline.
See **liquefied petroleum gas.**

buyback (n.), **buy back** (v.) The words refer to a company's repurchase of stock, usually on the open market. Often, a buyback is an attempt to bolster the share price by reducing the *float,* or number of shares available in public circulation. A company may also buy back stock for its executive-compensation or employee stock-option plans.

buy out (v.), **buyout** (n. and adj.)

buy side (n.), **buy-side** (adj.) The terms refer to the mutual-fund and other fund managers who purchase securities. The *sell side* includes brokers and dealers.

by-election A special election held between regularly scheduled elections. The term is most often associated with special elections to the British House of Commons.

bylaw

bylines On staff-written articles, the line *Staff Reporter of The Wall Street Journal* usually follows the byline name for staff members of the print editions. Other lines include *The Wall Street Journal Online* and *Dow Jones Newswires.*

B

For correspondents and others not on the WSJ staff, the line *Special to The Wall Street Journal* is used after the byline.

On articles that take two or more bylines, at least one of the reporters must have been reporting in the city in order for us to use the city in the dateline.

If two byline reporters contributed from separate cities, a judgment should be made about whether it is more appropriate to use one city for the dateline or to use a byline box that can mention the two cities.

When more than two reporters are involved, use a byline box. If all reporters were in the city involved, use a dateline instead of providing the location in the box.

If only one reporter was in the city involved and the location of the other reporters is deemed unimportant, use the city in a dateline and omit the locations in the byline box.

If it is deemed important to mention the location of all the reporters, give the information in the byline box and omit the dateline. (The usual form for a byline box: *By Wall Street Journal staff reporters Gary Putka in Boston, Jonathan Eig in Chicago, Karen Blumenthal in Dallas and Carrie Dolan in San Francisco.*)

See **datelines** and **taglines.**

byproduct

byte A unit of measure of computer information, it typically consists of eight *bits,* or binary digits, equivalent to the average word. *Computer speed* is rated by the number of bits processed each second. *Storage units* rate their capacity by the number of bytes they can store. A *megabyte* is 1,048,576 bytes. A *gigabyte* is 1,024 megabytes, or 1,073,741,824 bytes.

Cc

cabdriver, cabby Not *cabbie.*

cabinet Lowercase it, including in references to a specific body of advisers heading executive departments for a president: *the president's cabinet, the Bush cabinet, cabinet ministers.*

See **departments** for a listing of U.S. cabinet departments.

cabinet titles

Capitalize the full title when used before a name: *Secretary of State Colin Powell.*

Lowercase in other uses: *Colin Powell, the secretary of state.*

Exception: *Paul O'Neill, the secretary of the Treasury; Paul O'Neill, the Treasury secretary* (because references to the federal *Treasury* are capitalized in our style). Also *Treasury Secretary Paul O'Neill.*

See **titles.**

cable television, cable TV

cache, cachet

A *cache* is a hidden reserve.

Cachet is evidence of authenticity or a mark of distinction.

cactus, cactuses

cadet *See* **military academies.**

cadmium It is a highly toxic minor metal used mainly in batteries and chemicals. Rechargeable batteries use cadmium, usually obtained as a byproduct of zinc refining.

Caesarean section

Cairns Group The group of 15 agricultural exporting countries considers agricultural trade policy for its members. Based in Sydney, Australia, the group comprises Argentina, Australia, Brazil, Canada, Colombia, Chile, Fiji, Indonesia, Malaysia, New Zealand, Paraguay, the Philippines, South Africa, Thailand and Uruguay.

caliber Use this form: a *.38-caliber pistol.*

See **weapons.**

California Abbreviate as *Calif.* after city names. Residents are *Californians.*

See **state names.**

California Air Resources Board The board sets standards in the state for various fuels, notably a low-sulfur diesel fuel known as *CARB diesel.*

California-Oregon border It is a main hub for electricity trading on the West Coast and a benchmark location in electricity pricing.

California Public Employees' Retirement System It is *Calpers* on second reference.

call In the securities business, it is an option to buy a security at a specific price, usually above the current price and usually within a limited period.

C

call up (v.), **call-up** (n. and adj.)

Caltex Petroleum Corp. Based in Irving, Texas, *Caltex* is a joint venture of Texaco Inc. and Chevron Corp. that operates in Asia, primarily in South Korea, Indonesia, Thailand and India.

Cambodia Use this name rather than *Kampuchea* in datelines. When *Kampuchea* is used in the body of a story, identify it as another name for *Cambodia.*

Cameroon Not *Cameroons, Cameroun*s or *Cameroun. See* **geographic names.**

campaign manager Don't treat as a formal title. Always lowercase.

See **titles.**

Canada *Montreal, Ottawa, Quebec* and *Toronto* stand alone in datelines. For all other datelines, use the city name in caps and the name of the province or territory spelled out in caps and lowercase.

The 10 provinces of Canada are Alberta, British Columbia, Manitoba, New Brunswick, Newfoundland (includes Labrador), Nova Scotia, Ontario, Prince Edward Island, Quebec and Saskatchewan.

The territories are the Yukon, the Northwest Territories, and Nunavut. Like provinces, they elect their own legislators and elect representatives to Parliament. But unlike provinces, they are administered by the federal government.

See **datelines.**

Canada goose Not *Canadian goose.*

Canadian Wheat Board It is a government agency that markets all exports of western Canadian wheat and barley.

canal Capitalize as integral part of a proper name: *the Suez Canal.*

Canal Zone It has passed out of existence.

cancel, canceled, canceling, cancellation

C&F *See* **cost and freight.**

cannon *See* **weapons.**

cannot

cant It refers to the distinctive stock words and phrases used by a particular sect or class.

See **dialect.**

Canton The city in China now is called *Guangzhou.*

cantor *See* **Jewish congregations.**

Canuck The term, meaning a Canadian and especially a French Canadian, is often considered a derogatory label. Avoid it except in formal names (the Vancouver Canucks, a professional hockey team) or in quoted matter.

See **nationalities and races.**

canvas, canvass

Canvas is a heavy cloth.

Canvass is a noun and a verb denoting a survey.

Caobisco It refers to *the European Association of the Chocolate, Biscuit and Sugar Confectionery Manufacturers,* based in Brussels. The acronym is acceptable on second reference.

cape Capitalize as part of a proper name: *Cape Cod, Cape Hatteras.* Lowercase when standing alone.

Cape Canaveral, Fla. Formerly Cape Kennedy. *See* **John F. Kennedy Space Center.**

capesize It describes the largest category of cargo ship, too big to travel through the Panama or Suez canal.

See **Panamax.**

capital, capitol

A *capital* is a city that is a seat of government, and it is always lowercase. *Capital* also is the money, equipment or property owned or used in business by a person or corporation. *Capital assets* are those that are not bought or sold in the normal course of business. They generally include such *fixed assets* as land, buildings, equipment and furniture. A *capital gain* or *capital loss* is the difference between what a capital asset cost and the price it brings when sold.

Capitol is uppercase when it refers to the specific building that houses the federal or a state government. But it is lowercase in general and plural references: *The capitols of New Hampshire and Vermont are landmarks.* Uppercase *Capitol Hill*, the name of the area around the federal Capitol.

capital account *See* **balance of payments.**

capitalization If the stylebook provides no relevant listing for a word or phrase, consult Webster's New World Dictionary. *See* **headline capitalization.**

PROPER NAMES: Capitalize common nouns such as *party, river, street* and *west* when they are an integral part of the full name for a person, place or thing: *Democratic Party, Mississippi River, Fleet Street, West Virginia.* But generally lowercase the common nouns when they stand alone in subsequent references: *the party, the river, the street.* Exceptions: Uppercase certain specific entities in second reference: *the World Series, the Series; the Kentucky Derby, the Derby; the Olympic Games, the Games; Wall Street, the Street.*

Lowercase the common-noun elements of a name in all plural uses: *the Democratic and Republican parties; the Hudson and Mississippi rivers; Main and State streets; the New York and American stock exchanges.*

Capitalize words derived from a proper noun that continue to depend on it for their meaning: *American, Christian, Christianity, English, French, Marxism, Dadaism, Shakespearean.*

Lowercase words derived from a proper noun that no longer depend on it for their meaning: *french fries, herculean, manhattan cocktail, quixotic, spartan, venetian blind.*

Verbs derived from proper nouns are usually lowercased: *anglicize.* But: *Americanize.*

Capitalize the first letter after a colon only if what follows the colon is a clause, with subject and verb.

In poetry, capital letters are used for the first words of lines or phrases that would not be capitalized in prose. *See* **poetry.**

COMPOSITIONS: Capitalize the main words in the names of books, movies, plays, poems, songs, radio and television programs and works of art. Generally follow the rules under **headline capitalization.** *See* also **composition titles.**

TITLES: Capitalize formal titles immediately before a name. Lowercase formal titles used alone or in constructions that set them off from a name by commas. Lowercase terms that are job descriptions rather than formal titles.

See **academic titles; cabinet titles; legislative titles; military titles; religious titles;** and **titles.**

Capline It is the major U.S. crude-oil pipeline from St. James, La., to Patoka, Ill.

captain *See* **military titles** for military and police usage of the word and its abbreviation, *Capt.*

Lowercase and spell out in uses such as *team captain Drew Martin.*

C

carat, caret, karat
Carats are used to indicate the weight of diamonds and other precious stones. A *carat* is equal to 200 milligrams.
Carets are used by writers and editors to mark insertions.
Karats are used to indicate the proportion of pure gold used with other metals in alloys.

CARB *See* **California Air Resources Board.**

carbon steel The term applies to most steel produced in the world. Carbon steel relies on the carbon content for structure.

carbine *See* **weapons.**

cardinal *See* **Roman Catholic Church.**

CARE The acronym is acceptable in all references for Cooperative for American Relief Everywhere.

careen, career *Careen* literally means to tilt or be tilted, and the verb *career* means to move at high speed. But *careen* now is considered acceptable in both meanings.

carefree

caretaker

car maker, car makers

Carnegie Mellon University No hyphen.

car pool (n.), **car-pool** (adj and v.), **car pooling** (n. and v.)

carry forward (v.), **carry-forward** (n. and adj.)

carry over (v.), **carry-over** (n. and adj.)

cargo (oil) market Also called *the bulk market,* it involves volumes of oil of 18,000 metric tons and above, as opposed to *the bunker market,* which trades smaller volumes.

carry In the securities business, it is the difference between financing costs and a security's yield. Dealers can make a profit when the security they hold yields more than the cost of financing it in the overnight repurchase-agreement market; this is called *positive carry.* When the financing cost is greater than the yield, the *carry* is said to be *negative.*

carrier A *carrier* is a company that transports people or products or, in the case of the telecommunications industry, messages. The owners of goods being carried are *shippers.*

carrying charge The total cost of storing a physical commodity over a period of time is the *carrying charge.* It includes storage charges, insurance, interest and opportunity costs.

carryover In agriculture, *carryover* refers to the part of the current crop production that will be carried to the next crop year, or that part of current supplies of commodity comprising stocks from the previous crop year's production.

cartridge *See* **weapons.**

cash flow It is usually defined as *earnings plus depreciation allowances and other charges.* The *other charges* may include such things as deferred taxes and amortization of goodwill generated by mergers, plus or minus changes in working-capital accounts such as inventories, accounts receivable and accounts payable. Because the definition of cash flow varies among industries, always specify when providing a definition that varies from the norm: *Cash flow in the cable industry is defined as . . .*

Highly leveraged companies in real estate, mineral exploration, broadcast/communications and other operations report *cash-flow earnings* to indicate how well they can service their debt. Cash-flow earnings in this case are also known as *Ebitda,* or *earnings before interest, taxes, depreciation and amortization.*

See **future cash flows.**

Cash Management Account This is a Merrill Lynch trademark. Use *asset-management account* as the generic equivalent.

cash-management (Treasury) bills They are short-maturity bills that the Treasury occasionally sells because it expects its cash balances to be low for a number of days.

cash market The term is used by futures traders to refer to the regular cash-for-goods market, as opposed to their market.

cash on delivery Use *c.o.d.* in all references.

caster, castor

Caster is a roller.

Castor is a bean.

catalog, cataloged, cataloger, cataloging, catalogist

catchup, catsup Use *ketchup* instead.

Caterpillar A trademark for the brand of tractors and machinery made by Caterpillar Inc., of Peoria, Ill.

cathode It is a flat, rectangular piece of metal refined by electrolysis. Copper is commonly traded and delivered in cathode form.

Catholic, Catholicism Use *Roman Catholic Church, Roman Catholic* or *Roman Catholicism* in first reference to those Christians led by the pope in Rome. Use *Catholic* in subsequent references.

Other denominations that refer to themselves as Catholic include some high-church Episcopalians and members of Eastern Orthodox churches.

See **Roman Catholic Church.**

Caucasian

cave in (v.), **cave-in** (n. and adj.)

CB *See* **citizens' band radio.**

CBOT *See* **Chicago Board of Trade.**

CBS Corp. It and its divisions, *CBS News, CBS Radio and CBS-TV,* are owned by Viacom Inc., New York.

CD It can refer to a *compact disc,* the audio recording, or to the banking *certificate of deposit,* so use the abbreviation carefully.

CD-ROM It stands for *compact disc read-only memory.*

cease-fire, cease-fires (n. and adj.), **cease fire** (v.)

celebrant, celebrator

A *celebrant* is someone who conducts a religious ceremony, such as a Mass.

Celebrator is the better term for a reveler.

cellphone The short form for *cellular telephone* is one word, but *cellular phone* is two.

Celsius Use this term rather than *centigrade* for the temperature scale that is part of the metric system. The Celsius scale is named for Anders Celsius, a Swedish astronomer who designed it. In this scale, zero represents the freezing point of water, and 100 degrees is the boiling point of water at sea level.

To convert to *Fahrenheit,* multiply a Celsius temperature by 9, divide by 5 and add 32.

See **Fahrenheit.**

C

cement Cement is the powder that is mixed with water, sand or gravel to make concrete. Pavements, blocks and driveways are made of *concrete,* not cement.

censer, censor, censure

A *censer* is a container in which incense is burned.

To *censor* is to prohibit or restrict the use of something.

To *censure* is to condemn.

center (v.) A debate *centers on* politics, for example, *not around* politics. However, a debate can *revolve around* politics.

Centers for Disease Control and Prevention The normal form for first reference is *the federal Centers for Disease Control and Prevention,* which is treated as a singular entity despite the plural *Centers.* In later references, use *CDC,* not CDCP. Situated in Atlanta and run by the U.S. Public Health Service, the organization and its individual centers work with state health departments to provide specialized services.

centi-

See **metric system** for words not listed individually.

centigrade See **Celsius.**

centimeter One-hundredth of a meter, or 0.4 inch. There are 10 millimeters in a centimeter. To convert to inches, multiply by 0.4.

See **meter; metric system; inch.**

central bank A bank having responsibility for controlling a country's monetary policy.

Central European Free Trade Association The trade bloc comprises Bulgaria, Czech Republic, Hungary, Poland, Romania, Slovakia and Slovenia.

Central Intelligence Agency *CIA* is acceptable in second references.

Central Standard Time (CST), Central Daylight Time (CDT) *See* **time zones.**

cents Use: *five cents, 12 cents.* Don't use the cent sign, even in headlines. For amounts over a dollar: *$1.01.*

Numerals alone, with or without a decimal point, may be used in tabular matter.

See **dollars and cents.**

century Lowercase it, spelling out numbers less than 10: *the first century, the 21st century.*

For proper names, follow the organization's practice: *21st Century Insurance Co.*

CEO The abbreviation for *chief executive officer* is acceptable in second references and in headlines. *See* **chief executive.**

Ceylonese *Sri Lanka,* formerly Ceylon, should be used in datelines after a city name. Its people may be referred to as *Ceylonese* (n. or adj.) or *Sri Lankans. Sri Lanka* may be used as an adjective. The language is *Sinhalese.*

CFA franc It is the unit of currency for the *French African Community,* which comprises Benin, Burkina Faso, Central African Republic, Chad, Equatorial Guinea, Gabon, Ivory Coast, Mali, Niger, Senegal and Togo.

See **World Currencies appendix.**

CFTC *See* **Commodity Futures Trading Commission.**

cha-cha

chaebol The Korean word for a large conglomerate company, it should be italicized on the first reference in an article.

chain In retailing terminology, it is a number of stores, restaurants or the like owned or franchised by one company.

chain saw

chair Don't use as a verb or as a synonym for *chairman* or *chairwoman,* except in quoted matter.

chairman, chairwoman Capitalize the words as formal titles before names: *Chairman Graham Goble; Graham Goble, the chairman; Chairwoman Roberta Gardner; Roberta Gardner, the chairwoman.* But: *meeting chairman Brodie Martin.*

A woman is either a *chairwoman* or a *chairman,* depending upon which term her organization prefers. Don't use *chair* or *chairperson* for a woman or man, except in a quotation.

In corporate contexts, generally use *chairman* instead of *chairman of the board,* unless the article involved also refers to the *chairman of the executive committee.*

See **titles.**

chaise longue (not lounge)

It means *long chair.*

chancellor Capitalize it when it is used as a formal title before a name of the head of a government or school system: *Chancellor Barbara Martin; the chancellor.*

See **titles.**

changeable

changeover

change up (v.), **change-up** (n. and adj.)

channel Capitalize it when used with a number: *Channel 4, Channel 13, the channels.*

chapter Capitalize *chapter* when used with a numeral in reference to sections of a book or legal code: *Chapter 1, Chapter 11, the chapters.*

character, reputation

Character refers to moral qualities.

Reputation refers to the way a person is regarded by others.

charges *See* **profit terminology.**

charge off (v.) To write off as a bad debt.

charge-off (n. and adj.) The term refers to a loan that no longer is expected to be repaid and that is written off as a bad debt.

Charleston, Charlestown, Charles Town

Charleston is the name of the capital of West Virginia and of a port city in South Carolina.

Charlestown is a section of Boston.

Charles Town is the name of a small city in West Virginia.

Chase Manhattan Corp. Based in New York, it is the parent company of Chase Manhattan Bank.

chat room It is a World Wide Web site that enables computer users to send messages to one another in an online conversation.

chauffeur

Chechnya The people are Chechens.

check up (v.), **checkup** (n.)

Chevy The nickname for *Chevrolet.*

Chicago The city in Illinois stands alone in datelines.

Chicago Board of Trade It is the main U.S. exchange for trading some financial and commodity derivatives, including Treasury bonds, grains and the Dow Jones Industrial Average index futures. Use *CBOT* in headlines and on second reference in text.

C

Chicago Board Options Exchange *CBOE* is acceptable on second reference and in headlines.

Chicago Mercantile Exchange A futures market, it trades meat, livestock and currency futures, as well as S&P 500 index futures. *Merc* is acceptable in second reference, rather than the abbreviation *CME.*

Chicano, Chicanos Because it sometimes is considered derogatory, the term should be used only advisedly as an alternative for *Mexican-American.*

See **nationalities and races.**

chief

Capitalize as a formal title before a name: *He spoke to Police Chief J. Paul Goble. He spoke to Chief J. Paul Goble of the New York police.*

Lowercase when it is not a formal title: *union chief* Gregory Langan.

See **titles.**

chief executive officer For a company's top officer, *chief executive* is often sufficient. But use the full title in cases where *CEO* is to be used in second reference.

chief justice Capitalize only as a formal title before a name: *Chief Justice William Rehnquist.* The officeholder is the *chief justice of the U.S.,* not of *the Supreme Court.*

See **judge** and **U.S. Supreme Court.**

chief petty officer *See* **military titles.**

chief warrant officer

See **military titles.**

chili, chilies *Chili* applies to the pepper and to *chili con carne.*

China When used alone, it refers to the mainland nation. Use it in datelines and other routine references. Use *People's Republic of China, Communist China, mainland China* or *Red China* only in direct quotations.

For datelines on stories from the island of Taiwan, use the name of a community and *Taiwan.* In the body of a story, use *Nationalist China* or *Taiwan* for references to the government based on the island. Use the formal name *the Republic of China* when it is required for precision.

Chinese The people of China are *Chinese.* Avoid the term *Chinaman,* which is considered patronizing.

Chinese names For most Chinese place names and personal names, use the official Chinese spelling system known as Pinyin: *Zhu Rongji.* The Chinese usually give the family name first (*Zhu*) followed by the given (*Rongji*). Second reference should be the family name only: *Mr. Zhu, or Prime Minister Zhu.* Use these Pinyin spellings for former leaders: *Mao Zedong* and *Zhou Enlai.*

Use the traditional American spellings for *China, Inner Mongolia, Shanghai* and *Tibet* and for *Chiang-Kai-shek* and *Sun Yat-sen.*

Some Chinese have westernized their names, putting their given names first. In general, follow an individual's preferences. Chinese women don't normally take their husbands' surnames; for married women, generally use *Ms.* with the surname after the first reference.

chip In electronics, it is a sliver of silicon with electronic elements built in. It is also known as a *microprocessor.*

chitchat

chop suey

chow *Chow* and *Dog Chow* are Ralston Purina Co. trademarks for pet foods.

Christian Church (Disciples of Christ) This is the formal name, including the parentheses. All members of the clergy may be referred to as *ministers.* The term *pastor* is substituted if the individual leads a congregation. On first reference, use *the Rev.* before an individual's name. On subsequent references, use *Mr., Miss, Mrs.* or *Ms.* before the last name.

See **religious titles.**

Christian Science Church

See **Church of Christ, Scientist.**

Christmas, Christmas Day, Christmas Eve Don't abbreviate to *Xmas* or any other form.

Christmas Island Differentiate between the two islands with the name. One is Australian, in the Indian Ocean; the other is known as Kiritimati, part of Kiribati, in the central Pacific.

chromium It is a lustrous, hard and brittle metallic element, found primarily in chromite. Resistant to tarnish and corrosion, it is a primary component of stainless steel and is used to harden steel alloys.

church

Capitalize as part of the formal name of a building, a congregation or a denomination; lowercase in other uses: *St. Paul's Church, the Roman Catholic Church, the Catholic and Episcopal churches, a Roman Catholic church, a church.*

Lowercase in phrases where the church is used in an institutional sense: *He believes in separation of church and state. The pope said the church opposes abortion.*

See **religious titles** and the entry for the denomination in question.

Churches of Christ It comprises independent congregations that have no overall governing boards, headquarters or clergy titles.

churchgoer

Church of Christ, Scientist The terms *Christian Science Church* and *Churches of Christ, Scientist* are acceptable in all references.

The church does not have clergy in the usual sense. Either men or women may hold the three principal offices: *reader, practitioner* and *lecturer.*

Church of England

See **Anglican Communion.**

Church of Jesus Christ of Latter-day Saints Note the *Latter-day.* The church may be called the *Mormon Church* in most references, but include the formal name in articles dealing primarily with the church. Don't apply the term *Mormon* in reference to any polygamous groups or other splinter organization.

CLERGY: All faithful males over the age of 11 are considered members of the priesthood. The only formal titles are *president* for the head of the First Presidency, the church's policy-making body, *bishop* and *elder,* which includes missionaries. Capitalize these formal titles before a name on first reference; use *Mr.* with the last name on second reference. The terms *minister* or *the Rev.* aren't used.

See **religious titles.**

CIA Acceptable in second references for *Central Intelligence Agency.*

Cia. and Cie. Use instead of *Compania* and *Compagnie* in names of foreign companies.

See **foreign companies.**

c.i.f. A shipping-rate abbreviation for *cost, insurance and freight.*

CIF *See* **cost, insurance and freight.**

cigarette

C

Cincinnati The city in Ohio stands alone in datelines.

CIO Use the abbreviation sparingly in second reference to a *chief information officer.*
See **AFL-CIO.**

circuit breakers The New York Stock Exchange's *circuit breakers* are thresholds to control dramatic market drops. They are set this way as percentages of the Dow Jones Industrial Average:

If the average falls by 10% during one session, the exchange's trading is halted for an hour if the drop occurs before 2 p.m., and for half an hour if the drop occurs between 2 p.m. and 2:30 p.m. No halt in trading is triggered by declines after 2 p.m.

If the index falls by 20% during one session, trading is halted for two hours before 1 p.m., for one hour between 1 p.m. and 2 p.m., and for the rest of the day after 2 p.m.

If the index falls by 30% during one session, trading is halted for the day

See also **Dow Jones Industrial Average; program trading.**

C.I.S. *See* **Commonwealth of Independent States.**

Citgo Petroleum Corp. It is the U.S. unit of Petroleos de Venezuela SA, Venezuela's state oil company.

Citigroup Inc. Based in New York, it was formed by the merger of *Citicorp* and *Travelers Group.* Citigroup is also is the parent of *Salomon Smith Barney Inc.* and *Citibank.*

cities and towns *See* **datelines** for guidelines on when they should be followed by a state or country name.

Capitalize official names, including separate political entities such as *West Palm Beach, Fla.*

The preferred form for the section of a city is lowercase: *the west end, northern Los Angeles.* But capitalize widely recognized names for the sections of a city: *South Side* (Chicago), *Lower East Side* (New York).

Spell out the names of cities except short forms used in direct quotes or in a casual, feature context: *A trip to Las Vegas and Los Angeles,* but *"We're going to Vegas and L.A."* *See also* **city** and **datelines.**

citizen, subject, national, native

A *citizen* is a member entitled to full civil rights of a nation either by birth or by naturalization. Because cities and states in the U.S. do not confer citizenship, don't use *citizen* in referring to their residents.

Subject is technically used when the government is headed by a king or other sovereign.

National is applied to a person residing away from the country of which he is a citizen, or to a person under the protection of a specified nation.

Native applies to an individual born in the given location.

citizens' band radio *CB* is acceptable on second reference.

city Capitalize *city* as an integral part of a proper name: *Kansas City, New York City, Oklahoma City, Jefferson City.* Lowercase elsewhere: *a Texas city, the city government; the city Board of Education;* and *city of* phrases: *the city of Boston.* An exception is *City of London. See* **London.**

Capitalize when part of a formal title before a name: *City Manager Gregory Langan.* Lowercase when not part of the formal title: *city Health Commissioner David Maj.*

See **city council** and **governmental bodies.**

city commission *See* **city council.**

city council Capitalize it as part of a proper name: *the Lancaster City Council.*

Retain the capitalization if the reference is to a specific council but the context does not require the city name: *LANCASTER, Pa.—The City Council . . .* Later in the story: *The City Council, the council.* Use the formal names of bodies not known as city councils: *the Miami City Commission, the City Commission, the commission.* Use *city council* in a generic sense for plural references: *the Tampa and Miami city councils.*

city editor Capitalize as a formal title before a name.

See **titles.**

city hall

Capitalize specific references with or without the name of a city: *Philadelphia City Hall, City Hall.* Lowercase plural uses: *the Philadelphia and New York city halls.*

Lowercase generic uses: *You can't fight city hall.*

citywide

civil, criminal Civil cases are divided into *causes of action; criminal cases* are divided into *counts.*

Make it clear in articles whether the suit is civil or criminal. Especially if you use the word *charge* in reference to a civil case, specify "in a civil complaint."

Civil War

class *Class A stock, Class B stock.* But *the company's only class of stock.* Also, *Class A shares, Class B shares.*

class-action suit It is a lawsuit consolidating similar complaints from a large number of plaintiffs. It isn't filed as such, but a court can certify the plaintiffs' cases as a single *class-action suit.* Until it gets certification, it is a *potential* or *prospective class-action suit.*

clean oils The term applies to distillate products such as gasoline, naphtha, jet fuel, as opposed to *dirty oils,* such as other fuel oils or crude oil. The distinction is used to assess the suitability of using tankers for certain cargoes.

clean up (v.), **cleanup** (n. and adj.)

clear-cut

clerical titles *See* **religious titles.**

Cleveland The city in Ohio stands alone in datelines.

client/server computing The term applies to the sharing or distribution of data and processing power among computers on a local-area network. The "clients" typically are desktop personal computers that request applications, data or files from more powerful computers, the servers.

clientele

climactic, climatic

Climactic refers to a climax.

Climatic refers to the climate.

cloak-and-dagger

Clorox The bleach-brand trademark is held by Clorox Co. of Oakland, Calif.

closed-end investment company It operates an investment fund with a limited number of shares outstanding, unlike a mutual fund, which creates new shares to meet investor demand.

closedown (n.)

closed shop

A *closed shop,* set up by an agreement between a union and an employer, requires workers to be members of the union before they may be employed.

A *union shop* requires workers to join the union within a specified period after they are employed.

An *agency shop* requires that the workers who don't want to join the union pay the union a fee instead of union dues.

C

closely held Companies are considered *closely held* if their stock and voting control are concentrated in the hands of a few investors, but the shares are still traded to a limited extent.

close-up (n. and adj.)

cloture Use *cloture,* not closure, for the parliamentary procedure for closing debate in the Senate.

clue Not *clew.*

CNBC The primary owner of the financial-news television network is General Electric Co., which also owns the NBC television network. Articles in the Journal dealing with CNBC should include this: *Dow Jones & Co., which publishes The Wall Street Journal, co-owns CNBC television operations in Asia and Europe, and provides news content to CNBC in the U.S.*

co- Retain the hyphen when forming nouns, adjectives and verbs that indicate occupation or status:

co-author (don't use as a verb)

co-respondent (in a divorce suit)

co-pilot	co-chairman
co-defendant	co-host
co-signer	co-owner
co-star	co-partner
co-worker	

(Several are exceptions to Webster's New World.)

Use no hyphen in other combinations:

coed	cooperate
cooperative	coeducation
coequal	coordinate
coexist	coordination
coexistence	

Cooperate, coordinate and related words are exceptions to the rule that a hyphen is used if a prefix ends in a vowel and the word that follows begins with the same vowel. But use *co-op* as a short form for *cooperative* (to distinguish it from the word *coop*).

Co. *See* **company names.**

coach Capitalize it as a title before a name: *Coach Drew Martin.* If a further description of the individual's duties is included before the title: *head coach Drew Martin; third-base coach Dave Maj.*

See **titles.**

coarse grains This applies to all grains except wheat and rice. The most common coarse grains are corn, barley, sorghum, oats and rye.

coast Capitalize *coast* when it refers to general regions of the U.S.: *the Atlantic Coast states, a Gulf Coast city, the West Coast, the East Coast.* Don't capitalize *coast* when it refers to smaller regions: *the Virginia coast.* Capitalize *the Coast* only if the reference is to the West Coast.

coastal waters

See **weather terms.**

coast guard Capitalize it when it refers to the U.S. force: *the U.S. Coast Guard, the Coast Guard, Coast Guard policy.* Don't use the abbreviation *USCG.* Use lowercase for similar forces of other nations.

See **military academies.**

Coast Guardsman Capitalize it in all references to men in the U.S. Coast Guard. Lowercase *guardsman* when it stands alone.

See **military titles.**

coastline

coattails

COB *See* **California-Oregon border.**

cobalt The minor metal is used in batteries, chemicals and super-alloys, such as high-grade steel for the aeronautics industry. It is obtained mostly as a byproduct of nickel production.

Cobol A computer programming language, *Cobol* is an acronym for Common Business-Oriented Language.

coca, coco, cocoa, cacao *Coca* is a tropical plant that yields cocaine. *Coco* is a palm tree that bears coconuts. *Cocoa* is a chocolate drink, made from *cacao* beans.

Coca-Cola Co. Its products include *Coca-Cola, Coke, diet Coke and Coca-Cola Classic.*

cocaine The slang term *coke* should appear only in quoted matter.

c.o.d. Acceptable in all references for *cash on delivery,* or *collect on delivery.*

coed The term is outdated in the meaning of a woman student in a coeducational school. Avoid it except in quoted matter.

As an adjective to refer to an institution or activity involving both sexes, the term may be used with discretion: a *coed dormitory,* a *coed activity.*

Coffee, Sugar & Cocoa Exchange

See **New York Board of Trade.**

cogeneration It is the process of simultaneously producing two useful energy forms, normally electricity and heat, from the same fuel source. It differs from normal central-utility methods, in which the heat created as a byproduct of electricity production is wasted because there isn't any practical way to deliver the heat to the utility's customers.

cohort Although it originally meant a band of people, it now is commonly used to mean an individual companion or associate. Because its connotation is often negative, use *cohort* advisedly.

Cold War Capitalize the reference to the period of antagonism between the U.S. and the Soviet Union after World War II.

collar In commerce, it is a supply contract between a buyer and seller of a commodity, whereby the buyer is assured that he will not have to pay more than some maximum price, and the seller is assured of receiving at least a minimum price.

See **program trading.**

collateral Stock or other property that a borrower is obliged to turn over to a lender if he is unable to repay a loan.

collectible

collective nouns Many words such as *group, committee* and *variety* that denote collections of people normally take singular verbs and pronouns. But exceptions abound. The sense of the sentence should determine the choice, depending on whether unity or plurality is being stressed: *The variety of employees shows the company's diversity. A variety of incentives and bonuses are attracting top managers.*

With words like *variety, number* and *total,* a rule of thumb is to use a singular verb when the article *the* precedes the noun and a plural verb when the article *a* is used.

With percentages, the succeeding noun often suggests a singular or plural verb: *About 20% of profit comes from continuing operations. About 20% of employees are eligible for bonuses.*

See **couple.**

college Capitalize only when part of a proper name: *Dartmouth College; the college.*

See **organizations and institutions.**

collide, collision At least two objects must be in motion before they can *collide.* An automobile may hit a utility pole, but it doesn't *collide* with it—unless the pole is mounted on a moving truck.

colloquial The term means the informal use of the language in speech or writing. It is not local or regional in nature, as dialect is.

Webster's New World Dictionary identifies many words as colloquial with the label *Colloq.* The label itself, the dictionary says, "does not indicate substandard or illiterate usage." But words considered colloquial should be used with discretion.

See **slang.**

Colombia The country in South America.

colon (:)

It is often used at the end of a sentence to introduce lists, tabulations or texts. The colon also is used for emphasis: *He had an overriding interest: journalism.*

Use the colon in listings such as time of day (*8:31 p.m.*), biblical and legal citations (*2 Kings 2:11*) and in Q and A formats:

Q: What was your position at the time?

A: I was a vice president.

Capitalize the first word after a colon only if a clause, with a subject and verb, follows: *He promised this: The company will make good on all the losses.*

The colon is used instead of a comma to introduce *longer quotations* within a paragraph or at the end of paragraphs that serve as introductions to paragraphs of quoted material.

Colons go outside quotation marks unless they are part of the quotation itself.

colonel

See **military titles.**

colonies, colonial Capitalize the words when they refer to the British dependencies in America that declared their independence in 1776. Capitalize *Colonial* in reference to the architectural style of the time.

Colorado Abbreviate it as *Colo.* after city names. Residents are *Coloradans. See* **state names.**

colorblind

colored Referring to skin color, it is considered derogatory in the U.S., except in the formal name National Association for the Advancement of Colored People. In parts of Africa, *colored* is used to denote people of mixed racial ancestry. Use this non-British spelling and explain the usage.

See **African.**

Columbus Day It is observed the second Monday in October.

combat, combated, combating

comedian Use for both men and women.

Comex *Commodity Exchange Inc.*, a division of the *New York Mercantile Exchange,* trades futures in gold, silver and copper. Note that platinum and palladium are *Nymex,* not Comex, contracts. When referring to the entire New York precious metals futures complex, use *Nymex* to encompass the two exchanges, but when referring to gold, silver and copper futures, use *Comex.*

comma (,)

NO SERIAL COMMA: Commas are used to separate elements in a series, but the so-called serial comma isn't used before the concluding conjunction in a simple series: *friends, Romans and countrymen.*

But a comma should be used before the concluding conjunction to avoid ambiguities and in complex series of phrases: *Companies must consider whether they can meet the stiff requirements, whether they have the financial resources, and whether their boards will ultimately approve.*

See **semicolon** for cases when elements of a series contain an internal comma.

WITH ADJECTIVES: Use commas to separate adjectives if the commas could be replaced by the word *and* without changing the sense: *a pensive, deliberate manner; a pretty, springlike day.*

Use no comma when the adjective directly before a noun is an integral part of the noun: *a low-price mutual fund, a major auto maker.*

APPOSITION: Use a comma to set off words or phrases placed next to other words or phrases of definition or identity: *The chief justice, William Rehnquist, spoke at the session. The election, a yearlong event, ended that night.*

Use of a comma in some of these instances depends on the facts:

They ate dinner with their daughter, Julia, and her daughter Tess. (This implies that they have only one daughter and that she has more than one daughter.)

They ate dinner with their daughter Julia and her husband, Greg. (This implies that they have more than one daughter and that Julia has only one husband.)

INTRODUCTORY PHRASES: A comma is usually used after phrases that precede the main clause of a sentence, but it may be omitted after short introductory phrases.

WITH DIRECT QUOTES: Use a comma to introduce a complete, short quotation within a paragraph: *Mr. Klemmer said, "She spent six months in Argentina and came back speaking English with a Spanish accent."* But use a colon to introduce longer quotations. *See* **colon.** After direct quotes, use a comma before the attribution: *"Consult my library," Roberta Gardner suggested.*

WITH HOMETOWNS: Use a comma to set off an individual's hometown when it is placed in apposition to a name: *James Goble, Detroit, and Betty Firm, Lancaster, Pa., attended.* However, the use of the word *of* without a comma between the individual's name and the city name is generally preferable: *James Goble of Detroit and Betty Firm of Lancaster, Pa., were there.*

WITH GEOGRAPHICAL NAMES: *His journey will take him from Galway, Ireland, to Lansing, Mich., and back. The Selma, Ala., group saw the governor.* But with the possessive, the comma is omitted: *Selma, Ala.'s bonds* (which is better expressed as *the bonds of Selma, Ala.*).

Use parentheses rather than commas if a state name is inserted within a proper name: *the Huntsville (Ala.) Times.*

IN DATES: *May 14, 1932, was his date of birth.* But without a day: *May 1932 . . .*

IN DIRECT ADDRESS: The comma is required: *Travelers, beware of rough roads. Readers, take heed.*

IN LARGE FIGURES: Use a comma for most figures higher than 999. An exception: market averages and indexes of less than 100,000: *The Dow Jones Industrial Average closed that month at 10966.22.* Other exceptions: street addresses *(1234 Main St.);* broadcast frequencies *(1460 kilohertz);* room numbers; serial numbers; telephone numbers; and years *(2003).*

PLACEMENT: Commas always go inside closing quotation marks, whether they are single, double or both together.

PER-SHARE DATA: In presenting company financial data, an example: *In the company's first quarter, ended April 30, profit was*

$8.7 million, or 20 cents a share, after special charges.

See **semicolon** and **essential clauses, nonessential clauses.**

commander

See **military titles.**

commander in chief No hyphens. Capitalize it only if used as a formal title before a name.

See **titles.**

commercial paper Short-term obligations used by industrial or finance companies to obtain cash. The borrower agrees to pay back a specified amount on a given date. Commercial paper is sold through dealers in the open market or directly to investors by the major sales-finance companies. Chief buyers are large corporations, colleges, pension funds and insurance companies.

commission house It is a concern that buys and sells commodities or futures contracts for the accounts of clients, charging the clients commissions.

commissioner Do not abbreviate. Capitalize when used as a formal title. *See* **titles.**

committee *See* **congressional committees and subcommittees.**

commodity In a market sense, it is a product of mining or agriculture before it has undergone extensive processing. In a general sense, it is anything that is bought or sold.

commodity futures Contracts to buy or sell given amounts of individual commodities at given prices within specified periods.

Commodity Futures Trading Commission *CFTC* is acceptable in headlines and in second reference in text. The agency is the main regulatory body for U.S. futures markets. It was established by Congress in 1974 to administer the Commodity Exchange Act. It publishes the Commitments of Traders report every two weeks, containing data on traders' positions from the previous two weeks.

Common Agricultural Policy It is the price stabilization program of the European Union.

Common Market It was the predecessor to the European Union.

common stock, preference stock, preferred stock When other classes of stock are outstanding, the holders of *common stock* are the last to receive dividends and the last to receive payments if the corporation is dissolved. The company may raise or lower dividends on common stock as the company's earnings rise or fall. When *preference stock* or *preferred stock* is outstanding and company earnings are sufficient, fixed dividends are paid to holders of the preference and preferred stock. In case of liquidation, holders of preference stock (also called *prior preferred stock*) receive priority over holders of preferred stock, who, in turn, receive priority over holders of common stock.

Commonwealth, the Formerly the British Commonwealth, this association of sovereign states recognizes the British sovereign as its head. Some also recognize the sovereign as head of their states; others do not.

Commonwealth of Independent States It is the proper name for the organization founded in 1991 by the former republics of the Soviet Union. They are: Armenia (adjectival form, *Armenian*), Azerbaijan (*Azerbaijani*), Belarus (*Belarussian*), Estonia (*Estonian*), Georgia (*Georgian*), Kazakhstan (*Kazak*), Kyrgyzstan (*Kyrgyz*), Latvia (*Lat-*

vian), Lithuania (*Lithuanian*), Moldova (*Moldovan*), Russia (*Russian*), Tajikistan (*Tajik*), Turkmenistan (*Turkmen*), Ukraine (*Ukrainian*) and Uzbekistan (*Uzbek*).

communism, communist Lowercase *communism.* Capitalize *Communist* when referring to members or activities of the Communist Party.

See **political parties and philosophies.**

commutation

See **pardon, parole, probation.**

company names Consult the company, the company's annual report or Standard & Poor's Register of Corporations if in doubt about a formal name not listed below.

But if the company has more than four letters capitalized in any single word, arbitrarily capitalize only the first letter: *Legent Corp.*, not *LEGENT Corp.*

An exception is *USLife* for *USLIFE.*

Always abbreviate *Co., Cos., Corp., Inc., Ltd.*, with company names. Don't use the *Inc.* or *Ltd.* if it follows a *Co.* or *Corp.*

Always use *U.S.* instead of *United States* in company names.

Always use an *ampersand* instead of *and* in the names of companies, partnerships, stores and shops.

In company names containing a comma, the comma is dropped in short-form second references and headlines: *Goldman Sachs* for *Goldman, Sachs & Co.*

Drop punctuation marks or symbols that occur before the *Inc.* or *Co.*, such as the exclamation mark in *Yahoo! Inc.* and the question mark in *Guess? Inc.* This style rule doesn't affect marks or symbols in the middle of company names, such as the asterisk in *E*Trade.*

See **foreign-company names.**

comparable-store sales Also known as *same-store sales,* they are a more-reliable measure of a retailer's sales trends than total sales. While total sales account for sales in all of a company's stores, *comparable-store sales,* expressed as a percentage gain or decline, represent only the changes in sales at the stores currently in operation that were also operating a year earlier (or sometimes longer, depending on a company's definition). Major retailers report their monthly sales on the first Thursday of the following month.

compared to, compared with

Use *compared to* when the purpose is to liken dissimilar things, often fancifully: *He compared the stock market to a hockey game.*

Use *compared with* to express similarities or differences: *GM had sizable earnings, compared with a loss a year ago.*

compatible

complacent, complaisant

Complacent means self-satisfied.

Complaisant means eager to please.

complement, compliment

Complement denotes completing or something that is complete: *The ship has a full complement of sailors. The acquisition complements the company's business.*

Compliment is a verb or noun meaning praise: *The captain complimented the sailors. They showed no emotion as they listened to his compliments.*

component Avoid the word in favor of the word *part,* except when referring to parts being made into larger components.

compose, comprise, constitute

Compose means to create or put together. It is commonly used in both the active and passive voices: *Fifty states compose the U.S.; the U.S. is composed of 50 states.*

Comprise means to contain, to include all or embrace. Use it only in the active voice, followed by a direct object: *The U.S. comprises 50 states.* Don't say *The U.S. is comprised of 50 states.* Note that the whole comprises the parts, not vice versa.

C

Constitute, in the sense of form or make up, often is the best word if neither *compose* nor *comprise* seems to fit: *Fifty states constitute the U.S. A collection of animals can constitute a zoo.*

See **include.**

composite trading Among stocks that are listed on the New York and American stock exchanges, *composite trading* includes the transactions that took place not only on those exchanges but also on the five regional exchanges: the Boston, Chicago, Cincinnati, Philadelphia and Pacific exchanges. It also includes trading by Nasdaq market makers authorized to trade in Big Board and Amex issues.

Regular, or primary, trading on the New York and American exchanges closes at 4 p.m. Eastern time. But regular trading on the Pacific exchange continues until 4:50 p.m. Eastern time, on the Philadelphia Exchange until 4:15 and on the Chicago exchange until 4:30. Nasdaq market makers authorized to deal in NYSE and Amex issues can also trade the shares later than the 4 p.m. New York market close.

Thus, a stock can close at a given price in NYSE composite trading at 4 p.m. but still change significantly in price in later trading on the composite tape because of trading on the regional exchanges and trading by the Nasdaq market makers. The tape of composite trading thus technically ends at 6:35 p.m. but the Journal's stock tables use the "4 p.m. composite price" only. (Highlights of any trading after 4 p.m. are available to the staff on the Journal's Late-Trading Snapshot on the NewsNet intranet after 6:35 p.m. for inclusion in news articles.)

So-called *crossing sessions,* which continue on the NYSE until 5:15 p.m., can change the volume figures up to that time. In this trading, transactions must be at the 4 p.m. prices.

See **third market.**

composition titles The following applies to anthems, book titles, movie titles, play titles, poem titles, opera titles, song titles, television program titles, the titles of lectures and speeches, and works of art.

—Capitalize the principal words, including prepositions and conjunctions of four or more letters.

—Capitalize articles—*the, a, an*—and prepositions and conjunctions of fewer than four letters if they fall at the beginning or end of the title.

—Put quotation marks around all except the Bible and the names of books that are reference works.

EXAMPLES: *"The Star-Spangled Banner," "Time After Time," the NBC-TV "Today" program, the "CBS Evening News."*

Reference works: *Jane's All the World's Aircraft; Encyclopaedia Britannica; Webster's New World Dictionary.*

compound adjectives
See **hyphen.**

compound nouns If they aren't listed in this book or Webster's New World Dictionary, make them two words: *pocket phone.*

comprise
See **compose, comprise, constitute.**

Comptometer A trademark for an adding machine.

comptroller
See **controller.**

computer Categories of computers in descending order of computing power: supercomputer, mainframe, minicomputer, workstation, desktop, laptop, notebook and palmtop.

computer storage capacity *Kilo-*, *mega-*, *giga-* and *tera-* are prefixes used with *bit* or *byte* to measure capacities.

A *kilobyte* is 1,000 bytes; a *megabyte* is a million bytes; a *gigabyte*, a billion bytes; a *terabyte*, a trillion; a *petabyte*, a quadrillion; and an *exabyte*, a quintillion bytes.

For perspective, a novel may be about one *megabyte*, and the entire Library of Congress is 10 *terabytes* of information.

concrete
See **cement.**

condensate In the petroleum industry, it is a liquid hydrocarbon mixture defined either as ultra-light crude or natural gasoline. Australia, Indonesia, Malaysia, New Zealand, Thailand and the United Arab Emirates produce significant volumes.

Conference Board An independent business-research group.

confess, confessed Use the words carefully.
See **admit.**

Congo Its capital is Kinshasa. In datelines, give the name of the city followed by *Congo:*

KINSHASA, Congo—

In stories, use *the Congo* or *Congo* as the construction of a sentence dictates. It formerly was known as *Zaire.*

The *Republic of Congo*, a neighboring nation, has Brazzaville as its capital.

Congo River

Congress Capitalize *Congress* when it refers to the U.S. Senate and House of Representatives. Although *Congress* is sometimes used as a substitute for *the House,* it is more properly reserved for reference to the Senate and the House together.

Capitalize *Congress* also if referring to a foreign body that uses the term, or its equivalent in a foreign language, as part of its formal name: *the Argentine Congress, the Congress.*

See **foreign legislative bodies.**

Lowercase *congress* when it is used as a synonym for *convention* or in second reference to an organization that uses the word as part of its formal name: *the Congress of Racial Equality, the congress.*

congressional Lowercase unless part of a proper name: *congressional salaries, the Congressional Quarterly, the Congressional Record.*
See **Medal of Honor.**

congressional committees and subcommittees *The Senate Banking and Currency Committee, the Banking Committee, the committee, an Appropriations subcommittee.* But when a subcommittee has a proper name of its own: *the Senate Permanent Subcommittee on Investigations.*

congressman, congresswoman
See **legislative titles.**

Congress of Racial Equality *CORE* is acceptable on second reference.

Connecticut Abbreviate as *Conn.* after city names. Residents are *Connecticuters.*
See **state names.**

connote, denote
Connote means to suggest or imply something beyond the explicit meaning.

Denote means to give an explicit sign or definition.

consensus

conservative
See **political parties and philosophies.**

consortium The plural is *consortia.*

constitute
See **compose, comprise, constitute.**

C

constitution

Capitalize references to the U.S. Constitution: *He supports the Constitution.* When referring to constitutions of other nations or of states, capitalize only with the name of a nation or a state: *the French Constitution, the Massachusetts Constitution, the nation's constitution, the state constitution, the constitution.*

Lowercase in other uses: *the organization's constitution.*

constitutional Lowercase: *constitutional amendment.*

consulate Capitalize it with the name of a nation; lowercase without it: *the French Consulate, the U.S. Consulate, the consulate.*

consul, consul general, consuls general Capitalize the words when used as a formal title before a name. *See* **titles.**

consumer credit This refers to loans extended to individuals or small businesses, usually on an unsecured basis, providing for monthly repayment. It is also known as *installment credit* or *personal loans.*

consumer-price index A statistical measure of the average of prices of a specified set of goods and services purchased by wage earners in urban areas. Generally use the abbreviation *CPI* only in quoted or tabular matter.

See **cost of living.**

Consumer Product Safety Commission

Contac A trademark for a brand of decongestant capsule.

contagious

contemptible

contiguous The 48 states besides Alaska and Hawaii are referred to as the *contiguous U.S.*, rather than the continental U.S.

continent The seven continents, in order of their land size: Asia, Africa, North America, South America, Europe, Antarctica and Australia.

Capitalize *the Continent* and *Continental* only when using as synonyms for *Europe* or *European.* Lowercase in other uses such as: *the continent of Europe, the European continent, the African and Asian continents.*

continental Use *contiguous U.S.* rather than continental U.S. for the 48 states besides Alaska and Hawaii.

Continental Divide It is the ridge along the Rocky Mountains that separates rivers flowing east from those that flow west.

continental shelf, continental slope Lowercase. The *shelf* is the part of a continent that is submerged in relatively shallow sea at gradually increasing depths, generally up to about 600 feet below sea level.

The *continental slope* begins at the point where the descent to the ocean bottom becomes very steep.

continual, continuous

Continual means a steady repetition: *The merger has been the source of continual litigation.*

Continuous means uninterrupted, steady, unbroken: *The rainfall that day was continuous.*

contractions Negative verbs are contracted whenever possible: *didn't* instead of *did not.* (Exceptions are made in cases such as formal declarations.) The contractions help prevent errors where *not* is accidentally dropped or typed as *now.* But avoid awkward contractions such as *mayn't.*

Generally avoid positive contractions, especially those such as *he's* that can have two meanings (*he is* or *he has*).

When using an apostrophe with a pronoun, as in a quotation, double-check to be sure that the meaning calls for a contraction: *you're, it's, who's,* rather than a possessive: *your, its, whose.*

contrasted to, contrasted with

Use *contrasted to* when the intent is to assert without the need for elaboration that two items have opposite characteristics: *He contrasted the appearance of the house today to its ramshackle look last year.*

Use *contrasted with* when indicating that two or more items are being juxtaposed to illustrate similarities or differences: *He contrasted the Republican platform with the Democratic platform.*

See **compared to, compared with.**

control, controlled, controlling

controller This is generally the proper term for financial officers of businesses and for other positions such as air-traffic controllers.

Comptroller is generally the accurate term for government financial officers: *the comptroller of the currency, the state comptroller.*

Capitalize *comptroller* and *controller* when used as the formal title before a name. Use lowercase otherwise.

See **titles.**

controversial An overused word; try to avoid it.

convention

Capitalize it as part of the name for a specific national or state political convention: *the Democratic National Convention, the Republican State Convention.*

Lowercase it in other uses: *the national convention, the state convention, the convention, the annual convention of the American Medical Association.*

convertible bond Holders of these bonds may exchange them for a set number of the issuing company's shares at a predetermined price. Because the bond has a call option on the company's equity, a *convertible bond* carries a much lower interest rate than traditional debt and is therefore a cheap way for a company to raise debt financing.

See also **call** and **options.**

convict (v.) Follow it with the preposition *of,* not *for: He was convicted of murder.* Don't use the term in referring to a verdict in a civil suit.

convince, persuade

Convince may be followed by an *of* phrase *(The company convinced him of his importance)* or a *that* clause *(The company convinced him that he should quit).* But it should *not* be followed by a *to* infinitive *(The company convinced him to quit).*

Persuade, however, is acceptable in all three usages.

cookie In computer lingo, a *cookie* is a file stored on a hard drive that contains information about an individual computer user. The file becomes available to a server as the user connects to a Web site.

cooperate, cooperative But *co-op* as a short form of *cooperative.*

Cooperative for American Relief Everywhere

See CARE.

coordinate, coordination

Coordinated Universal Time This term has replaced Greenwich Mean Time for the world standard, with the advent of more-accurate atomic clocks.

See **time zones.**

C

cop A colloquialism for a police officer, it is often better avoided except in quoted matter.

Copenhagen The capital of Denmark stands alone in datelines.

copper It is the benchmark base metal on the London Metal Exchange. It is widely used in the construction and electronics industries.

copper cake It is a byproduct of electrolytic zinc refining, usually containing a fair amount of cobalt.

copter The short form for *helicopter* is acceptable as a noun or adjective.

copydesk

copy editor *See* **titles.**

copyright (n., v., adj.) It entails the exclusive rights of artists, authors, composers, publishers and others to the contents of pieces of work, protecting them from plagiarism or imitation.

The disclosure was made in a copyright story.

Use *copyrighted* only as the past tense of the verb: *He copyrighted the article.*

co-respondent The term for a third party in a divorce action has a hyphen.

Corn Belt The region in the north-central Midwest where much corn and cornfed livestock are raised. It extends from western Ohio to eastern Nebraska and northeastern Kansas.

corporation An entity that is treated as a person in the eyes of the law. It is able to own property, incur debts, sue and be sued.

Abbreviate as *Corp.* in the names of companies and government agencies.

See **company names.**

corps Capitalize when used with a word or a figure to form a proper name: *the Marine Corps, the Signal Corps.*

Capitalize when standing alone only if it is a shortened reference to *U.S. Marine Corps.*

The possessive form is *corps'* for both singular and plural: *one corps' location, two corps' assignments.*

corral, corralled, corralling

Corsica Use instead of *France* in datelines on stories from communities on this island.

Cortes The Spanish parliament.

See **foreign legislative bodies.**

cost and freight A commodity quoted *C&F* includes the cost of shipment from its origin, but excludes insurance.

cost of living The amount of money needed to pay taxes and to buy the goods and services deemed necessary to make up a given standard of living, taking into account changes that may occur in tastes and buying patterns.

The term often is treated incorrectly as a synonym for the *consumer price index,* which does not take taxes into account and measures only price changes, keeping the quantities constant over time.

Hyphenate when used as a compound modifier: *The cost of living went up, but he didn't receive a cost-of-living adjustment.*

See **consumer price index.**

cost, insurance and freight The seller assumes those costs when a price is quoted *CIF.* Other costs, such as customs and tariffs, are either assumed by the buyer or negotiated separately.

Cotton Belt The region in the South and Southeastern sections of the U.S. where much cotton is grown.

council, councilor, councilman, councilwoman The terms refer to meetings and those who meet.

See **legislative titles.**

Council of Economic Advisers A group of advisers who help the U.S. president prepare his annual economic report to Congress and recommend economic measures to him.

counsel, counseled, counseling, counselor, counselor-at-law

To *counsel* is to *advise.*

A *counselor* is one who advises.

A *counselor-at-law* is a lawyer.

See **lawyer.**

counter- The rules in **prefixes** apply. Practically all combinations are without hyphens.

Some examples:

counteract	counterrevolution
counteroffer	countermove
countercharge	counterspy

countryside

county

Capitalize it when it is part of a proper name: *Dade County, Fla., Lancaster County, Pa.*

Capitalize the full names of county governmental units: *the Dade County Commission, the commission; the Lancaster County Commissioners, the commissioners.*

Capitalize *county* as part of a formal title before a name: *County Manager John Smith.* Lowercase when it is not part of the formal title: *county Health Commissioner Frank Jones.*

Avoid *county of* phrases where possible, but when necessary, always lowercase: *the county of Westchester, N.Y.*

Lowercase plural combinations: *Westchester and Rockland counties.*

Apply the same rules to similar terms such as *parish.*

See **governmental bodies.**

county court In some states, a *county court* is the administrative body of the county and is presided over by a "county judge" who is not a judge in the traditional sense but the chief administrative officer of the county. The terms should be explained if they are not clear in the context.

coup d'etat *Coup* is usually sufficient. It connotes a successful overthrow. *Putsch, uprising* or *rebellion* is preferred in reference to a coup that hasn't succeeded.

couple When used in the sense of two people, *couple* takes plural verbs and pronouns: *The couple were married Saturday and left Sunday on their honeymoon. They will return in two weeks.*

In the sense of a single unit, use a singular verb: *Each couple was asked to give $10.*

couple of The *of* is necessary. Never use *a couple tomatoes* or a similar phrase. The phrase takes a plural verb in constructions such as: *A couple of tomatoes were stolen.*

coupon *See* **loan terminology.**

course numbers Use Arabic numerals and capitalize the subject when used with a numeral: *History 6, Philosophy 209.*

court decisions Use figures and a hyphen: *The Supreme Court ruled 5–4, a 5–4 decision.* The word *to* is not needed. *See* **numbers.**

courtesan, courtier

A *courtesan* is a mistress of a man of wealth or nobility.

A *courtier* is an attendant at a royal court or an inveterate flatterer.

courtesy titles *See* **Mr., Mrs., Miss, Ms.**

C

courthouse Capitalize with the name of a jurisdiction: *the Lancaster County Courthouse, the U.S. Courthouse.* Lowercase in other uses: *the county courthouse, the courthouse, the federal courthouse.*

Court House is used in the proper names of some communities: *Cape May Court House, N.J.*

court-martial, court-martialed, courts-martial.

court names Capitalize the full proper names of courts at all levels.

Retain capitalization if *U.S.* or a state name is dropped: *the U.S. Supreme Court, the Supreme Court, the Massachusetts Superior Court, the state Superior Court, the Superior Court, Superior Court.*

For other federal courts: *Second District Court, Eighth U.S. Circuit Court of Appeals.* Be sure to provide the location, whether or not you use the full formal name: *The federal district court in Tallahassee, Fla.*

For additional details on federal courts, see **judicial branch** and separate listings under **U.S.** and the court name.

See **judge** for guidelines on titles before the names of judges.

Court of St. James's Note the *'s*. It is the formal name for the royal court of the British sovereign. Derived from St. James's Palace, the former scene of royal receptions.

courtroom

cover up (v.), **coverup** (n. and adj.) *He tried to cover up the scandal. He was prosecuted for the coverup.*

crackerjack, Cracker Jack The capitalized trademark represents a glazed popcorn.

crack up (v.), **crackup** (n. and adj.)

cracking, cracker

In the petroleum industry, *cracking* is a refining process used to break down the heavier components of crude oil into lighter products, increasing the yield of value-added and higher-priced light products.

A *cracker* is a secondary refining unit.

crash In the stock market, it refers to a precipitate decline in prices, usually accompanied by a sharp decline in economic activity.

credit ratings *See* **bond ratings.**

Credit Suisse First Boston *CSFB* is acceptable in second reference to the unit of Credit Suisse Group of Zurich.

credit-worthy, credit-worthiness

crescendo It is an *increasing* or a *buildup.* Don't use it to mean a loud point or climax.

criminal

See **civil, criminal.**

crisis, crises

crisscross

criterion, criteria

Croatia The people are *Croats.* The adjective is *Croatian.*

cross-examine, cross-examination

cross-eye (n.), **cross-eyed** (adj.)

crossover (n. and adj.)

cross trade It is a broker's offsetting match of the buy order of one customer against the sell order of another, or the match of a trade made by a broker with that of his customer. The practice is legal only if the broker first offers the security or commodity publicly at a price higher than the bid.

crude oil A mixture of mostly hydrocarbon compounds pumped from the Earth's crust, *crude oil* is the raw material in the oil refining. With a sulfur content of less than 1.5%, it is called *sweet crude;* with 1.5% sulfur or more, it is *sour crude.* Saudi Arabia is the world's largest crude-oil producer.

CSX Corp. The railroad and container-shipping company is based in Richmond, Va.

cuckoo clock

cult Because of its pejorative overtones, generally avoid using the word in reference to specific groups except in an attributed quotation.

cumulative voting In elections of some corporate directors: Each share has as many votes as there are directors to be elected, and holders may distribute these votes as they wish.

cup Equal to eight fluid ounces. The approximate metric equivalent is 240 milliliters, or 0.24 liter.

To convert to liters, multiply by 0.24.

See **liter.**

cupful, cupfuls

cure-all

currencies

See **World Currencies appendix.**

currency

See **foreign money.**

currency depreciation, currency devaluation A nation's money *depreciates* when its value falls in relation to the currency of other nations or in relation to its own prior value.

A nation's money is *devalued* when its government deliberately reduces its value in relation to the currency of other nations.

When a nation *devalues* its currency, the goods it imports become more expensive, while its exports become less expensive abroad and thus more competitive.

See **revalue.**

current assets

See **assets.**

curtain raiser

Cusip number An identifying number for securities, it stands for *Committee on Uniform Securities Identifying Procedures.*

customs Capitalize *U.S. Customs Service,* or simply *the Customs Service.* Lowercase elsewhere: *a customs official; he went through customs.*

cut back (v.), **cutback** (n. and adj.) *He cut back his son's allowance. The cutback date is Monday.*

cyberspace The term, popularized by William Gibson in the novel "Neuromancer," refers to the digital world of computer networks. *Cyber-* prefixes in general are overused.

cyclone *See* **weather terms.**

Cyclone It is a trademark for a brand of chain-link fence.

cynic, skeptic

A *cynic* is a disbeliever.

A *skeptic* is a doubter.

czar Use this spelling, not *tsar.* Lowercase except before the name of a former Russian ruler: *Czar Boris, the czar; the energy czar.*

Czech Republic Its capital is Prague.

Dd

Dacron It is a trademark for a brand of polyester fiber.

Dada, Dadaists Capitalize references to the art movement.

DaimlerChrysler AG The German auto company's U.S. headquarters is in Auburn Hills, Mich.

dalai lama The *dalai lama* is the traditional high priest of Lamaism, a form of Buddhism practiced in Tibet and Mongolia. The *dalai lama* is a title rather than a name, but it is used alone when referring to the man. Capitalize in references to the holder of the title: *The Dalai Lama spoke to the gathering.*

Dallas The city in Texas stands alone in datelines.

dam Capitalize it when it is part of a proper name: *Hoover Dam.*

damp (v.) When the economy or whatever is being checked or cooled, it is *damped,* as a furnace is damped—not *dampened.*

Danish pastry

Dardanelles, the Not *the Dardanelles Strait.*

Dark Ages The period from the sack of Rome in A.D. 476 to the end of the 10th century. This period in Europe was characterized by intellectual stagnation, widespread ignorance and poverty.

dark horse

dash (—) Dashes can be used to mark an abrupt change in thought in a sentence or an emphatic pause: *GM offered a plan—it was termed unprecedented—to raise revenue.*

Use a dash before an author's or composer's name at the end of a quotation: *"Who steals my purse steals trash."—Shakespeare.*

USE IN DATELINES: *NEW YORK—The city is facing a crisis.*

IN TICKOFFS: Dashes are often used instead of bullets or numbers to introduce individual items in a list. Capitalize the first word following the dash in these cases, whether or not it starts a sentence: *The company provided several reasons for its action:*

—Its revenue has been falling.

—It is considered a takeover target.

—It needs to raise additional funds.

data A plural noun, it takes plural verbs and pronouns.

databank, database

datelines Datelines on articles should contain a city name, entirely in capital letters, followed in most cases by the name of the state, country or territory where the city is situated, in caps and lowercase.

U.S. DATELINES: The cities below should stand alone, without state designations, in datelines, headlines and articles. Factors influencing the selection include the population of the city and its metropolitan region and the uniqueness of its name.

ATLANTA	MILWAUKEE
BALTIMORE	MINNEAPOLIS
BOSTON	NEW ORLEANS
CHICAGO	NEW YORK
CINCINNATI	OKLAHOMA CITY
CLEVELAND	PHILADELPHIA
DALLAS	PHOENIX
DENVER	PITTSBURGH
DETROIT	ST. LOUIS
HOLLYWOOD	SALT LAKE CITY
HONOLULU	SAN ANTONIO
HOUSTON	SAN DIEGO
INDIANAPOLIS	SAN FRANCISCO
LAS VEGAS	SEATTLE
LOS ANGELES	WASHINGTON
MIAMI	

Articles from all other U.S. cities should have both the city and the state name in the dateline, including *KANSAS CITY, Mo.*, and *KANSAS CITY, Kan.*

Spell out *Alaska, Hawaii, Idaho, Iowa, Maine, Ohio, Texas* and *Utah.* Abbreviate others as listed in this book under the full name of each state.

Use *Hawaii* on all cities outside Honolulu. Specify the island in the text if needed.

FOREIGN CITIES: These locations outside the U.S. stand alone in datelines, articles and headlines:

AMSTERDAM	BERLIN
BEIJING	BONN
BRASILIA	MONACO
BRUSSELS	MONTREAL
BUCHAREST	MOSCOW
BUDAPEST	NEW DELHI
BUENOS AIRES	OSLO
COPENHAGEN	OTTAWA
DUBLIN	PARIS
FLORENCE	PRAGUE
FRANKFURT	QUEBEC
GENEVA	RIO DE JANEIRO
GIBRALTAR	ROME
GUATEMALA CITY	SAN MARINO
THE HAGUE	SHANGHAI
HAVANA	SINGAPORE
HONG KONG	STOCKHOLM
JERUSALEM	TEL AVIV
KUWAIT CITY	TOKYO
LISBON	TORONTO
LONDON	VATICAN CITY
LUXEMBOURG	VENICE
MACAO	VIENNA
MADRID	WARSAW
MEXICO CITY	ZURICH
MILAN	

Use UNITED NATIONS alone, without an *N.Y.* designation, in articles from U.N. headquarters.

CANADIAN DATELINES: Datelines on articles from Canadian cities other than Montreal, Ottawa, Quebec and Toronto should contain the capitalized city followed by the name of the province in capitals and lowercase. Do not abbreviate any province or territory name.

OTHER CITIES: Stories from cities outside the U.S. that do not stand alone in datelines should contain the name of the country or territory.

CHOICE OF NAMES: In most cases, the name of the nation in a dateline is the conventionally accepted short form of its official name: *Argentina,* for example, rather than *Republic of Argentina.* (If in doubt, look for an entry in this book. If none is included, follow Webster's New World Dictionary.)

Special cases:

Instead of *United Kingdom,* use *England, Northern Ireland, Scotland* or *Wales.*

For divided nations, use the commonly accepted names: *North Vietnam, South Vietnam,* after city names. Use the full names in headlines as well.

Use the article with *El Salvador* and some island chains. Don't use the article with *Ivory Coast.*

Some overseas territories and other areas that aren't independent nations nevertheless have commonly accepted identities used in datelines. Examples:

Bermuda	Martinique
Corsica	Puerto Rico
Faeroe Islands	Sardinia
Greenland	Sicily
Guadeloupe	Tibet
Guam	

dateline selection

For relatively short articles that *do not take bylines,* use the dateline of the city where the company is based or the action is occurring. (But company briefs do not take datelines.)

For articles *with bylines or byline boxes,* don't use a dateline unless at least one of the byline reporters was reporting in the city. *See* **bylines.**

A reporter's presence in the dateline city to report the story is required in byline articles. If there is any doubt about this, an editor should err on the conservative side by dropping the dateline.

Articles assembled from several cities by a number of reporters normally carry no datelines or individual bylines at the top of the article, but a byline box or a credit line *A Wall Street Journal News Roundup.* Such articles may contain wire-service material, with appropriate credit.

When a wire-service article is used, the dateline contains the appropriate logo followed by a dash, as *NEW YORK (AP)—.*

See **bylines** and **taglines.**

dates Always use Arabic figures, without *st, nd, rd* or *th.*

See **months** for examples and punctuation guidelines.

daughter-in-law, daughters-in-law

Daughters of the American Revolution *DAR* is acceptable on second reference.

day-care center

daylight time

Capitalize it when linking the term with the name of a time zone: *Eastern Daylight Time,* or *Central, Mountain or Pacific Daylight Time.*

Lowercase *daylight-saving time* (note the hyphen and the singular *saving*) and *daylight time* whenever it stands alone. But uppercase the abbreviation without points: *EDT, CDT, MDT, PDT,* after the first reference to a given time zone.

A federal law specifies that daylight time applies from 2 a.m. on the first Sunday of April until 2 a.m. on the last Sunday of October in areas that do not specifically exempt themselves.

daylong

days of the week Don't abbreviate them, except when necessary in tabular matter.

See **time element.**

daytime

day to day, day-to-day Hyphenate the construction as a compound modifier before a noun: *They have extended the contract on a day-to-day basis.* But: *The terms are enforced day to day.*

day trading It refers to the establishing and offsetting of the same futures-market position within one day, or the buying and selling of a security in a single day.

D-Day It was June 6, 1944, the day the Allies invaded France at Normandy in World War II. By extension, it is any major turning point.

DDT Use in all references for the insecticide *dichloro diphenyl trichloroethane.*

de- The rules in **prefixes** apply. Do not hyphenate unless the base word begins with an *e* or with a capital letter: *decode, deactivate, de-emphasize, de-Stalinization.*

dead center

dead end (n.), **dead-end** (adj.) *The company reached a dead end, with many dead-end jobs.*

Dead Sea Scrolls

deadweight tonnage It refers to a ship's capacity to carry cargo.

deaf Don't apply the term to those who are simply *hard of hearing.*

deal Use the noun cautiously, as it can connote connivance.

dealer *Dealers,* as opposed to *brokers,* act as principals in transactions, buying and selling for their own accounts.

See **broker, brokerage** entry.

dean

Capitalize it only as a formal title before a name: *Dean John Madeira.*

dean's list *He is on the dean's list. She is a dean's-list student.*

deathbed (n. and adj.)

debenture *See* **loan terminology.**

debt In the context of the securities markets, it refers to *bonds, notes, mortgages* and other *debt instruments,* or forms of paper showing amounts owed.

See **equity.**

debtholders

debt ratings *See* **bond ratings.**

debut Its use as a verb has become acceptable: *The show debuts on Saturday.* But avoid the verb forms *debuting* and *debuted.* Use *opening* or *opened* or the like instead.

decades Use Arabic figures to indicate decades of history. Use an apostrophe to indicate numerals that are left out: show plurals by adding the letter "s": *the 1890s, the '90s, the Gay '90s, the 1920s, the mid-1930s.*

December *See* **months.**

decimals Use figures for numbers that contain decimals: *5.3 shares of stock, 0.2 share of stock.* Note the the use of "0" if no other digit appears before the decimal point. But: a *.22-caliber rifle.*

See **dollars and cents.**

decimate It originally referred to the killing of every 10th man, as the Romans did to punish mutinous legions. The meaning has since been broadened to refer to any large-scale destruction, principally of lives.

Deepfreeze It is a trademark for a brand of home freezer. Use two words for an extended postponement: *The plan is in the deep freeze.*

default It refers to a failure to meet a financial obligation or payment of principal or interest when due. It also refers to a breach of the terms of a note or mortgage.

defendant

defense Don't use it as a verb.

defense attorney Always lowercase and don't abbreviate.

See **attorney** and **titles.**

Defense National Stockpile Center This Virginia-based section of *the Defense Logistics Agency* buys and sells commodities from stockpiles maintained for strategic purposes.

defense spending *Military spending* is usually the more precise term.

deferred charges Expenditures that aren't directly applicable to an accounting period, although they may have been made in that period. These expenditures are carried to the balance sheet as a temporary asset and written off against future revenue.

deficit A *deficit* or loss *widens* or *narrows.* Don't use *increase* or *decline* or the like to describe a deficit.

See **profit terminology.**

deflation A decline in the general level of prices for goods and services. It is the opposite of inflation. *Disinflation,* by comparison, is the *slowing* of price increases.

defuse, diffuse

Defuse means to remove the fuze from an explosive devise, or generally to make harmless or less harmful.

Diffuse means to scatter, or as an adjective scattered or long-winded.

degrees *See* **academic degrees.**

deity Lowercase.

See **gods and goddesses** and **religious references.**

Delaware Abbreviate as *Del.* after a city name. Only Rhode Island is smaller in area. Residents are *Delawareans.*

See **state names.**

delegate The formal title applies to members of the lower houses of some legislatures. Capitalize the word only before their names.

See **legislative titles.**

Lowercase in other uses: *convention delegate Eric Martin.*

delivery (of futures contracts) Generally, *delivery* refers to the change of ownership or control of a commodity under terms established by the exchange on which the contract is traded. The commodity ordinarily must be placed in an approved warehouse, precious-metals depository or other storage facility for inspection, after which the facility issues a receipt or due bill that becomes a transferable *delivery instrument.* After receiving the delivery instrument, the new owner typically has these choices: take possession of the physical commodity; deliver the instrument into the futures market to offset a short position; or sell the instrument.

Delmarva Peninsula The peninsula between Chesapeake Bay and the Atlantic Ocean consists of Delaware and parts of Maryland and Virginia.

Delta Air Lines

demagogue Not *demagog.*

democrat, democratic, the Democratic Party, the party

See **political parties and philosophies.**

D

Democratic Governors' Conference Note the apostrophe.

Democratic National Committee In second reference: *the committee* is preferable to the abbreviation *DNC.*

demolish, destroy Both mean to do away with something completely. Something cannot be partly *demolished* or *destroyed.* It is redundant to say *totally demolished* or *totally destroyed.*

demurrage charge It is the fee for holding a vessel or freight car longer than the time allotted for loading or unloading.

denote

See **connote, denote.**

Denver The capital of Colorado stands alone in datelines.

depart *He will depart from La Guardia Airport.* Don't drop the preposition.

departments The federal government departments as we refer to them are: *Agriculture Department; Commerce Department; Defense Department (the Pentagon* is acceptable in second references and headlines); *Department of Energy (DOE* is acceptable in second references and headlines); *Education Department; Department of Health and Human Services (HHS* is acceptable in second references and headlines); *Department of Housing and Urban Development (HUD* is acceptable in second references and headlines); *Interior Department; Justice Department; Labor Department; State Department; Department of Transportation (DOT* is acceptable in second references and headlines); *Treasury Department;* and *Department of Veterans Affairs.*

Lowercase *department* in plural uses, but capitalize the proper-name element: *the Labor and Justice departments.* A shorthand reference (in a quotation only) to the proper-name element is capitalized: *The president said, "State and Justice must resolve their differences."* But: *Colin Powell, the secretary of state; Ann Veneman, the agriculture secretary.*

In *the Treasury,* referring to the Treasury Department, *Treasury* is capitalized, just as *the Pentagon* is: *The decision was made by the Treasury secretary, Paul O'Neill.* Lowercase *the department* whenever it stands alone.

Don't abbreviate *department* in any usage, except in graphics where space is limited. *See* **academic departments.**

dependent (n. and adj.)

depletion It is the gradual exhaustion of a natural resource. The *depletion allowance* is a reduction in taxable income based on a formula for excluding any return of capital from the proceeds of natural-resource operations.

depositary receipt

See **American depositary receipt.**

depreciation In finance, it is the amortization of fixed assets, such as plants and equipment, so as to allocate the cost over their depreciable life. It reduces taxable income.

In economics, it is the wearing out of capital goods, such as plant and equipment, through use and over time.

In the foreign-exchange market, it is the weakening in value of a currency against another currency in free trading.

See **amortization** and **devaluation, revaluation.**

depression Capitalize *Depression* and the *Great Depression* when referring to the worldwide economic slump that began with the stock-market collapse of Oct. 28–29, 1929, and continued through most of the 1930s.

Lowercase *depression* in other uses.

deputy Capitalize as a formal title before a name.

See **titles.**

de rigueur It is *fashionable* to spell it correctly.

derivative A financial contract whose value is designed to track the return on stocks, bonds, currencies or some other benchmark. *Derivatives* fall into two broad categories—*forward*-type contracts and *option*-type contracts—and may be listed on exchanges or traded privately.

OTC derivatives are those that are transacted "over-the-counter," or off organized exchanges, and usually by telephone. A *swap* is a forward-type derivative contract in which two parties agree to exchange streams of payments over time according to a predetermined rule. In an *interest-rate swap,* one party agrees to pay a fixed interest rate in return for receiving a floating interest rate from another party. An *equity-index swap* may involve swapping the returns on two different stock-market indexes, or swapping the return on a stock index for a floating interest rate.

derivative suit It is a suit brought by a shareholder for the benefit of the mutual fund or corporation rather than himself. If damages are assessed, they go to the corporation or fund and not to the shareholder.

-designate Hyphenate: *chairman-designate.* Capitalize only the first word if used as a formal title before a name.

See **titles.**

desktop

See **computer.**

destroy, demolish Both mean to do away with something completely. Something cannot be partly *demolished* or *destroyed.* It is redundant to say *totally demolished* or *totally destroyed.*

detective Don't abbreviate. Capitalize before a name only if it is a formal rank.

See **titles.**

detente

Detroit The city in Michigan stands alone in datelines.

deutsche mark The German currency usually is called simply the *mark.*

devaluation, revaluation; depreciation, appreciation The two sets of terms refer to movements in currencies. Use *depreciation* and *appreciation* to describe changes in currency exchange rates that occur among freely trading currencies, such as the dollar and yen, through trading in the foreign-exchange market. *Devaluation* and *revaluation,* describing official changes in currency-exchange rates or exchange-rate targets, are possible only for currencies whose exchange rates central banks control or target. *Devaluation* means the currency adjustment causes it to lose buying power against other currencies. *Revaluation* causes the currency to gain buying power against other currencies.

devil But capitalize *Satan.*

Dexedrine It is a trademark for *dextroamphetamine sulfate.*

dialect It is language peculiar to a region or a group, usually in matters of pronunciation or syntax. Avoid using dialect in quoted matter unless it is clearly pertinent to a story, because it can imply the speaker's usage is substandard or illiterate.

dialogue

diarrhea

Dictaphone It is a trademark for a brand of dictation recorder.

dictionary For spelling, style and usage questions not covered in this stylebook, consult Webster's New World Dictionary, Fourth College Edition. If it provides different spellings in separate entries (*tee shirt* and *T-shirt*, for example), use the spelling that is followed by a full definition (*T-shirt*). If it provides definitions under two different spellings for the same sense of a word, either use is acceptable.

See **geographic names.**

die-hard (n. and adj.)

diesel fuel It is a middle distillate often known as *No. 2* or *heating oil.*

Diet Generally use *the Japanese parliament* instead, in references to the body.

See **foreign legislative bodies.**

diet Coke, diet Pepsi But *Diet-Rite* soft drinks.

dietitian Not *dietician.*

different It usually takes the preposition *from,* not *than.* The exceptions involve cases where *than* introduces a condensed clause: *English in America is spoken with a different accent than in England.* This is a simpler way of saying: *English in America is spoken with an accent different from the one spoken in England.*

differ from, differ with

To differ from means to be unlike.

To differ with means to disagree.

diffuse *See* **defuse, diffuse.**

diffusion indexes They compare the number of survey participants reporting increases with the number who say conditions were unchanged or reporting decreases. They don't measure the magnitude of the changes. Formulas for computing diffusion indexes can vary. The U.S. National Association of Purchasing Management and its regional groups use diffusion indexes in surveys of business activity. The Federal Reserve Bank of Philadelphia uses them in its periodic surveys of regional business.

digital video disc *DVD* is acceptable on second reference. It is similar to a CD-ROM, but able to hold more music, video or data.

dilemma It means more than a problem. It implies a choice between two unattractive alternatives.

diluted earnings Companies are required to report a figure for earnings per share on a *basic* basis as well as on a *diluted* basis. The *diluted basis* is calculated on the highest number of common shares that would be outstanding if certain convertible issues were converted into common. Use the *diluted* figure in articles, as it is the more-conservative measure of earnings. When a company reports a loss, the *diluted* and *basic* per-share figures should normally be the same.

See earnings per share in the **profit terminology** entry.

dimensions Use numerals and spell out inches, feet, yards, etc., to indicate *depth, height, length* and *width.* Hyphenate adjectival forms before nouns.

EXAMPLES: *He is 5 feet 6 inches tall; the 5-foot-6-inch man; the 5-foot-6 man; the 5-foot man; the basketball team signed a 7-footer. The car is 17 feet long, 6 feet wide and 5 feet high. The rug is 9 feet by 12 feet; the 9-by-12 rug. The storm left 5 inches of snow on the ground.*

Diners Club Use no apostrophe, in keeping with the practice the company has adopted for its public identity. Only its incorporation papers still read *Diners' Club.*

diocese Capitalize as part of a proper name: *the Diocese of Rochester, the Rochester Diocese, the diocese.*

See **Episcopal Church** and **Roman Catholic Church.**

dip (n. and v.) It refers to a decline followed by a rise. It isn't a synonym for decline.

direct foreign investment

See **balance of payments** *(capital account).*

direct-reduced iron Made from iron ore by removing the oxygen, it is a feedstock in the steelmaking processes.

directions and regions In general, lowercase *north, south, northeast, northern,* etc., when they indicate compass direction; capitalize these words when they designate regions.

DIRECTIONS: *The car drove west on the turnpike. The storm is moving east.*

REGIONS OF THE U.S.: *The cold front that developed in the Midwest is spreading eastward. It will bring showers to the East Coast by morning and to the entire Northeast later in the day. The Western states won't be affected. The teacher has a Southern accent, although she is a Northerner. Eastern nations are opening their doors to Western businessmen.*

REGIONS ABROAD: Capitalize political entities and commonly used names: *Northern Ireland, South Vietnam, the South Pacific, Western Europe, Eastern Europe, Southeast Asia.* But: *southern France, eastern Canada.*

WITH STATES AND CITIES: Usually lowercase the compass points when they describe a section of a state or city: *western Pennsylvania, southern Atlanta.* But capitalize them in referring to widely known sections: *Southern California, Northern California, the South Side of Chicago, the Lower East Side of New York.* If in doubt, use lowercase.

director The formal title for the individuals who head *the Federal Bureau of Investigation* and *the Central Intelligence Agency.* Capitalize when used immediately before their names or those of others for whom *director* is a formal title: *former FBI Director J. Edgar Hoover.* Most uses of *director,* however, involve an occupational description not capitalized in any use: *company director David Maj.*

See **titles.**

directors In corporations, they are usually *nominated* by the chairman to stand to be *elected* by stockholders at the annual meeting, or they are *named* or *appointed* by the chairman to fill an empty seat or an unexpired term.

dirty oils

See **clean oils.**

dis- Solid: *dismember, dissemble, disservice, dissuade, dissymmetry.*

disability, disabled The terms are preferred in reference to physical or mental conditions that once were described as *handicaps.*

disburse, disperse

Disburse means to pay out.

Disperse means to scatter.

disc, disk

Use *disc* as the industry does in references to a phonograph record, *compact disc, videodisc* and *disc jockey.* Also use *disc* in *disc brakes* and *disc harrows.*

Use *disk* in references to the computer storage devices *floppy disks* and *hard disks,* as well as in references to *spinal disks.*

discount

In finance, the term can mean:

The difference between a bond's current market price and its face or redemption value.

The manner of selling securities such as Treasury bills, which are issued at less than face value and redeemed at face value.

The relationship between two currencies. *The French franc sells at a discount to the dollar.*

If the stock market has already taken into account the benefit of a company's introduction of a new product, for instance, the news is said to have been *discounted.*

The method whereby interest on a bank loan or note is deducted from the selling price.

The reduction in the selling price of merchandise or a percentage off the invoice price in exchange for quick payment.

discount rate It is the rate of interest charged by the Federal Reserve on loans it makes to banks and other depository institutions. The *discount rate* has an influence on the rates the institutions then charge their customers.

discount window It refers to the system the Federal Reserve uses to lend reserves to commercial banks.

discreet, discrete

Discreet means prudent, circumspect: *"I'm afraid I was not very discreet," she wrote.*

Discrete means detached, separate: *There are four discrete sounds from a quadraphonic system.*

diseases Don't capitalize *arthritis, emphysema, leukemia, malaria, migraine, pneumonia,* etc. But: *Bright's disease, Parkinson's disease,* etc.

disinflation It is the slowing of price increases. It usually occurs during a recession, when retailers are unable to pass higher prices along to consumers. By comparison, *deflation* is an actual *decline* in price levels.

disinterested, uninterested

Disinterested means impartial, which is usually the better word to convey the thought.

Uninterested means that someone lacks interest.

disintermediation It refers to the withdrawal by savers of their deposits in financial intermediary institutions, such as banks and savings-and-loan associations, for the purpose of direct investment in debt securities, such as U.S. Treasury bills. It occurs in varying degrees when rates of return on direct investments rise above rates paid on savings deposits.

disk

See **disc, disk.**

diskette It is a synonym for *floppy disk.*

disk operating system A set of programs for IBM-compatible computers that control communications between computer components. *DOS* is acceptable on second reference. *MS-DOS* is the Microsoft version.

Disney Walt Disney Co., based in Burbank, Calif., operates the ABC Television Network, the Disneyland theme park in California, Walt Disney World in Florida and produces motion pictures.

dispel, dispelled, dispelling

disposable personal income The income that a person retains after deductions for income taxes, Social Security taxes, property taxes and other payments such as fines and penalties to various levels of government.

Disposall It is a trademark for a type of mechanical garbage disposer.

dissociate Not *disassociate.*

distillate fuel, distillates The umbrella groupings refer to home-heating oil and diesel fuel, the so-called middle of the barrel in the refining process.

district Always spell it out. Capitalize it when forming a proper name: *the Second District.*

district attorney Don't abbreviate it. Capitalize it as a formal title before a name: *District Attorney Greg Langan.* Use *DA* (no periods) only in quoted matter.

See **titles.**

district court

See **court names** and **U.S. District Court.**

District of Columbia Abbreviate it as *D.C.* when the context requires that it be used in conjunction with Washington. Spell it out when *District of Columbia* is used alone. *The district,* rather than *D.C.,* should be used in subsequent references.

ditto marks They can be made with quotation marks, but their use in newspapers, even in tabular material, is confusing. Don't use them.

dive, dived, diving Not *dove* for the past tense.

divest It takes the preposition *of.* A company doesn't *divest* a unit, it *divests itself of* a unit.

dividend Corporations distribute *dividends* on a per-share basis to stockholders as a return on their investment, usually on a quarterly, semiannual or annual basis. When reporting a dividend, also report the *payment date* (the date on which the company will distribute the dividend to shareholders) and the *record date* (the cutoff date for determining the shareholders who will receive the dividend).

A *stock dividend* usually is expressed as a percentage. A *10% stock dividend* means a holder of 100 shares receives 10 additional shares as a dividend.

See **profit terminology.**

division A corporate *division* normally is a wholly owned operation of a parent company with all the departments necessary to operate independently of the parent. Lowercase *division* in corporate uses: *the Chevrolet division of General Motors.*

divorce, divorcee Avoid the terms as nouns applied to individuals. If marital status is clearly relevant, simply state the man or woman *is divorced* or *has been divorced*—or that his or her marriage *ended in divorce.*

Dixie cup It is a trademark for a paper drinking cup.

DNA It may stand alone in references to *deoxyribonucleic acid,* the cell matter that contains the genetic code.

DNS It stands for *domain name system,* an international network of Internet domain servers, names and addresses.

doctor The abbreviation *Dr.* should be used in second reference as a title before the names of those who are generally called doctor in their professions in the U.S.: *Presenting the paper was Monica Goble, a cardiologist. Dr. Goble is affiliated with the Medical College of Virginia.*

If appropriate in context and if the individual desires it, *Dr.* is thus used after the first reference before the names of individuals who hold Ph.D.s and other doctoral degrees. Holders of Ph.D.s in the academic world, for example, often prefer to be called *doctor.* It usually isn't necessary to specify that the degree is a Ph.D., M.D. or other degree. But because the public tends to identify *Dr.* with physicians, if the individual's specialty isn't clear in context, mention it as quickly as possible.

In a general academic context, for instance, in reference to a liberal-arts professor who holds a Ph.D. in education or history, it usually is sufficient to call the individual either *Dr.* or *Prof.,* without specifying the degree he or she holds. But if it is relevant in a scientific context, say whether the Ph.D. holder's field is anatomy, for instance, or botany. Thus: *Dr. Pauling, a chemist; Dr. Watson, a biologist; Dr. Goble, a cardiologist; Dr. Wenger, a chiropractor; Dr. Madeira, an optometrist.*

The Rev. Martin Luther King Jr. on subsequent references is *Dr. King.*

Generally, try to establish the person's preference for using the title. Unless you know the person has a doctorate or other qualifying degree that he or she prefers to use, use *Mr., Miss, Mrs.* or *Ms.*

If the individual's only doctorate is an honorary one, do not use *Dr.,* except in a quotation. Lawyers, despite their J.D. degrees, aren't called *doctor.*

In general references to M.D.s, it is more precise to use *physicians* rather than *doctors.* The phrase *doctors and dentists,* for instance, would better be *physicians and dentists.*

dollar-cost averaging It is the systematic purchasing of fixed dollar amounts of securities, rather than fixed numbers of shares, at regular intervals. The dollars thus buy more shares when the price is low and fewer shares when the price is high.

dollars and cents *Five cents, 12 cents*; but *$5, $12.* Also, *$100,000, $10.2 million, $10.22 billion, $10.223 trillion.* Dollar figures are generally rounded off as above—to one decimal place for millions, two decimal places for billions and three for trillions—instead of using the exact figure. But the precise figures can be used when necessary, to differentiate between two nearly identical sums, for example, and in bond-page stories.

Use unrounded figures for precision in calculating percentage changes—such as the increase or decrease in a company's profit.

Use a singular verb with specified dollar amounts: *He said $400,000 is being spent on the project.*

It is permissible to use such forms as: *a million-dollar sale.*

Don't use *c* or a *cent sign* for cents, even in headlines.

Don't use hyphens between dollar figures and the word *million* or *billion.*

See **stock prices.**

domain name In a Web-site address, it is what appears directly after the @ sign. It includes a suffix defining *.com* for commerce, *.edu* for education, *.gov* for government, *.org* for organization and *.non* sometimes for individuals.

See **DNS.**

domino, dominoes

door to door, door-to-door Hyphenate when used as a compound modifier: *He is a door-to-door salesman.* But: *He went door to door.*

DOS

See **disk operating system.**

do's and don'ts

dot-com As a noun or adjective, it refers to companies that do business mainly on the Internet.

doughnut Not *donut,* except in proper names.

Douglas fir

dove A bird. The past tense of *dive* is *dived.*

Dow Jones & Co. It publishes The Wall Street Journal and its international and online editions, Barron's and SmartMoney magazines and other periodicals, Dow Jones Newswires, Dow Jones Indexes and the Ottaway group of community newspapers. Dow Jones is co-owner with Reuters Group of Factiva and with NBC of the CNBC television operations in Asia and Europe. Dow Jones also provides news content to CNBC and radio stations in the U.S.

Dow Jones Industrial Average The stock-market indicator comprising 30 of the leading issues. Editors of The Wall Street Journal administer it. Always use the full term on first reference in stories. On subsequent references, use *Dow industrials, industrials* or *blue chips.* Use *the Dow* and *the DJIA* sparingly in text and headlines.

-down Follow Webster's New World. Some examples, all nouns or adjectives:

breakdown	countdown
rundown	sitdown

All are two words when used as verbs.

down- The rules in **prefixes** apply, meaning no hyphen.

Some examples:

downswing	downgrade
downtown	downtrend
downtime	

Down East Use only in reference to Maine, and make the reference clear in context.

download The term refers to copying a file from one computer to another.

down payment *Down* is an adjective, not a prefix, in this case.

downplay Avoid it in favor of *play down.*

downsize It is a euphemism. Use *retrench* or the like instead.

downstate Lowercase: *downstate New York.*

Down syndrome Not *Down's,* for the chromosomal disorder first reported in 1866 by J. Langdon Down.

downtick

See **program trading.**

Down Under It refers to Australia, New Zealand and environs.

Dr.

See **doctor.**

draft beer Not *draught beer.*

dragon bonds They are debt securities issued in Asia that target investors in the region outside Japan. Debt is usually issued in U.S. dollars but may also be issued in other major currencies.

DRAM The acronym stands for *dynamic random access memory.* Provide the definition.

drama

See **composition titles.**

Dramamine It is a trademark for a brand of motion-sickness remedy.

dramatic, dramatically Use the words sparingly. Price increases, for instance, aren't *dramatic.* Generally, words like *marked, substantial* or *unexpected* are preferred.

Drambuie It is a trademark for a brand of Scottish liqueur.

Dripolator It is a trademark for a brand of drip coffeemaker.

drive *See* **addresses.**

drive-in (n.)

drop out (v.), **dropout** (n.)

D

drought

drowned, was drowned If a person suffocated in water or other liquid, the individual *drowned.* Saying that someone *was drowned* implies that another person caused the victim to drown.

Dr Pepper The trademark has no period after *Dr* for the brand of soft drink.

Drug Enforcement Agency *DEA* is acceptable in second reference.

drugs Because the word *drugs* has come to be used as a synonym for narcotics in recent years, the word *medicine* is frequently the better term to specify that an individual is taking medication.

drugstore

drunk, drunken

Drunk is the adjective used after noun: *He was drunk.*

Drunken is the adjective used before nouns: a *drunken driver, drunken driving.*

dry-clean (v.), **dry cleaning** (n.), **dry-cleaning** (adj.)

DSL It stands for *digital subscriber line,* and it is used for high-speed access to the Internet over the telephone network.

Dublin The Irish capital stands alone in datelines.

due-diligence meeting In the securities business, officials of an entity that is issuing securities meet with members of the syndicate distributing the securities to discuss the terms of the issue, contents of a prospectus and the final agreement between the parties.

In acquisitions, a *due-diligence meeting* is held to let an acquiring company look at a target's books as a condition of the pending deal.

due to Many consider it substandard to use *due to* except in an adjective sense: *His absence was due to illness. Absence* is the modified noun. Not: *He was absent due to illness,* which uses *due to* adverbially.

duel It is a contest between two people. Three people or entities cannot duel.

duffel Not *duffle.*

duke, duchess

See **nobility.**

dumb For a person who is *mute,* or *cannot speak,* the term is considered pejorative.

dumping In international trade, it is the selling of a product in a foreign market at a price lower than in the domestic price.

Dumpster It is trademark for a large metal trash bin.

DuPont Co. Use this rather than the longer name for E.I. du Pont de Nemours & Co. Most members of the family spell the surname *duPont.*

durable goods They are products such as machinery and household furnishings that are considered useful for at least three years.

duration In the debt-securities market, it refers to the average number of years it takes to receive the interest and principal from a bond or portfolio of bonds. The cash flows are discounted to present value based on current interest rates. Longer durations have greater sensitivity to interest-rate changes.

Duration is a more precise measurement than *maturity,* which considers only the principal payment.

See **maturity.**

dust storm *See* **weather terms.**

Dutch auction It is so called because, as in flower auctions in the Netherlands, the sellers set prices that they will accept. Traditionally, the prices are lowered until the sellers sell all the flowers they want to sell.

In the U.S. corporate world, a *Dutch-auction tender offer* is used by a company that wants to buy back a large number of shares from holders in a shorter time than it legally could on the stock markets (and with less risk of running up the price). The company states the number of shares it will buy during a stipulated period, just as in a conventional tender offer. But instead of stating a single purchase price, the company sets a price range within which stockholders can tender their shares. The highest price within that range necessary to acquire all the shares the company wants becomes the purchase price for all the shares.

Dutch/Holland
See **Netherlands.**

Dutch oven, Dutch treat, Dutch uncle

DVD It stands for *digital video disc* (or *digital versatile disc*). It is a disc for recording images, sound or data. It is similar to a CD-ROM, but more versatile.

dyeing, dying
Dyeing refers to changing colors.
Dying refers to death.

Ee

e- The prefix *e-* stands for *electronic* and refers to Internet business transactions. The constructions, such as *e-business, e-tickets* (for airline trips), *e-banking, e-commerce* and *e-tailing,* have become hackneyed, so use them sparingly.

each It takes a singular verb when it is the subject of a clause: *Each of the companies is contributing to the effort.* But when *each* comes after a plural subject, it doesn't govern the verb: *The companies each are contributing to the effort.*

each other, one another Two people walk with *each other.* More than two walk with *one another.*

Either phrase may be used when the number is indefinite: *We help each other. We help one another.* For the possessive, *each other's possessions.* Not *each others' possessions.*

eager

See **anxious.**

earl, countess

See **nobility.**

earmark

earnings

See **profit terminology.**

earth Generally lowercase it, but capitalize it when referring to it as a planet: *The pattern applies to Mars, Jupiter and the Earth. The astronauts returned to Earth. He tries to move heaven and earth.*

See **planets.**

earthquakes The National Earthquake Information Service operated by the U.S. Geological Survey in Golden, Colo., keeps records on earthquakes.

Magnitudes are calculated from ground motion recorded on seismographs. The scales in use are all similar, so it is usually unnecessary to mention the scale. The Richter Scale is no longer widely used. Instead, list magnitudes simply as *magnitude 5.8,* for example.

A quake of magnitude 2.5 is the smallest normally felt by humans; 4 can cause moderate damage; 5, considerable damage; 6 to 7, heavy damage and 8 tremendous and widespread damage.

OTHER TERMS: The word *temblor* (not *trembler*) is a synonym for earthquake.

The word *epicenter* refers to the point on the Earth's surface above the underground center, or focus, of an earthquake.

east, eastern

See **directions and regions.**

Easter, Easter Sunday, Easter egg, Easter lily

E

Eastern Hemisphere The half of the Earth made up primarily of Africa, Asia, Australia and Europe.

Eastern Orthodox churches These include the Greek Orthodox Church, the Russian Orthodox Church and the Orthodox Church in America, which don't recognize papal authority over them. Their national or archdiocese leaders have the title *metropolitan* or *patriarch.* Other clergy are *archbishops, bishops, priests* and *deacons.* Use *the Rev.* in first reference to priests and *Father* in subsequent references. Use *Deacon* before the name of a deacon in all references. Archbishops are either *the Rt. Rev.* or *the Most Rev.* in second reference.

See **religious titles.**

Eastern Rite churches The term applies to Catholic churches organized along ethnic lines. They recognize the authority of the pope but have considerable autonomy. A married man may be ordained, but marriage is not permitted after ordination.

See **Roman Catholic Church.**

Eastern Shore A region on the east side of Chesapeake Bay, including parts of Maryland and Virginia.

Eastern Shore is *not* a synonym for *East Coast.*

Eastern Standard Time (EST), Eastern Daylight Time (EDT)

See **time zones** and **daylight-saving time.**

Eastman Kodak Co. *Kodak* is acceptable on second reference and in headlines.

easygoing

Ebita, Ebitda

Ebita stands for earnings before interest, taxes and amortization.

Ebitda stands for *earnings before interest, taxes, depreciation and amortization.* It is a pretax income figure reported by highly leveraged companies to indicate their ability to service their debt.

See **cash flow** and **profit terminology.**

ECN

See **electronic communications network.**

E. coli This abbreviation is acceptable in all references for *Escherichia coli,* a bacterium that contaminates food and water.

ecology It refers to the relationship between organisms and their surroundings. It isn't synonymous with *environment,* which refers to conditions affecting organisms.

economics Use singular verbs and pronouns when *economics* means the *science* but plural ones when it means *financial considerations* or *economically significant aspects* (an exception to Webster's New World Dictionary): *Economics is the dismal science. The economics of our business aren't what they used to be.*

Ecuador, Ecuadorean

editor Capitalize *editor* before a name only when it is an official corporate or organizational title. Don't capitalize as a job description.

See **titles.**

editorial, news In references to a newspaper, reserve *news* for the news department, its employees and news articles. Reserve *editorial* for the department that prepares the editorial page, its employees and articles that appear on the editorial page or pages.

editor in chief Don't use hyphens. Capitalize when used as a formal title before a name: *Editor in Chief Horace Greeley.*

See **titles.**

EEA
See **European Economic Area.**

EEOC
See **Equal Employment Opportunity Commission.**

effect
See **affect, effect.**

EFTA
See **European Free Trade Association.**

e.g. The abbreviation represents the Latin words *exempli gratia,* meaning *for example.*

Eglin Air Force Base, Fla. Not *Elgin.*

either Use it to mean *one or the other,* not *both.* For example: *There are arguments on both sides.* Not: *There are arguments on either side.*

either . . . or, neither . . . nor The nouns that follow do not constitute a compound subject; they are alternative subjects and require a verb that agrees with the nearer subject. *Neither they nor he is going. Neither he nor they are going.*

El Al Israeli Airlines An *El Al airliner* is acceptable in any reference.

elderly The terms *elderly* and *senior citizen* aren't appropriate to refer to anyone under 65 and shouldn't be used casually to refer to anyone of any age. If possible, provide the person's age instead. *Elderly* may be used, however, to refer to the demographic group: *health care for the elderly.*

-elect Always hyphenate and lowercase: *President-elect Langan.*

Election Day

Electoral College But *electoral vote(s).*

electrical, electronic *Electronic* suggests a flow of electrons through semiconductor or other field, so the term applies to devices such as computers that aren't simply *electrical.*

electrical steel It is steel that includes silicon. The silicon content allows the steel to minimize energy loss during electrical applications.

electric power grid It is a complex system of electric power lines and substations that support delivery of electricity generated by linked power plants. The U.S. has three separate grids joined by transmission lines: one serves west of the Rocky Mountains, another serves east of the Rockies, and the third serves most of Texas.

electrocardiogram *EKG* is acceptable on second reference.

electronic communications network An *ECN* is a screen-based order-matching system through which individuals and institutions can trade securities directly without a market maker or floor specialist as intermediary. The largest is Instinet Corp., which trades primarily Nasdaq stocks.
See **after-hours trading.**

ellipsis (...) It consists of three periods and is placed flush between two words, without open spaces.

If a period or other punctuation follows the ellipsis, attach the mark without leaving a space. Avoid overusing the ellipsis in quotations; paraphrasing is usually the better alternative.

El Nino, La Nina *El Nino* is the warm (and frequently wet) weather system originating in the southern Pacific that affects weather conditions in the Americas. The name means *Christ child* in Spanish; Peruvian fishermen gave it the name when they first noticed the event around Christmas 1982.

E

La Nina, meaning little girl, is applied to a phenomenon in which tropical waters in the Pacific Ocean turn unusually cold, affecting weather patterns.

El Salvador The use of the article in the name of this nation helps to distinguish it from its capital, *San Salvador.* Use *Salvadoran(s)* in references to citizens of the nation.

e-mail This is acceptable in first reference to electronic mail or an electronic message. Related electronic terms such as *e-commerce* and *e-shopping* are acceptable, but avoid overusing them.

embargo It is any restriction on trade. It is usually applied to goods entering or leaving a country.

See **boycott.**

embarrass, embarrassment

embassy

An *embassy* is the official residence of an ambassador in a foreign country and the office that handles the political relations of one nation with another.

A *consulate,* the residence of a consul in a foreign city, handles the commercial affairs and personal needs of citizens of the appointing country.

Capitalize with the name of a nation; lowercase without it: *the French Embassy, the U.S. Embassy, the embassy.*

See **consulate.**

emcee, emceed, emceeing A colloquial verb and noun best avoided.

emerging markets The term refers to economies that are making a transition to market economics from state control or shelter. Use the plural form, for an *emerging market* also can mean a developing industry sector such as artificial intelligence in computer software.

Avoid the term *emerging nations* because those newly adapting to market economics usually have long been sovereign states.

emeritus To indicate retired professors and others, *emerita* is sometimes used for women, but *emeritus* is usually used for both: *David Maj, emeritus professor of philosophy. Professor emeritus* is also acceptable.

emigrate, immigrate One who leaves a country *emigrates* from it. One who comes into a country *immigrates.*

The same principle holds for *emigrant* (*emigre*) and *immigrant.*

Emmy, Emmys The annual awards by the Academy of Television Arts and Sciences.

emoticon Also known a *smiley face,* it is a typographical symbol used to indicate mood or appearance, as :-), often appearing sideways.

Empirin A trademark for a brand of aspirin compound.

employee

Employee Stock Ownership Plans Known as *ESOPs,* the plans provide tax advantages when companies give shares to their employees. Under the plans, a trust is created, and banks make loans to the trust to buy the company's stock. As the company makes payments to the trust to retire the debt, the trust allocates the stock to employees.

employment report The Labor Department's employment report, usually released on the first Friday of the month, is considered the first official look at U.S. economic activity in the preceding month. Critical components are the *civilian unemployment rate, nonfarm payrolls, average hourly earnings* and *factory workweek.*

empty-handed

enact
See **adopt, approve, enact, pass.**

encyclopedia But follow the spelling of the formal names: *Encyclopaedia Britannica.*

ended, ending Use *ended* to refer to a financial period in the past. Use *ending* to refer to a current or future financial period: *the quarter ended* [last] March 31; the *quarter ending* [next] Sept. 30.

enforce But *reinforce.*

England, English
See **datelines** and **United Kingdom.**

English muffin, English sparrow, English setter

enormity It denotes wickedness or outrageousness in addition to size.
Use *enormousness* to mean great size alone.

Enovid A trademark for a brand of oral contraceptive. It may also be called *norethynodrel with mestranol.*

enquire, enquiry The preferred words are *inquire, inquiry.*

enroll, enrolled, enrolling

en route Always two words.

ensign
See **military titles.**

ensure, insure, assure
Use *ensure* to mean guarantee: *Steps were taken to ensure accuracy.*
Use *insure* for references to insurance: *The policy insures his life.*
Use *assure* in referring to people: *I assured him of my loyalty.*

enthuse A back formation from *enthusiasm* that is generally frowned upon. Use the verb only in quotes.

entitle, title
Use *entitle* when a *right* is involved: *Employees were entitled to two weeks' vacation.*
Use *title* to mean *to give a title to: They titled the magazine SmartMoney.*

E

envelop, enveloping, enveloped (v.), **envelope** (n.)

environment See ***ecology.***

Environmental Protection Agency *EPA* is acceptable on second reference.

envoy It is not a formal title. Lowercase it.
See **titles.**

epicenter The point on the Earth's surface above the underground center, or focus, of an earthquake.
See **earthquakes.**

epidemiology

Episcopal Church The term is acceptable in all references to the *Protestant Episcopal Church,* the U.S. component of the Anglican Communion.

Its clergy comprises *bishops, priests, deacons* and *brothers.* A priest who heads a parish is a *rector* rather than a pastor. The term *minister* is seldom used. In first reference to bishops, use the word before the individual's name: *Bishop James Paul Goble. The Rt. Rev.* is an alternative title for U.S. bishops. In first references, use *the Rev.* before the name of a priest. In second reference to a male priest, use *Father* before the last name unless the individual prefers *Mr.* For second reference to a woman priest, use *Miss, Mrs.* or *Ms.* before the woman's last name, depending on her preference.

See **Anglican Communion** and **religious titles.**

Episcopal, Episcopalian Use *Episcopalian* only as a noun referring to a member of the Episcopal Church: *He is an Episcopalian.* The adjective *Episcopal* is capitalized to refer to the church.

equal adjectives
See **comma.**

Equal Employment Opportunity Commission *EEOC* is acceptable on second reference.

equal, equaled, equaling

Equal Rights Amendment *ERA* is acceptable on second reference if the context is clear.

equator Always lowercase it.

equipment trust certificates Debt instruments that carriers use to finance the purchase of equipment with the equipment as collateral.

equity When used in a financial sense, *equity* means the value of property beyond the amount that is owed on it. In the context of the securities markets, it refers to the stock-ownership interest of shareholders.
See **debt.**
A *stockholder's equity* in a corporation is the value of the shares he holds. A *homeowner's equity* is the difference between the value of the house and the amount of the unpaid mortgage.

Erisa Acronym for the *Employee Retirement Income Security Act,* passed in 1974, that gives governmental jurisdiction over the establishment, operation and funding of most nongovernmental pension and benefit plans.

escalator Formerly a trademark, it has become a generic term.

escalator clause A clause in a contract providing for increases or decreases in wages, prices, etc., based on fluctuations in the cost of living, production, expenses, etc.

escapee Either *escaped convict* or *fugitive* is preferable.

Eskimo, Eskimos Some prefer the term *Inuit* for these native peoples in northern North America, and it is an acceptable alternative.

ESOP
See **Employee Stock Ownership Plans.**

espresso The coffee is *espresso,* not *expresso.*

essential clauses, nonessential clauses Both *essential* and *nonessential clauses*—sometimes called *restrictive* and *nonrestrictive clauses*—provide additional information about a word or phrase in a sentence. But an *essential clause* cannot be eliminated without changing the meaning of a sentence.

COMMAS: An *essential clause* isn't set off from the rest of the sentence by commas: *Reporters who do not read the stylebook should not criticize their editors.* Here, only one class of reporters, those who do not read the stylebook, are admonished not to criticize their editors. The *who . . . stylebook* phrase is essential to the meaning of the sentence.

A *nonessential clause,* however, *is* set off by commas: *Reporters, who do not read the stylebook, should not criticize their editors.* Here, the writer is saying that all reporters as a class should not criticize their editors. The *who . . . stylebook* phrase could be deleted and the central meaning of the sentence would remain intact.

USE OF *WHO*, *THAT*, *WHICH*: When an essential or nonessential clause refers to a human being or an animal with a name, it preferably should be introduced by *who* or *whom.*

See **who, whom.**

That is the preferred pronoun to introduce essential clauses referring to an inanimate object or an animal without a name. *Which* is the only acceptable pronoun to introduce a nonessential clause that refers to an inanimate object or an animal without a name.

See **that (conjunction)** for guidelines on the use of *that* as a conjunction.

estimate (n. and v.) *Projection* and *project* are the preferred words in references to future periods in the context of budgets and earnings.

ethanol It is a fuel mixture using ethyl, produced from corn.

ethnic Use the word only as an adjective: *ethnic group.*

ethyl tertiary butyl ether It is an oxygenate used in cleaner-burning gasoline. It is made from corn and is considered a renewable resource, as opposed to petroleum products, which aren't renewable.

Eurasian It refers to people of mixed European and Asian descent.

euro The common currency for nations in Europe is lowercase, and the plural is *euros.* The 12 nations in the European Union that have adopted the euro as of 2002 are: Austria, Belgium, Finland, France, Germany, Greece, Ireland, Italy, Luxembourg, the Netherlands, Portugal and Spain. (The three that haven't adopted it are Britain, Sweden and Denmark.) Don't refer to the euro as Europe's *single* currency, which is a misnomer.

Use *European cents* instead of *eurocents* for the denominations, although the coins are inscribed with *eurocents.*

Eurobond The term refers to debt publicly issued in bearer form outside the home market of the currency of denomination and outside the reach of national tax authorities. *Eurobond* terms typically include selling restrictions in the country of the currency.

Eurodollars They are U.S. dollars deposited in banks outside the U.S. The term refers only to the location of deposit. In all other ways, *Eurodollars* are no different from dollars deposited in the U.S.

They are also known as *offshore dollars* or, depending on where they are deposited, *Asian dollars.*

Euronext It was formed by the merger of the stock exchanges in Paris, Brussels and Amsterdam. The New York Stock Exchange and Euronext are partners in the *Global Equity Market,* or *GEM,* formed for joint trading of global companies' securities.

European Bank for Reconstruction and Development The London-based development bank's shareholders include European Union members, the U.S. and many countries of the former Soviet bloc.

European Central Bank It is based in Frankfurt. With the central banks of the nations participating in the economic and monetary union, it forms the European System of Central Banks. It dictates monetary policy for the euro zone, with the primary objective of maintaining price stability.

See **euro** and **European economic and monetary union.**

European economic and monetary union This refers to the effort by European Union countries to establish a common monetary policy and closer economic-policy coordination. Effective Jan. 1, 1999, 11 E.U. member nations adopted the euro as their common currency, and the European Central Bank began setting monetary policy for the entire euro area. Greece joined in 2001.

The 12 members are Austria, Belgium, Finland, France, Germany, Greece Ireland, Italy, Luxembourg, the Netherlands, Portugal and Spain.

See also **euro** and **European Central Bank.**

E

European Economic Area It is a trade area comprising the members of the European Union and the European Free Trade Association, except Switzerland. *EEA* is acceptable in second reference in text.

European Free Trade Association Established in 1960 to bring about free trade in industrial goods and expansion of trade in agricultural goods, it is based in Geneva. Members are Iceland, Liechtenstein, Norway and Switzerland. Use the abbreviation *EFTA* sparingly.

European Monetary System Created in 1979 by the European Community, it attempts to stabilize currencies of member nations, the community now known as the European Union.

European Union *EU* is acceptable in second reference. The 15 members as of 2000: Austria, Belgium, Denmark, Finland, France, Germany, Greece, Ireland, Italy, Luxembourg, the Netherlands, Portugal, Spain, Sweden and the United Kingdom. The presidency of the EU rotates every six months. The executive body, in Brussels, is the *European Commission.* Founded to advance the economic integration of its member nations, the EU was formerly known as the European Community and before that the European Economic Community.

evangelical, evangelist Most conservative Protestants who consider themselves "born again" call themselves *evangelical* Christians rather than *fundamentalist* Christians.

An *evangelist* or *revivalist* is a preacher of the Christian gospel. When capitalized, *Evangelist* applies to one of the four men credited with writing the Gospels: *Matthew, Mark, Luke* and *John.*

eve Capitalize when used after the name of a holiday: *New Year's Eve, Christmas Eve.* But: *the eve of Christmas.*

even-steven Not *even-stephen.*

every day (adv.), **everyday** (adj.) *He goes to work every day. She wears everyday shoes.*

every one, everyone

Two words when it means each individual item: *Every one of the clues was worthless.*

One word when used as a pronoun: *Everyone wants his life to be happy.* Note that it is followed by singular verbs and pronouns.

ex-

Use no hyphen for words that use *ex-* in the sense of *out of: excommunicate, expropriate.* But see **ex-dividend.**

Hyphenate when using *ex-* in the sense of *former: ex-convict, ex-chairman.* Don't capitalize *ex-* when it is attached to a formal title before a name: *ex-President Clinton.* But *former* is preferred: *former President Clinton.*

exaggerate

except

See **accept, except.**

exclamation point (!) Use the mark sparingly to express a high degree of surprise, incredulity or other strong emotion. Use a comma or period instead after mild interjections.

Place the exclamation mark inside quotation marks when it is part of the quoted material: *"How extraordinary!" he exclaimed. "Never!" she shouted.* Place it outside quotation marks when it is not part of the quoted material: *How I hated "Moby Dick"!*

ex-dividend Stocks are usually traded *ex-dividend,* or without the declared dividend, four trading days before the stock-of-record date that determines the holders who will receive the dividend. Stock trades on the *ex-dividend date* generally are at lower prices, reflecting the absence of the dividend rights.

execute To *execute* a person is to kill him in compliance with a military order or judicial decision.

executive branch

executive director, executive secretary Capitalize them before a name only if they are formal titles.

See **titles.**

executor Use it for both men and women. It isn't a formal title, so lowercase it.

See **titles.**

exercise In options trading, it refers to the converting of an option into a position in the underlying future, security or commodity to which that option applies. For example: In exercising a call option on a gold futures contract (which gives the holder the right but not the obligation to buy the gold futures), the holder *exercises,* or converts, that right into an actual holding of gold futures.

exit The verb takes the preposition *from.*

exorcise, exorcism Not *exorcize.*

expel, expelled, expelling

See **call; option; put; strike price.**

Export-Import Bank *Ex-Im Bank* is acceptable in second reference and headlines.

Express Mail It is a trademark of the U.S. Postal Service.

extol, extolled, extolling

extra-

Do not use a hyphen when *extra-* means *outside of* unless the prefix is followed by a word beginning with *a* or a capitalized word:

extralegal	extramarital
extraterrestrial	extraterritorial

But:

extra-alimentary	extra-Britannic

Follow *extra-* with a hyphen when it is part of a compound modifier describing a condition beyond the usual size, extent or degree:

extra-base hit	extra-dry drink
extra-large book	extra-mild taste

extraordinary item In financial statements, it is a catch-all term for a one-time *gain* or *charge* that doesn't result from a company's regular operations. Examples are court judgments, employee layoff costs, penalties or windfalls from early debt payments, and gains or losses on sales of operating units.

See **profit terminology.**

extrasensory perception *ESP* is acceptable on second reference.

Exxon Mobil Corp. Its headquarters is in Irving, Texas.

eye Generally avoid as a verb.

eyestrain

eye to eye, eye-to-eye Hyphenate when used as a compound modifier: *an eye-to-eye confrontation.*

eyewitness *Witness* is usually sufficient.

Ff

FAA It stands for *Federal Aviation Administration.*

fabricator In the metals industry, it is a maker of intermediate products that doesn't also produce primary metal: a brass wire and rod mill, for example.

facade

face: in the face of Although some dictionaries say *in the face of* can mean either *in the presence of* or *notwithstanding,* use the expression only in the latter sense, to avoid confusion: *The market fell sharply in the face of strong economic reports.*

facilities It is an acceptable general alternative term for plants and other commercial buildings. But use the specific *plant, building* or *factory* when possible.

fact-finding (adj.)

Factiva The database information service is a joint venture of Dow Jones & Co. and Reuters Group PLC of Britain.

factors In the business world, they are companies that buy accounts receivable and take over the job of collecting the money due.

fade out (v.), **fade-out** (n.)

Faeroe Islands The group of Danish islands is in the northern Atlantic Ocean between Iceland and the Shetland Islands. Use a city name before Faeroe Islands in datelines. The people living there are *Faeroese.*

Fahrenheit This temperature scale, commonly used in the U.S., is named for Gabriel Daniel Fahrenheit, the German physicist who designed it. In the scale, the freezing point of water is 32 degrees and the boiling point is 212 degrees. When it is necessary to mention the scale, use this form: *78 degrees Fahrenheit.*

To convert to Celsius, subtract 32 from the Fahrenheit figure, multiply by 5 and divide by 9.

See **Celsius** and **Kelvin scale.**

fall

See **seasons.**

fallout

family relationships Capitalize words denoting family relationships only when they precede the name of a person or when they stand unmodified as a substitute for a person's name: *I wrote to Grandfather Smith. I wrote Mother a letter. I wrote my mother a letter.*

Fannie Mae It no longer formally calls itself the Federal National Mortgage Association.

The government-chartered association, listed on the New York Stock Exchange, buys Federal Housing Administration and other mortgages from banks and other lenders and packages them as investment securities. Its bonds are known on the markets pages as *Fannie Maes.*

FAQs The Internet term refers to *frequently asked questions,* a format used to summarize information on Web sites. Spell it out in copy.

Far East The eastern portions of the Asian continent: China, Japan, North and South Korea, Taiwan, Hong Kong and the eastern part of Russia.

Use *the Far East and Southeast Asia* when referring to a wider portion of eastern Asia including the Indochina Peninsula.

See **Asian subcontinent** and **Southeast Asia.**

far-flung (adj.)

Farm Belt

Farm Credit System The *Farm Credit System* is a federally chartered network of farmer-owned agricultural lenders. Unlike commercial banks, the Farm Credit System doesn't take deposits, but raises funds for lending by selling securities in the capital markets. Financial results for the system are reported by the affiliated *Federal Farm Credit System Funding Corp.*

Farmers Home Administration *FmHA* is acceptable on second reference, to distinguish it from the FHA, the Federal Housing Administration.

farmhand, farmhouse, farmland

far-off (adj.)

far-ranging (adj.)

far-reaching (adj.)

farrowing In the hog market, the term refers to giving birth. *Farrowing intentions,* or the number of births hog producers expect from their herds, are closely watched by the hog futures market at the Chicago Mercantile Exchange.

farsighted It means, literally or figuratively, that one can see things at a distance but has difficulty seeing them close at hand.

farther, further

Farther refers to physical distance: *He walked farther into the woods.*

Further refers to an extension of time or degree: *She will look further into the mystery.*

Far West The U.S. region is generally the area west of the Rocky Mountains.

FASB *See* **Financial Accounting Standards Board.**

fascism, fascist Capitalize the words only in reference to the onetime Italian Fascist Party and its members.

Father *See* **religious titles.**

father-in-law, fathers-in-law

Father's Day

Father Time

fatwa It is a decree by an Islamic religious leader.

fax The short form for *facsimile* is acceptable as a noun and as a verb.

faze, phase

Faze means to disturb or embarrass.

Phase is an aspect or stage.

FBI Acceptable in second reference for *Federal Bureau of Investigation.*

featherbedding It is the practice of using more workers than needed to handle a job. But use the word judiciously, as the matter usually is in dispute.

February
See **months.**

federal
Use a capital letter for the architectural style and for corporate or governmental bodies that use the word as part of their formal names: *the Federal Trade Commission.* (*See* separate entries for governmental agencies.)

Lowercase when used as an adjective to distinguish something from state, county, city, town or private entities: *federal assistance, federal court, the federal government, a federal judge.*

Federal Aviation Administration *FAA* is acceptable on second reference.

Federal Bureau of Investigation *FBI* is acceptable on second reference.

Federal Communications Commission *FCC* is acceptable on second reference.

federal court Always lowercase. The preferred form for first reference is to use the proper name of the court.

See entries under U.S. and the court name.

Don't create nonexistent entities such as *Manhattan federal court.* Instead, use *federal court in Manhattan* if the article clearly indicates the location is New York and not Kansas.

See **judicial branch.**

Federal Crop Insurance Corp.

Federal Deposit Insurance Corp. *FDIC* is acceptable on second reference.

Federal Energy Regulatory Commission This agency regulates interstate natural gas and electricity transactions. *FERC* is acceptable on second reference, but *the agency* or *the commission* is preferred.

Federal Farm Credit System Funding Corp.
See **Farm Credit System.**

F

federal funds It is money in excess of what the Federal Reserve says a bank must have on hand to back up deposits. The excess can be lent overnight to other banks that need more cash on hand to meet reserve requirements. The interest rate on these loans, which is regulated by the Federal Reserve's Open Market Committee through the purchase and sale of Treasury bills, is the *federal-funds rate.*

Federal Highway Administration Reserve *FHA* abbreviation for the *Federal Housing Administration.*

Federal Home Loan Bank system It is a credit reserve system for the thrift industry. Its job is to enhance and stabilize the flow of mortgage credit to the public.

Federal Home Loan Mortgage Corp. *Freddie Mac* has become its official name.
See **Freddie Mac.**

Federal Housing Administration *FHA* is acceptable in second reference.

Federal Maritime Commission

Federal Mediation and Conciliation Service

Federal National Mortgage Association This name is no longer used.
See **Fannie Mae.**

Federal Open Market Committee It is the policy-making arm of the Federal Reserve. Its voting panel comprises the seven governors of the Fed, the president of the Federal Reserve Bank of New York and four presidents from the other 11 regional district banks. District bank presidents serve on a rotating basis. The rotation changes in January. Nonvoting presidents are members of the *FOMC* and participate in discussions of policy. The committee meets eight times a year to plot monetary strategy.

F

Federal Register This publication, issued every workday, is the legal medium for recording and communicating the rules and regulations established by the executive branch of the federal government. Individuals or corporations cannot be held legally responsible for compliance with a regulation unless it has been published in the *Register.*

In addition, executive agencies are required to publish in advance some types of proposed regulations.

Federal Reserve System, Federal Reserve Board On first reference in text, use *Federal Reserve;* for headlines and second reference in text, *the fed* is acceptable.

The *Federal Reserve System,* established in 1913, is the central banking system of the U.S. It consists of 12 district banks, each with a private-sector board of directors and each with a president. Commercial banks in each Federal Reserve district hold stock in the district's Federal Reserve bank.

The *Federal Reserve Board* in Washington governs the Federal Reserve System. Its seven members are appointed by the U.S. president, subject to U.S. Senate confirmation, and serve 14-year terms. The U.S. president chooses one of the governors to be chairman for a four-year term. The board supervises the banking system by issuing regulations controlling the activities of bank holding companies, and it also issues regulations implementing U.S. laws regulating banking. It holds a voting majority at meetings of the influential Federal Open Market Committee, which exercises control over the supply of credit in the banking system. The Fed board also sets reserve requirements for national banks and state-chartered banks that own stock in Federal Reserve Banks. The board also approves applications from regional banks to change the *discount rate.* There is no Federal Reserve Board of San Francisco; there is, however, a Federal Reserve Bank of San Francisco. When writing about a regional Fed bank, be specific: *a study by the Federal Reserve Bank of New York* (on second reference in text: *the New York Fed*).

See **Federal Open Market Committee** and **federal funds.**

Federal Reserve terminology

See **discount window; matched sale-purchase transactions; outright purchase or sale; repurchase agreements.**

Federal Trade Commission *FTC* is acceptable on second reference.

FedEx Corp. It is based in Memphis, Tenn.

feedstock In the petroleum business, *feedstock* is the raw material supplied to refining or petrochemical units. Crude oil is the most widely used feedstock for refineries. Petrochemical plants use naphtha and other feedstocks.

felony, misdemeanor A *felony* is a serious crime. A *misdemeanor* is a minor offense against the law. A fuller definition of what constitutes a felony or misdemeanor depends on the governmental jurisdiction involved.

At the federal level, a *misdemeanor* is a crime that carries a potential penalty of no more than a year in jail. A *felony* is a crime that carries a potential penalty of more than a year in prison. Often, however, a statute gives a judge options such as imposing a fine or probation in addition to or instead of a jail or prison sentence. A *felon* is a person who

has been convicted of a felony, regardless of whether the individual actually spends time in confinement or is given probation or a fine instead. *Convicted felon* is a redundancy.
See **prison, jail.**

Ferris wheel

ferryboat

fertility rate As calculated by the federal government, it is the number of live births per 1,000 females 15 through 44 years old.

fewer, less Use *fewer* for number, *less* for aggregates or quantity. *Fewer than three seats were lost by the Democrats. Less than $50 is in the bank.*
But with *one*, phrase it *One seat fewer was lost.*

fiance (man), fiancee (woman)

fiberglass, glass fiber Use either of these forms. Avoid generic use of Fiberglas, which is a trade name.

fiber optics *Fiber-optic* technology—note the adjective is *optic*—involves the use of optical fiber to transmit large amounts of data at high speeds.

fief Not *fiefdom.*

field house

FIFO It stands for the *first-in, first-out* system of inventory accounting. Don't use *FIFO* without including the definition in the text.
See **LIFO.**

figuratively, literally
Don't use *literally* to mean *figuratively.* Don't say: *He literally exploded at the news.*

figure The symbol for a number: *the figure 5.*
See **numbers.**

figure skating

filet, fillet
Filet mignon is a preparation of beef tenderloin.
Fillet is deboned fish.

filibuster *To filibuster* is to make long speeches to obstruct the passage of a bill. A senator who uses this tactic is also a *filibuster,* not a filibusterer.

Filipinos The people of the Philippines.

fillet Deboned fish.
See **filet.**

film, filmmaker, filmmaking

film ratings
See **movie ratings.**

***Financial* Accounting Standards Board** FASB is acceptable in second reference. The accounting industry's self-regulatory organization is responsible for creating "generally accepted accounting principles."

fiord Not *fjord.*

fire (v.) Because *firing* of employees can connote dismissal for cause, restrict use of the word to instances where poor performance or infractions of company rules are alleged.
See **lay off.**

firearms
See **weapons.**

firefighter This is the preferred term to describe a person who fights fires.

firm A business partnership is correctly referred to as a *firm.* Brokerage firms that have otherwise incorporated continue to be called *firms.* But generally don't use *firm* in references to an incorporated business entity, except in headlines. Use *the company* or *the corporation* instead.

first class, first-class Hyphenate as a modifier before a noun: *The hotel was first class. It was a first-class hotel.*

first degree, first-degree Hyphenate as a modifier before a noun: *The burns were first degree. They were first-degree burns.*
See **burns.**

first family Always lowercase.

first lady The news pages lowercase it in all references to the wife of a chief of state or a governor, but the editorial pages uppercase it.

first-mortgage bond It is secured by real estate or equipment. A corporate bond, it shouldn't be confused with securitized home or commercial loans that make up the mortgage market.

first quarter, first-quarter Hyphenate as a modifier before a noun: *The earnings were for the first quarter. The first-quarter earnings rose.*

fiscal policy, monetary policy
Fiscal policy involves taxation and spending of governments.
Monetary policy involves interest rates or minimum reserve requirements of central banks.

fiscal year It is the 12-month period that a corporation or a governmental body uses for bookkeeping purposes. Fiscal years for our purposes are expressed according to when the year ends: The year ending March 31, 2002, is *fiscal 2002.* When referring to an entity's fiscal year, always indicate when it begins or ends. The federal government's fiscal year runs from Oct. 1 to Sept. 30. When the entity's fiscal year is the January–December calendar year, the term *fiscal* isn't necessary.

fitful It means restless, not a condition of being fit.

fixed-income investment It is a bond or other security that pays a fixed rate of return or a preferred stock that pays a fixed dividend.

flack, flak
Flack is slang for press agent and is usually considered pejorative. Use it advisedly.
Flak is antiaircraft fire, hence figuratively a barrage of criticism.

flag Among other meanings, a *flag* is a newspaper's *nameplate* carried at the top of page one.
See **masthead.**

flagpole, flagship

flail, flay
To flail is to swing the arms widely or to strike or beat.
To flay is, literally, to strip off the skin by whipping. Figuratively, *to flay* means to tongue-lash a person.

flair, flare
Flair is conspicuous talent.
To flare is to blaze up with sudden, bright light or to burst out in anger. A *flare* is a flame.

flak
See **flack, flak.**

flare up (v.), **flare-up** (n.)
See **flair, flare.**

flat-rolled steel
See **steel.**

flaunt, flout

To flaunt is to make an ostentatious or defiant display: *She flaunted her beauty.*

To flout is to show contempt for: *He flouts the law.*

flautist The preferred word is *flutist.*

fleet *The Sixth Fleet.* Lowercase *fleet* whenever it stands alone.

flier, flyer

A *flier* is a handbill, an aviator or a person who flies.

Flyer is used in the formal names of some fast buses and trains.

flimflam, flimflammed

flip-flop

float

In *banking,* it is the time between the deposit of a check in a bank and the availability of the funds to the depositor. Commercial banks receive interest-free credit from the Federal Reserve for these checks in *float* between banks.

In *securities matters,* it is the number of shares of a company that are outstanding and available for trading by the public. It includes shares the company doesn't hold in its treasury, those that aren't tied up in stock option plans, as well as those that aren't tied up in trust by an institution or investor. A *small float* means the stock will be more volatile, because any large order to buy or sell shares can greatly influence the stock's price.

floods, flood stage

See **weather terms.**

floor leader Treat it as a job description, lowercased, rather than a formal title: *Republican floor leader Trent Lott.*

See **titles.**

Florence The city in Italy stands alone in datelines.

Florida Abbreviate as *Fla.* after city names. Residents are *Floridians.*

See **state names.**

Florida Keys A chain of small islands extending southwest from the southern tip of mainland Florida.

Cities, or the islands themselves, are followed by *Fla.* in datelines: *KEY WEST, Fla.*

flounder, founder *To flounder* is to move about clumsily. Because *to founder* often means to become disabled or sink, the word is best avoided in any context that isn't meant to suggest demise.

flout

See **flaunt, flout.**

fluid ounce Equal to 1.8 cubic inches, two tablespoons or six teaspoons. The metric equivalent is approximately 30 milliliters.

To convert to milliliters, multiply by 30 (3 ounces × 30 equals 90 milliliters).

See **liter.**

fluorescent

flutist The preferred term, rather than *flautist.*

flyer *See* **flier, flyer.**

FM This is the preferred term in all references for the *frequency modulation* system of radio transmission.

FOB *See* **free on board.**

-fold *Twofold, fourfold, tenfold.* But use numerals and a hyphen for numbers over ten: *12-fold.*

folk singer, folk song

following *He has a large following. He is following his conscience. The following statement was made.*

As a preposition, *following* connotes *as a result of.* Thus: *Following two days of negotiations, the strike was settled.* But *after* is usually preferred: *He spoke after dinner.*

follow up (v.), **follow-up** (n. and adj.)

F

food In general, lowercase the names of foods, but capitalize trade names and most proper nouns or adjectives that occur in a name. Some names that include a proper noun or adjective: *baked Alaska, Brussels sprouts, French dressing, Irish potatoes, Russian dressing, Swiss cheese.*

A few names have acquired a meaning independent of a proper noun or adjective and are no longer capitalized: *bologna, french fries, manhattan cocktail.* Follow Webster's New World, using the form listed first. The same rules apply to foreign names of food: *mousse de saumon* (salmon mousse), *salade Russe* (Russian salad).

Food and Agriculture Organization It is a U.N. agency, based in Rome.

Food and Drug Administration *FDA* is acceptable on second reference.

foot The metric equivalent of a foot is 30.48 centimeters. For conversions to centimeters, multiply by 30.48.

To convert to meters, multiply by 0.3.

See **centimeter, meter, metric system** and **dimensions.**

foot-and-mouth-disease Use this form rather than *hoof-and-mouth disease,* except in quoted matter.

forbear, forebear

To forbear is to avoid or shun.

A *forebear* is an ancestor.

forbid, forbade, forbidding They take the preposition *to.*

force majeure It refers to conditions permitting a company to deviate from the strict terms of a contract because of an event or effect that can't be reasonably anticipated or controlled.

Ford Motor Co. Use *Ford,* not *FMC,* on second reference. It is based in Dearborn, Mich. When necessary, differentiate between Ford, the parent, and Ford division, the largest unit.

fore- The rules in the **prefixes** entry apply, but in general, no hyphen:

forebrain
forefather
foregoing

These nautical terms are exceptions:

fore-topgallant
fore-topmast
fore-topsail

forecast Use *forecast* also for the past tense, not *forecasted.*

See **weather terms.**

forego, forgo

To forego means to go before, as in *foregone conclusion.*

To forgo means to abstain from.

foreign companies

Below are some foreign corporate designations, with explanations. Note that we drop PLC, Inc. and Ltd. when they follow Co. or Corp.: *Saatchi & Saatchi Co.,* not *Saatchi & Saatchi Co. PLC.* But two corporate designations are sometimes used, as noted.

We no longer use periods with many of the abbreviated designations.

AB It stands for *Aktiebolag,* with the names of Finnish and Swedish shareholder companies often appearing before the name.

AG For *Aktiengesellschaft,* after German, Austrian and Swiss shareholder company names.

AS For *Aksjeselaskap,* with Norwegian shareholder companies, *Aktieselskab* with Danish companies and *Anonim Sirketi* with Turkish companies.

A/S For *Aksjeselaskap,* with Norwegian companies.

Bhd. For *Berhad,* after public limited companies with more than 50 shareholders in Malaysia. For the few companies designated *Corp. Bhd.,* keep both designations.

BV For *Besloten Vennootschap met beperkte Aansprankelijkheid,* with Dutch company names.

Cia. For *Companhia* in Brazil and Portugal, *Compania* in Spanish-speaking countries.

Cie. For *Compagnie,* in French-speaking countries.

GmbH For *Gesellschaft mit beschrankter Haftung,* in German-speaking countries.

KG *Kommanditgesellschaft,* in Austrian and German company names.

KGaA For *Kommanditgesellschaft aufAktien,* in German-speaking countries.

KK For *Kabushiki Kaisha,* with Japanese companies. Most bigger Japanese companies use *Co., Corp.* or *Ltd.* The exceptions are mainly smaller companies that don't use English translations for their names. They use *KK,* either before or after the company name. It translates as *Co. Ltd.*

LLC For *Limited Liability Company.*

L.P. For *Limited Partnership.*

Ltd. For *Limited,* mainly with British companies.

mbH For *mit beschrankter Haftung,* in German-speaking countries.

NL For *No Liability,* in Australia.

NV For *Naamloze Vennootschap,* with Dutch companies, often before the name. Some private Indonesian companies, particularly trading companies, still carry this Dutch designation.

Oy For *Osakeyhtioe,* with Finnish shareholder companies, before or after name.

PCL For *Public Company Limited,* in Thailand.

PLC For British *Public Limited Companies.*

PT For *Perseroan Terbatas,* designating limited-liability companies in Indonesia that may or may not have a stock-exchange listing. The designation precedes the company name.

Pte. For *Private,* with Singapore companies and some others.

Pte. Ltd. For *Private Limited,* with companies in Singapore. Use both designations.

Pty. Ltd. For *Proprietary Limited.* Designates private companies in Australia. Use both designations.

SA For *Societe Anonyme,* with French-language names.

SA For *Sociedad Anopmina,* with Latin American company names.

SC For *Societe Cooperative,* with French-language names.

Sdn. Bhd. For *Sendirian Berhad,* with most private companies in Malaysia. Use both designations.

SNC For *Societe en Nom Collectif,* designating a *general partnership,* with French-language names.

SpA For *Societa per Azioni,* designating an Italian stockholder company.

SRL For *Societa a Responsibilita Limitata,* designating a closely held, nonstockholder company, usually not as big as an *SpA.*

foreign currency

See **foreign money** and **World Currencies** appendix.

foreign exchange, foreign-exchange market

Foreign exchange refers to money instruments used to make payments between countries.

The *foreign-exchange market* is the market in which foreign currencies are bought and sold and exchange rates between currencies are determined.

foreign governmental bodies
Capitalize the names of specific foreign governmental agencies and departments, either with the name of the nation or without it if clear in the context: *the French Foreign Ministry, the Foreign Ministry.*

Lowercase *the ministry* or similar term when standing alone.

Foreign Legion Capitalize in reference to the French force.

foreign legislative bodies
In general, capitalize the proper name of a specific legislative body abroad, whether using the name in the native language or the English equivalent: *In Rome, Parliament acted quickly on the matter.*

Lowercase *parliament, congress, national assembly* or similar term when used generically to describe a body for which the foreign name is being given: *the Diet, Japan's parliament.* But capitalize *parliament* or similar term when it is used instead of the foreign name: *The meeting occurred in the Japanese Parliament.*

PARLIAMENTS: The name is used in Australia, Canada, Denmark, Finland, France, India, Ireland, Italy, New Zealand, Norway, Poland and the United Kingdom. *Parliament* applies as well to the Diet, the Cortes in Spain and the Knesset in Israel.

PLURALS: Lowercase *parliament* and other terms in plural constructions: *the British and French parliaments.*

NATIONAL ASSEMBLIES: Nations in which *national assembly* is the name include: Bulgaria, Congo, Czechoslovakia, Egypt, Hungary, Nepal, Pakistan, Portugal, Tunisia, Uganda and Zambia.

Lowercase *assembly* when used as a shortened reference to *national assembly.* In many countries, *national assembly* is the name of a unicameral legislative body. In some, such as France, it is the name for the lower house of a legislative body known by some other name, such as *parliament.*

foreign money When amounts of foreign money are listed in spot-news articles involving such things as acquisitions and earnings reports, a translation into dollars should generally be provided in the first reference, using a foreign-exchange ratio taken from the Exchange Rates table in the Journal on the day the article is being prepared: *The company had a loss of 540 million French francs ($70 million).* Use the dollar figures in headlines as well.

In these news articles, after providing the dollar conversion in the first reference, generally use just the foreign-money figure. But in instances where billions of yen, say, are mentioned in the first reference and hundreds of yen or less in a subsequent reference, provide additional dollar-equivalent translations, as a help to the reader.

In the cases of Canadian, Australian or Hong Kong dollars, don't use the dollar sign on the initial reference: *The bid was 45 Australian dollars (US$20) for the shares.* (Note that in this use only, *US* has no periods.) In subsequent references: *The new price was A$25* (or *C$25* or *HK$25*).

EXCEPTIONS: In references to the cost of products or services abroad and normally in page-one and other feature articles, use just the dollar equivalents, which are more meaningful to most readers. The foreign-currency figures are a distraction in contexts other than corporate financial news.

See **dollars and cents** and **World Currencies** appendix.

BRITISH: Use the pound sign (£) for the British *pound,* but spell out all other foreign-currency names.

CHINESE: Use *yuan* rather than *renminbi* for the currency of China.

GERMAN: Use *mark* instead of *deutsche mark* or *D-mark* for the German currency, except in quotes.

IRISH: The Irish currency is the Irish *pound,* also called the *punt.* Northern Ireland's currency is the British *pound.*

foreign names

For foreign place names that aren't included in the stylebook, use the primary spelling in Webster's New World Dictionary. If it has no entry, follow the National Geographic Atlas.

For personal names, follow the individual's preference for an English spelling if it can be determined. Otherwise:

Use the nearest phonetic equivalent in English if one exists: *Alexander Solzhenitsyn,* for example, rather than *Aleksandr,* the spelling that would result from a translation of the Russian letters into the English alphabet.

If a name has no close phonetic equivalent in English, express it with an English spelling that approximates the sound in the original language.

foreign words Some foreign words and abbreviations have been universally accepted into the English language: *post-mortem; versus, vs.; et cetera, etc.* They may be used without explanation if they are clear in the context. But foreign words that haven't received such wide acceptance generally should be avoided in favor of their English equivalents: *forbidden* instead of *verboten, expert* instead of *maven.*

For foreign words included in Webster's New World Dictionary, use italics on first reference if the word is italicized in the listing there.

foreman, forewoman

foresee Generally use *see* instead.

foreword Unlike a book's *preface,* a *foreword* is written by someone other than the book's author.

formal titles *See* **titles.**

former Always lowercase. But retain the capitalization of a following formal title that is used immediately before a name: *former President Clinton.*

Formica A trademark for laminated plastic.

Formosa

See **Taiwan.**

Formosa Strait Not the *Straits of Taiwan.*

formula, formulas

forsake, forsook, forsaken

fort Don't abbreviate in names of cities or military installations.

In datelines for cities:

FORT LAUDERDALE, Fla.—

In datelines for military installations:

FORT BRAGG, N.C.—

fortnight *Two weeks* is preferred over *fortnight* in American usage.

fortuitous Although use of *fortuitous* to mean fortunate has found its way into most dictionaries, the primary meaning of fortuitous is *by chance.* And the distinction is worth preserving.

Fortune 500 The 500 leading U.S. industrial companies, based on revenues, as compiled by Fortune magazine.

fortuneteller, fortunetelling

forty, forty-niner But *the San Francisco 49ers.*

forward Not *forwards.*

foul, fowl

Foul means offensive, out of line.

A *fowl* is a bird, especially the larger domestic birds used as food: chickens, ducks, turkeys.

founder, flounder *To flounder* is to move about clumsily. Because *to founder* often means to become disabled or sink, the word is best avoided in any context that isn't meant to suggest demise.

F

Four-H Club *4-H Club* is preferred when it doesn't start a sentence. Members are *4-H'ers.*

401(k) The employer-sponsored salary-deferral plan that allows employees to contribute a portion of gross salary to a savings plan or company profit-sharing plan. Substantial tax penalties are applied if the funds aren't kept in the plan until the employee reaches age 59½ or retires or leaves the company.

four-star general

Fourth Estate Capitalize the term for journalism and journalists. Edmund Burke is said to have called the reporters' gallery in Parliament a "Fourth Estate." The three estates of English society were the Lords Spiritual (the clergy), the Lords Temporal (the nobility) and the Commons (the bourgeoisie).

Fourth of July, July Fourth

fowl (sing. and pl.) The term applies to birds, especially those used as food: chickens, ducks and turkeys.

fractions

When they stand alone, without whole numbers, generally spell out and hyphenate fractions: *two-thirds, seven-eighths, eight-tenths.* For denominations of more than 10, use figures: *5/11ths, 7/32nds.* When the fractions appear with whole numbers, use the figures: *4½, 8¼, 75¾.* Decimals can be used alternatively, except when comparisons are made with other fractions.

See **stock prices.**

fragment, fragmentary

Fragment describes a piece or pieces broken from the whole: *She sang a fragment of the song.*

Fragmentary describes disconnected and incomplete parts: *Early returns were fragmentary.*

frame up (v.), **frame-up** (n.)

franchisee, franchiser

A *franchisee* is one who is granted a franchise.

A *franchiser* is one who grants franchises, or marketing rights, to another.

Frankfurt The German city stands alone in datelines.

fraternal organizations and service clubs

Capitalize the formal names: *American Legion, Lions Club, Rotary Club.*

Capitalize the formal titles of officeholders when used before a name. *See* **titles.**

Capitalize also words describing membership: *Legionnaire, Rotarian.*

Freddie Mac This has become the formal name of the Federal Home Loan Mortgage Corp. The publicly held, government-chartered company has two businesses: It buys home mortgages from lending institutions to hold in its portfolio and it issues securities backed by pools of mortgages that it guarantees. Although Freddie Mac is not a federal agency, bond-market investors often refer to Freddie Mac securities as *agency debt.*

free (adj., adv. and v.) It is not a noun, so *for free* is a solecism. Drop the *for.*

free-for-all (n. and adj.)

free-lance (v. and adj.), **free-lancer** (n.)

free on board A commodity purchased *FOB,* or *free on board,* must be transported from the origin at the buyer's expense.

freeware It is Web jargon for free software.

freewheeling

Free World The term is imprecise and subjective, though it was widely used during the Cold War. In the news pages, use it only in quoted matter.

freeze-dry, freeze-dried, freeze-drying

French Canadian, French Canadians Use them without a hyphen, an exception to the normal practice in describing a dual ethnic heritage.

French Foreign Legion

Retain capitalization if shortened to *the Foreign Legion.*

Lowercase *the legion* and *legionnaires.* Unlike the American Legion, for example, the French Foreign Legion is a military group.

french fries The term isn't capitalized.

See **capitalization.**

frequency modulation *FM* is preferable in all references.

Friday

See **days of the week.**

Friends General Conference, Friends United Meeting

See **Quakers.**

Frigidaire It is a trademark for a brand of refrigerator.

Frisbee A trademark for a plastic disk thrown as a toy.

front line (n.), **front-line** (adj.)

front page (n.), **front-page** (adj.) At the Journal, it is usually called *page one,* which is also hyphenated as a modifier.

front-runner

fruits

See **food.**

FTP It stands for *file transfer protocol,* a common procedure for transferring files on the Internet. Explain it if you use it.

fuchsia The plant and its color were named for the German botanist Leonhard Fuchs.

fulfill, fulfilled, fulfilling

full- Hyphenate when used to form compound modifiers before a noun:

full-dress	full-scale
full-page	full-length
full-fledged	full-time

But don't hyphenate when the modifiers appear after the word they modify: *This was a full-time job. The job was full time.*

fulsome It means *revolting, disgusting* and *excessive.* Don't use it to mean lavish, profuse.

fundamentalist In Christian allusions, use it only to refer to people who define themselves that way.

See **evangelical.**

In Islam and some other religions, *fundamentalism* refers to doctrinal conservatism.

fund raising (n.), **fund-raising** (adj.), **fund-raiser** (n.) *Fund raising is difficult, so they hired a fund-raiser to plan a fund-raising campaign.*

furlough

further
See **farther, further.**

fuse, fuze
A *fuse* is an electrical safeguard.
Fuze is the preferred spelling for a device for detonating explosives.

fuselage

fusillade

future cash flows Unlike regular cash flows, *future cash flows* of divested divisions or product lines are actual cash from selling products or services that will generally be used to cover debt service. Future cash flows, unlike traditional cash flow, can include receivables.

futures *See* **commodity futures.**

FYI It means *for your information.* But don't use it in news copy.

Gg

G *See* **movie ratings.**

G-3 *The Group of Three* leading industrial nations comprises the U.S., Japan and Germany.

G-7 *The Group of Seven* leading industrial nations comprises Canada, France, Germany, Italy, Japan, the United Kingdom and the U.S.

G-8 *The Group of Eight* leading nations (note the omission of *industrial*) comprises the G-7 plus Russia.

G-10 *The Group of 10* leading industrial nations has 11 members: the G-7 plus Belgium, the Netherlands, Sweden and Switzerland.

G-15 *The Group of 15* developing nations is an advisory trade body comprising 16 "southern" nations: Algeria, Argentina, Brazil, Chile, Egypt, India, Indonesia, Jamaica, Kenya, Malaysia, Mexico, Nigeria, Peru, Senegal, Venezuela and Zimbabwe.

G-22 *The Group of 22* industrial and developing nations was formed in 1997, after the start of the Asian economic crisis. Still called G-22, it has 26 members: Argentina, Australia, Belgium, Brazil, Canada, China, France, Germany, Hong Kong, India, Indonesia, Italy, Japan, Malaysia, Mexico, Netherlands, Poland, Russia, Singapore, South Africa, South Korea, Sweden, Switzerland, Thailand, United Kingdom and U.S.

G-24 *The Group of 24*, whose official name is *the Inter-Governmental Group of 24 on International Monetary Affairs*, was created in 1972 by 77 developing countries. The group was given responsibility for representing their interests in negotiations over international monetary matters. The group meets twice yearly under the auspices of the International Monetary Fund. Its members are: Algeria, Argentina, Brazil, Colombia, Congo, Egypt, Ethiopia, Gabon, Ghana, Guatemala, India, Iran, Ivory Coast, Lebanon, Mexico, Nigeria, Pakistan, Peru, Philippines, Sri Lanka, Syria, Trinidad and Tobago and Venezuela. In addition, China attends group meetings.

Gadhafi, Col. Moammar The Libyan head of state.

gaff, gaffe

A *gaff* is a hook used to land a fish, or a pole on the mast of a ship.

A *gaffe* is a blunder.

gage, gauge

Gage, seldom used, is a security or pledge—or a variety of plum.

A *gauge* is an instrument or means for measuring or evaluating. *Gauge* also designates the bore size of shotguns.

gaiety

gale *See* **weather terms.**

gallon Equal to 128 fluid ounces. The metric equivalent is approximately 3.8 liters.
To convert to liters, multiply by 3.8.
See **imperial gallon; liter; metric system.**

Gallup Poll It is run by the Gallup Organization in Princeton, N.J.

G

galvanizing It is the process by which steel is coated with a layer of zinc to provide the steel with greater corrosion resistance.

game names They don't require quotation marks: *Monopoly, Sonic the Hedgehog, Pictionary.*

game plan

gaming Use *gambling* instead, except in proper names or in quotations.

gamma testing In the development of new software, *gamma testing* is a third stage sometimes conducted after the alpha and beta testing, as a precaution just before commercial marketing.

gamut, gantlet, gauntlet
A *gamut* is a complete range or extent (as a scale of notes).
A *gantlet* is a flogging ordeal, literally or figuratively.
A *gauntlet* is a glove thrown down to issue a challenge. *To take up the gauntlet* means to accept the challenge.

gamy, gamier, gamiest

gantlet
See **gamut, gantlet, gauntlet.**

garnish, garnishee *Garnishee* (*garnisheed, garnisheeing*) is the better verb in the sense of putting a lien on a debtor's property or wages to satisfy a debt. As a noun, *garnishee* identifies the individual who was served with the *garnishment.*

gas Never use for gasoline, even in headlines, except in such idioms as *gas-guzzling cars* and *gas stations.*

GATT
See **World Trade Organization.**

gauge
See **gage, gauge.**

gauntlet
See **gamut, gantlet, gauntlet.**

gay (n. and adj.) Use *gay* instead of *homosexual* in reference to political and social issues (or use *lesbian* for women specifically). Use *homosexual* for men and women in regard to sexual and psychological matters.

GDP *See* **gross domestic product.**

gel As a verb meaning solidify, *jell* is preferred.

gender, sex Although *gender* originally applied only to the grammatical classification of words, it now may be used instead of the word *sex* in idioms such as *gender gap,* and to prevent ambiguity or double meanings.

General Accounting Office This federal agency, which is the investigative arm of Congress, may be referred to as *the GAO* in second reference.

General Agreement on Tariffs and Trade
See **World Trade Organization.**

general assembly
See **legislature** for its treatment as the name of a state's legislative body. Capitalize when it is the formal name: *the General Assembly of the World Council of Churches.*

General Electric Co. *GE* is acceptable in second reference. It is based in Fairfield, Conn.

General Electric Co. PLC It is based in London. Use *the PLC* on first reference and call it *GEC* on later references. Specify that it isn't related to the U.S. General Electric Co.

general, general of the army
See **military titles.**

general manager Capitalize only as a formal title before a name.
See **titles.**

General Motors Corp. *GM* is acceptable on second reference. It is based in Detroit.

general-obligation bond It is a bond secured by the full faith and credit of an issuer with taxing power. Issuance usually requires voter or legislative approval.
See **loan terminology.**

General Services Administration *GSA* is acceptable on second reference.

Generation X The term applies to people born from 1965 to 1980, after the baby boom. Also: *Gen X* and *Gen Xers.*

Generation Y The term applies to people born in 1980 or thereafter.

Geneva The Swiss city stands alone in datelines.

gentile Generally, any person not a Jew; often, specifically a Christian. But to Mormons it is anyone not a Mormon.

gentleman Don't use as a synonym for *man.*
See **lady.**

geographic names The authority for spelling place names in the 50 U.S. states and territories is the U.S. Postal Service Directory of Post Offices, but don't use the postal abbreviations for states.

See **state names** for the abbreviations and the rules for using them. *Saint* normally is abbreviated *St.* in place names, but *Sault Ste. Marie* is an exception. Don't abbreviate *Fort* or *Mount: Fort Lauderdale, Mount Holyoke.*

FOREIGN LOCATIONS: Spell foreign place names as they are listed in this book or the first listing in Webster's New World College Dictionary.

For names of former Soviet republics, see **Commonwealth of Independent States.** If neither the stylebook nor the dictionary has an entry, use the first-listed spelling in the National Geographic Atlas.

See **addresses; capitization, datelines;** and **directions and regions** for additional guidelines.

Georgia Abbreviate the state as *Ga.* when it follows a city name. Residents are *Georgians.*
See **state names.**

Georgia, Republic of
See **Commonwealth of Independent States.**

germanium The minor metal is used in the electronics sector. It is obtained mostly from the refining of copper, zinc and lead.

German measles Also known as *rubella.*

getaway

get-together (n.)

ghetto, ghettos Don't use *ghetto* indiscriminately as a synonym for the sections of cities inhabited by minorities or the poor.

gibe (v. and n.), **jibe** (v.)

To gibe means to taunt: *They gibed her about her height.* A *gibe* is a taunt.

To jibe in sailing means to shift direction;

colloquially, it means to agree: *They jibed across the wind. Their alibis didn't jibe.*

Gibraltar, Strait of Gibraltar

Gibraltar, the British crown colony off Spain, stands alone in datelines.

The body of water linking the Mediterranean Sea and the Atlantic Ocean is *the Strait of Gibraltar* (not Straits).

GI Bill of Rights This refers to laws passed after World War II, mainly to help finance education of veterans.

G

gigabyte It equals a billion bytes.

See **computer storage capacity.**

Gila monster

gilt In the commodities business, a *gilt* is a young female hog.

Ginnie Mae

See **Government National Mortgage Association.**

ginning It is a process involving the separation of cotton fibers from the seed and combing the finished fibers.

girl Use *girl* in reference only to the very young. Also, use *saleswoman,* not salesgirl.

girlfriend, boyfriend

glamour It is one of the few *-our* endings still used in American English. But the adjective is *glamorous.*

global bond It is a bond that is registered and can be sold immediately without any restriction to U.S. investors. The issue usually is at least $500 million.

Global Depositary Receipts They are similar to American Depositary Receipts, which allow companies outside the U.S. to list their stock in the U.S. *Global Depositary Receipts* allow companies in the U.S., Europe, Asia and Latin America to list their stock in various markets around the world. Companies in emerging markets such as India, China and Brazil are the prime issuers of GDRs.

See **American Depositary Receipts.**

Global Equity Market The New York Stock Exchange and Euronext are partners in the *Global Equity Market,* or *GEM,* formed for joint trading of global companies' securities. Euronext comprises the merged stock exchanges in Paris, Brussels and Amsterdam.

globe-trotter, globe-trotting

GmbH Follows some German company names.

See **foreign companies.**

GMT Greenwich Mean Time is no longer used.

See **Coordinated Universal Time** and **time zones.**

go-between (n.)

godchild, goddaughter, godfather, godliness, godmother, godsend, godson Always lowercase.

gods and goddesses

Capitalize *God* in references to the deity of all monotheistic religions. Capitalize all noun references to the deity: *God the Father, Holy Ghost, Holy Spirit,* etc. Lowercase personal pronouns: *he, him, thee, thou.*

Lowercase the words *gods* and *goddesses* in references to the deities of multitheistic religions.

See **religious references.**

gold Commercially, it is used mostly in electronics, jewelry and coins.

gold loan It is the financing of a gold-related project or business. It provides a combination of cheap funding and built-in hedging.

golden parachute It refers to a lucrative contract given to a top executive to generate lavish benefits in case the job is lost in a takeover.

Goldman Sachs Group Inc. The brokerage firm is based in New York.

goodbye

Good Conduct Medal

Good Friday

Goodrich *BFGoodrich Co.* of Charlotte, N.C., is in the aerospace and specialty-chemicals business. Its onetime tire brand name and retail tire stores are owned by Michelin SA of France.

good, well

Good, an adjective, means something is better than average. *Good* is properly used as an adjective sentences with linking verbs, such as *The future looks good.*

Well, as an adjective, means suitable, proper, or healthy. As an adverb, *well* means in a satisfactory or skillful manner.

goodwill (n. and adj.) It is the amount by which the purchase price exceeds the fair value of an acquired company's net assets. Formerly, accountants used the term *goodwill* to refer to an intangible business asset, such as a well-regarded business name, brand, or symbol, acquired in a merger. But under revised guidelines, the intangible assets such as trademarks, brands, patents, symbols, franchise rights, and licenses have been grouped under their own line item as *identifiable intangible assets* rather than being included in the goodwill line. Upon undertaking an acquisition, a company adjusts the carrying amounts for the the acquired company's assets and liabilities, to bring them in line with fair-market values.

GOP The term *GOP* as a synonym for the Republican Party is to be used only in direct quotations, and then explained as standing for *Grand Old Party.*

gorilla An ape. Not to be confused with a *guerrilla,* an unorthodox soldier.

Gospel, gospel Capitalize *Gospel* and *Gospels* when referring to any or all of the first four books of the New Testament: *the Gospel of St. John, the Gospels.* Lowercase in other references: *gospel singer.*

government Never abbreviate: *the federal government, the state government, the U.S. government.*

governmental bodies

Generally capitalize on first reference: *the Pennsylvania Department of Human Resources, the Lancaster City Council, the Chicago Fire Department.*

For federal government, *see* **departments.**

Retain capitalization in referring to a specific body if the dateline or context makes the name of the nation, state, county, city, etc., unnecessary: *the State Department* (in a story from Washington); *the Department of Human Resources* or *the state Department of Human Resources* (in a story from Pennsylvania); *the City Council* (in a story from Lancaster); *the Fire Department* or the *the city Fire Department* (in a story from Chicago).

Lowercase further condensations of the name: *the department, the council.*

For additional guidance, *see* **assembly; city council; committee; congress; federal; legislature; house of representatives; senate; U.S. Supreme Court.**

GENERIC REFERENCES: Words capitalized as part of a proper name are lowercased as plurals and when they don't refer to a specific body. *The town doesn't have a fire department. Several city councils will provide funds. He will address both houses of the New York and New Jersey legislatures.*

FOREIGN BODIES: The same principles apply. *See* **foreign governmental bodies** and **foreign legislative bodies.**

government, junta, regime

A *government* is an established system of political administration: *the U.S. government.*

A *junta* is a group or council that often rules after a coup. It becomes a government after it establishes an administration.

Regime is a synonym for *political system: a democratic regime,* an *authoritarian regime.*

Don't use *regime* to mean a specific government or junta.

An *administration* comprises officials who make up the executive branch of a government: *the Bush administration.*

Government National Mortgage Association *Ginnie Mae* is acceptable for most references. This government-owned corporation is part of the Department of Housing and Urban Development. It was split off from Fannie Mae in 1968, to take over such functions as special assistance, management and liquidating. Ginnie Mae's mission is also to make real-estate investment more attractive to institutional investors. Its debt trades in the mortgage-securities market.

governor Capitalize and abbreviate as *Gov.* or *Govs.* when used as a formal title before one or more names. Lowercase and spell out in all other uses.

But for members of boards of governors, *governor* isn't considered a formal title: *Supporting the move was Fed governor Wayne Angell.*

See the next entry and **titles.**

governor general It is the title for Britain's representatives in Canada and elsewhere. Don't abbreviate it.

grade, grader Hyphenate: *fourth-grade student,* a *fourth-grader,* a *10th-grader.*

graduate (v.) It is acceptable to say someone *graduated from a school* or he *was graduated from the school.* But one does not *graduate high school.*

graffiti The singular is *graffito,* but *graffiti* is often used as a singular in reference to the practice of drawing on walls and vehicles: *Graffiti has almost been eliminated.*

grain (weight) This is smallest unit in the system of weights in the U.S. It was originally defined as the weight of one grain of wheat. It takes 437.5 grains to make an ounce.

See **ounce (weight)** and **pound.**

gram It is the basic unit of weight in the metric system. It is the weight of one cubic centimeter of water at 4 degrees Celsius. A gram is about one-28th of an ounce.

To convert to ounces, multiply by 0.035.

See **metric system.**

grammar

Granada, Grenada *Granada* is a city in Spain; *Grenada* is a Caribbean island.

granddad, granddaughter, grandfather, grandmother, grandson

grand jury Always lowercase: a *Los Angeles County grand jury, the grand jury.*

Grand Slam It is capitalized in reference to the four major tournaments in golf and tennis—the U.S. Open, the British Open, the Masters and the PGA championship in golf and the Australian Open, the French Open, Wimbledon and the U.S. Open in tennis.

grant-in-aid, grants-in-aid

grantor trust The nontaxable *grantor trust* often is used as a vehicle for issuing asset-backed securities.

See **asset-backed securities.**

grass roots (n.), **grass-roots** (adj.)

gravity

In the petroleum industry, *gravity* refers to the density of a crude oil or oil product. On the gravity scale used in the U.S., the American Petroleum Institute's *API scale,* water is 10. Lighter measurements are above 10, and heavier measurements are below 10. (The *specific-gravity scale* is opposite to API scale.)

gray Not *grey.* But: *greyhound.*

great- Hyphenate *great-grandfather, great-great-grandmother,* etc.

Great Britain *Britain* is preferable in all references. It comprises England, Scotland and Wales. The United Kingdom comprises Britain and Northern Ireland.

See **United Kingdom.**

Great Depression

See **depression.**

greater Capitalize when used to define a community and its surrounding region: *Greater Boston.*

Great Lakes They are Lake Erie, Lake Huron, Lake Michigan, Lake Ontario and Lake Superior.

Great Plains Capitalize *Great Plains* or *the Plains* when referring to the U.S. prairie lands that extend from North Dakota to Texas and from the Mississippi River to the Rocky Mountains.

Greek Orthodox Church

See **Eastern Orthodox churches.**

green card It is a registration card granting an alien permission to live and work in the U.S.

greenmail The jargon term is applied to the practice whereby outsiders buy blocks of a company's stock and then entice the company to buy the shares back at a premium to avoid a takeover. If you use the term, provide an explanation of it.

G

green-shoe clause In the financial world, it is a provision in an underwriting agreement. It provides that, if public demand for a new issue of securities is exceptional, the issuer will authorize additional shares to be distributed by the *syndicate* of investment bankers who are purchasing the issue for resale to the public.

Greenwich Mean Time (GMT) It has been replaced by Coordinated Universal Time.

See **time zones.**

Grenada The Caribbean island.

See **Granada, Grenada.**

grisly, grizzly

Grisly is horrifying.

Grizzly means grayish and refers to the *grizzly bear.*

gross Don't use as a verb.

gross domestic product The total value of goods and services produced in a nation. It replaced *gross national product* as the Commerce Department's main measure of U.S. economic output. *GDP* is acceptable on second reference.

gross national product The total value of a nation's output of goods and services, including what the nation produces abroad. *GNP* is acceptable on second reference.

Groundhog Day It is Feb. 2.

groundskeeper

groundswell

groundwater

G

group It normally takes singular verbs and pronouns: *The group is reviewing its position.* But *see* **collective nouns.**

Group of Seven It comprises the U.S., Canada, France, Germany, Italy, Japan, and the United Kingdom. *G-7* is acceptable on second reference.

For *Group of Three,* etc., *see* **G-3; G-7; G-8; G-10; G-15; G-22.**

grow One *grows* crops or plants or a beard. *Growing* a business or a company or the economy is jargon, so confine that usage to quotations.

grown-up (n. and adj.)

G-string, G-suit

Guadalupe It is in Mexico.

Guadeloupe The city in the West Indies uses this spelling. Other cities in Central and South America use the spelling *Guadelupe.*

Guam The capital of the U.S. territory is Hagatna (formerly Agana).

guarantee Preferred to *guaranty,* except in some proper names.

guardsman *See* **National Guard** and **Coast Guardsman.**

Guatemala City It stands alone in datelines.

gubernatorial

guerrilla An unorthodox soldier who attacks government or military units. A *terrorist* attacks civilians.

guest Don't use as a verb except in quoted matter.

guild shop

See **closed shop.**

guilty Only in criminal actions do defendants plead *guilty* or *not guilty.* Be careful with recording the *not-guilty* pleading to avoid inadvertently dropping the *not.* Generally say instead that the defendants are *acquitted.*

Don't use the word *guilty* in civil-case decisions. Judges or juries in civil cases *rule against* or *rule in favor* of defendants.

See **legal terminology.**

Gulf Coast Capitalize when referring to the region of the U.S. and Mexico lying along the Gulf of Mexico.

See **coast.**

Gulf Cooperation Council A group comprising the six Arab nations of Bahrain, Saudi Arabia, Oman, Kuwait, Qatar and the United Arab Emirates. All except Oman and Bahrain are also members of the Organization of Petroleum Exporting Countries. Council representatives meet regularly to discuss issues such as regional energy policy and security.

Gulf Stream But the racetrack is *Gulfstream Park.*

gunbattle, gunboat, gunfight, gunfire, gunpoint, gunpowder

gung-ho A colloquialism.

guns

See **weapons.**

guru

gut Confine the verb form to the meaning *remove the intestines.* Use *burned out the interior of* or *destroyed the interior of* to describe damage done by a fire.

gypsy, gypsies Capitalize references to the ethnic group or its members, also called *Romany* or *Roma.* Lowercase otherwise: *gypsy cab, gypsy-cab driver, gypsy moth.*

Hh

Häagen-Dazs Co. The ice-cream company is a unit of Grand Metropolitan PLC.

habeas corpus The writ or petition is filed to seek the prompt release of someone in custody. It compels those detaining the person to justify their action.

hacker In the computer world, the term for an accomplished software strategist has come to imply mischievous or illegal manipulating of the software. Use the term carefully.

Hades But lowercase *hell*.

hajj, hajji

A *hajj* is a pilgrimage to Mecca, required of every Muslim.

A *hajji* is a Muslim who has made the pilgrimage.

Hague, The The city in the Netherlands stands alone in datelines.

hailstorm

half The preposition *of* is optional: *half the time* or *half of the time.*

half- Follow Webster's New World Dictionary. Hyphenate if not listed there.

Words without a hyphen:

halfback	halfhearted
halftone	halftrack

Also: *halftime,* an exception to the dictionary in keeping with widespread practice in sports copy.

Two words:

half brother	half sole (n.)
half size	half note
half dollar	half tide

With a hyphen:

half-baked	half-sole (v.)
half-life	half-hour
half-moon	half-truth
half-cocked	

half-mast, half-staff

On ships and at naval stations, flags are flown at *half-mast.*

Elsewhere, flags are flown at *half-staff.*

hallelujah But the spelling *alleluia* is preferred for Catholic prayer usage.

Halley's comet After Edmund Halley, an English astronomer who predicted the comet's appearance once every 75 years. Last seen in 1986.

Halloween

halo, halos

handgun

hand-held

handicap, handicapped Avoid the words in references to physical or mental conditions.
See **disabled.**

handmade

handpicked

hands off, hands-off Hyphenate it when it is used as a compound modifier: *He kept his hands off the matter, but his hands-off policy wasn't appreciated.*

hand to hand, hand-to-hand, hand to mouth, hand-to-mouth Hyphenate the terms when they are used before the noun they modify.

hangar, hanger
A *hangar* is a building for aircraft.
A *hanger* is used to hang clothes.

hang, hanged, hung
One *hangs* a picture, a criminal or oneself.
For past tense or the passive, use *hanged* when referring to executions or suicides, but otherwise use *hung.*

hangover

hanky-panky

Hanukkah The Jewish Festival of Lights is an eight-day commemoration of the rededication of the temple by the Maccabees after their victory over the Syrians. It usually occurs in December, but sometimes in late November.

hara-kiri

harass, harassment

hard drive In a computer *hard drive,* data are written onto and read from rotating disks with magnetic coating.

hard-liner

hardware Computer components such as disks, disk drives, display screens, keyboards, printers and chips.
See **software.**

harebrained

harelip

Havana The capital of Cuba stands alone in datelines.

Hawaii Don't abbreviate. Residents are *Hawaiians.*
Honolulu stands alone in datelines. Use *Hawaii* after all other cities in datelines, specifying the island in the text if necessary.
Honolulu is on Oahu, the most populous of the eight major islands. The largest island is Hawaii, also called the Big Island. The other six: Kahoolawe, Kauai, Lanai, Maui, Molokai and Niihau.
See **datelines** and **state names.**

Hawaiian Airlines

Hawaiian Standard Time There is no daylight-saving time in Hawaii.

H-bomb Use *hydrogen bomb* unless a direct quotation is involved.

headline capitalization
Generally lowercase: *a, an, and, as, at, but, by, for, if, in, of, off, on, or, out, the, to* (as a preposition or an infinitive), *up* and *yet* (as a conjunction). But capitalize them when they start a line or when the prepositions are an integral part of the verb: *Hold Out, Take Up.* Apply this test: Capitalize the preposition if the verb involved has no object, or if the

preposition can be placed after the verb's object without changing the meaning: *Send In the Marines* can be reworded *Send the Marines In,* so the preposition is uppercased.

Capitalize the prepositions when they are used as adjectives or adverbs: *He Travels With the In Crowd; The Fire Was Out by That Time; We're Off to See the Wizard*; or as nouns: *That Left Him an Out; That Is a Big If Since the Rate Rise; The Boxer Came To.*

Capitalize prepositions and conjunctions that end a headline or a headline segment: *What This World Is Coming To; This 'Surprise' Was Anything But.*

Generally capitalize after hyphens: *Ex-Chairman, Cease-Fire.* But: *Co-op.* Capitalize any word after a colon.

Lowercase *a.m.* and *p.m.*

headline guidelines

Don't start any section of the head (flashline, top, deck or barline) with a numeral or a dollar figure.

But numerals may be used, even for one through nine, elsewhere in the headline if the numerals aren't mixed with spelled-out numbers in the same headline.

Ordinal numerals may be used within headlines only to designate calendar or fiscal quarters and halves, in the guidelines above: *1st Quarter, 2nd Half, 3rd Period.* But: *First Act, Eighth Year.*

Don't start any section of the head with a verb that omits a subject: *Pays $82 Million for Gotham Co.*

Try to include all auxiliary verbs (*Is* and *Are*) in headlines, and especially try never to omit the auxiliary verb of the second phrase of a headline: *Gotham Co. Lays Off 2,000 After Plant Is Struck.*

Use the present tense except when the headline itself makes clear that the event was in the past: *Gotham Co. Reports Earnings Fell in First Quarter. Gotham's First-Quarter Earnings Fell.* But: *Gotham's Earnings Fall After Strike.*

Use single quotes rather than double quotes in headlines and subheads.

Don't put an adjective on one line and the noun it modifies on another.

Don't put a possessive on one line and the word it modifies on another.

Don't put a preposition on one line and its object on another.

Don't put part of the verb on one line and the rest on another.

Don't round off dollar figures more than the story does.

Overworked verbs to try to avoid in headlines: *eye, nod* (as in *gives nod to*), *mull, OK.*

H

headlong

head-on (adj., adv.)

headquarters It may take either a singular or a plural verb.

Don't use *headquarter(ed)* as a verb. Use *based* instead.

health care (n.), **health-care** (adj.)

hearing examiner A job description, not a formal title. Lowercase.

See **administrative law judge.**

hearsay

heating oil No. 2 fuel oil, a distillate fuel oil, is used for domestic heating and in some commercial and industrial burners.

See **diesel.**

heaven

heavenly bodies

Capitalize the proper names of planets, stars, constellations, etc.: *Mars, Arcturus, the Big Dipper, Aries. See* **earth** and **planet**.

For comets, capitalize only the proper-noun element of the name: *Halley's comet.*

Lowercase *sun* and *moon,* but if their Greek names are used, capitalize them: *Helios* and *Luna.*

hectare A unit of surface measure in the metric system equal to 10,000 square meters.

A *hectare* is equal to 2.47 acres, 107,639.1 square feet, or 11,959.9 square yards.

To convert to acres, multiply by 2.47.

See **acre** and **metric system.**

hedge funds The private investment partnerships for large investors seek quick profits by putting huge sums in global currency, bond and stock markets.

hedging In commerce, it involves the buying or selling of a product or a security to offset a possible loss from price changes on a future corresponding purchase or sale.

In commodities trading, dealers *hedge* against falling prices of a product by selling it for future delivery. For example, a miller who buys wheat to convert to flour will sell a similar quantity of wheat he doesn't own at a price near the price he paid for his wheat. He will agree to deliver it at the same time that his flour is ready for market. If at that time the price of wheat, and therefore flour, has fallen, he will lose on the flour but can buy the wheat at a low price and sell it at a profit. If prices have risen, he will make an extra profit on his flour that he will have to sacrifice to buy the wheat for delivery. Either way, he has protected his profit or narrowed his loss.

he, him, his, thee, thou Personal pronouns referring to the deity are lowercase.

heights

See **dimensions.**

heliport

hell But capitalize *Hades.* Use *hell of a* rather than *helluva.*

helter-skelter

hemisphere Capitalize *Northern Hemisphere, Western Hemisphere,* etc. Lowercase *hemisphere* in other uses: *the Eastern and Western hemispheres, the hemisphere.*

hemorrhage, hemorrhoid

an herb, a herbal tea As illogical as it may seem, the *h* in *herb* is silent, but the *h* in *herbal* is sounded.

here Don't overuse the word as a means of referring to the dateline city of an article. It is often redundant or confusing.

heroin The narcotic, originally a trademark.

hertz This term, the same in singular or plural, has been adopted as the international unit of frequency equal to one cycle per second. In contexts where it would not be understood by most readers, it should be followed by a parenthetical explanation: *15,400 hertz (cycles per second).*

Don't abbreviate.

he, she

See **his, her.**

Hewlett-Packard Co. *H-P* is acceptable on second reference and in headlines, but *Hewlett* is a preferred short form for headlines. The maker of computer systems and printers is based in Palo Alto, Calif.

hideaway

hi-fi

highflier, highflying

high school, high-school diploma Not *high-school degree.*

highway designations *U.S. Highway 1, U.S. Route 1, Route 1, state Route 34, Interstate Highway 95, Interstate 95.* On second reference for an interstate: *I-95.*

When a letter follows a number, capitalize it but don't use a hyphen: *Route 9W.*

highway patrol Capitalize it in the formal name of a police agency: *the New York Highway Patrol, the Highway Patrol.* Lowercase *highway patrolman* in all uses.

See **state police.**

hijack (v.), **hijacking** (n. and adj.)

hike Don't use as a synonym for raise or rise.

Hindi, Hindu *Hindi* is the language, *Hindu* the religion.

his, her Use the pronoun *he* or *his* when an indefinite antecedent may be male or female: *A doctor listens to his patients.* (Not *his or her patients.*)

Often, however, the better choice is a slight revision of the sentence: *Doctors listen to to their patients.*

Hispanic (n. and adj.) Although *Latino* is also used, especially in the Southwest, *Hispanic* is generally the preferred reference to those of any race descended from a Spanish-speaking culture or from any area of Latin America. But use *Latino* to refer to a specific group that prefers the term. If possible, use a more specific term, such as *Cuban* or *Puerto Rican.*

historic, historical

A *historic* event is an important occurrence, one that stands out in history.

Historical means concerned with history or occurrences in the past. Because the *h* is pronounced, use the article *a: a historic occasion.*

history Avoid the redundancy *past history.*

hit-and-run (n. and adj.)

hitchhike, hitchhiker

HIV It refers to the *human immune-deficiency virus that causes AIDS.* Either define it or call it the AIDS virus. Don't use the redundancy *HIV virus.*

See **AIDS.**

hoard, horde

A *hoard* is a supply kept in reserve; *to hoard* is to form such a supply, usually secretly.

A *horde* is a moving crowd.

Hobson's choice It is an apparent free choice that actually is no choice. Don't confuse it with a *dilemma* or *quandary.*

See **dilemma.**

Ho Chi Minh City This became the name of the former Saigon after the Vietnamese Communist takeover in 1975. But the old name remains in popular use.

hodgepodge

Hodgkin's disease Thomas Hodgkin, an English physician, first described the disease of the lymph nodes.

ho-hum

holding company It is a company whose principal assets are the securities it owns in companies that actually provide goods or services. The usual reason for forming a *holding company* is to enable one corporation and its directors to control several companies by holding a majority of their stock.

hold on to Not *hold onto.* In a headline, the O in *on* is uppercase, as part of the verb.

hold up (v.), **holdup** (n. and adj.)

holidays, holy days Capitalize them: *New Year's Eve, New Year's Day, Groundhog Day, Easter Sunday, Memorial Day, Fourth of July,* etc.

Holland/Dutch
See **Netherlands.**

Hollywood Stands alone in datelines.

holocaust Capitalize it in reference to the Nazi extermination of Jews in World War II. Lowercase it or find a better word in other references to other massacres or firestorms.

Holy Communion, Communion
See **sacraments.**

Holy Father The preferred form is *the pope* or *the pontiff,* or the individual's name: *Pope John Paul II.*

Holy See It refers to the headquarters of the Roman Catholic Church in Vatican City.

Holy Spirit The term is preferred over *Holy Ghost* in most cases.

Holy Week The week before Easter.

home builder, home buyer, but **homemade, homeowner**

home in on Not *hone* in on.

home page It is the introductory screen of a site on the Internet or an intranet.

hometown
See **comma** for guidelines on how to list a hometown after an individual's name.

homicide, murder, manslaughter
Homicide applies to a killing of a person.

Murder is malicious and premeditated homicide.

Manslaughter is homicide without malice or premeditation.

Avoid saying a victim was *murdered* until someone has been convicted of the crime.

See **execute** and **assassin, killer, murderer.**

Hong Kong It stands alone in datelines.

Honolulu The capital of Hawaii stands alone in datelines.

honorariums Not *honoraria,* for the plural of *honorarium.*

honorary degrees All references to honorary degrees should specify that the degree was honorary. Don't use *Dr.* before the name.

hooky Not *hookey.*

hopefully Strict constructionists use *hopefully* only in the sense of *in a hopeful manner (He started the mission to China hopefully)* and object to the use of *hopefully* in the sense of *it is hoped (Hopefully, the law will be passed).* So it is hoped that we will generally avoid it in favor of constructions such as *Congress hopes* or *most people hope.*

horde, hoard
A *horde* is a moving crowd.

A *hoard* is a supply kept in reserve; *to hoard* is to form such a supply, usually secretly.

horizontal portal It is a broad-interest Internet portal such as Yahoo! Portals geared to users with specific interests are *vertical portals.* Don't use the terms without explaining them.

horsepower

horse races Capitalize their formal names: *Kentucky Derby, Preakness, Belmont Stakes.*

horses' names Capitalize them.
See **animals.**

host Its use as a verb has become acceptable.

hotel
Capitalize it as part of the proper name of a specific hotel: *the Waldorf-Astoria Hotel.* But: *It was a Hilton Hotel.*

hot issue It usually refers to a stock that rises sharply in price immediately after being offered publicly for the first time.

House of Commons, House of Lords They are the two houses of the British Parliament. In second reference: *Commons* or *the Commons,* or *the Lords.*

house of representatives Capitalize it when referring to a specific government body: *the U.S. House of Representatives, the Massachusetts House of Representatives, the U.S. House, the Massachusetts House.*
See **organizations and institutions.**

housewife *Homemaker* is the term preferred by many women.

Houston The city in Texas stands alone in datelines.

Hovercraft A trademark for a vehicle that travels on a cushion of air.

howitzer
See **weapons.**

html It stands for *hypertext markup language,* the system used to create documents on the World Wide Web.

http In the world of the Web, it stands for *hypertext transfer protocol.*

hub In the cyber world, it is a device that splits one network cable into a number of cables, each connecting to an individual computer. *E-mail hub* refers to a processing center where telecom messages and servers converge, much like airplanes converging an airline's hub city.

HUD It is acceptable in second reference for *the Department of Housing and Urban Development.*
See **departments.**

human, human being Either is acceptable.

Humphrey-Hawkins Act Formally, it is *the Full Employment and Balanced Growth Act of 1978.* It specifies that the primary objectives of U.S. economic policy should be maximum employment, stable prices and moderate long-term interest rates. The act requires the chairman of the Federal Reserve to testify to Congress twice a year (by Feb. 20 and by July 20) on the state of the economy and the conduct of monetary policy.

hurly-burly

hurricanes Don't personalize hurricanes in using the names assigned to them. *Earlier, Hurricane Betsy changed course and devastated the coast.* Not: *Betsy behaved capriciousy and took a devastating turn.* For pronoun references to hurricanes, use *it,* not *she* or *he.*

hush-hush

Hyannis Port, Mass.

hydro- The rules in **prefixes** apply, but in general, no hyphen: *hydroelectric, hydrophobia.*

hyper- The rules in **prefixes** apply, but in general, no hyphen: *hyperactive, hypercritical.*

hyperlink It is a link from an Internet page to another page in the document, as a newspaper's home page with a link to its editorial page.

hypertext It is a system of linking electronic documents.

hyphen (-) Use hyphens to avoid ambiguity or to form a single idea from two or more words.

COMPOUND MODIFIERS: When a compound modifier—two or more words that express a single concept—precedes a noun, use hyphens to link all the words in the compound except the adverb *very* and all adverbs that end in *ly: first-quarter earnings,* a *bluish-green dress,* a *full-time job,* a *well-known man,* a *better-qualified woman,* a *know-it-all attitude,* a *very good time,* an *easily remembered rule.*

The hyphen is helpful to quick understanding even in some frequently used compound modifiers: *high-school students, real-estate dealers, stock-market rally, federal-funds rate.*

Exceptions: Latin and other foreign terms that aren't ordinarily hyphenated: *pro bono, per capita.* And modifiers and nouns that appear together unhyphenated in the dictionary: *carpal tunnel syndrome.*

Many combinations that are hyphenated before a noun are not hyphenated when they occur after a noun: *The earnings rose in the first quarter. The rate for federal funds. The dress, a bluish green, was attractive on her. She works full time. His attitude suggested that he knew it all.*

But when a modifier that would be hyphenated before a noun occurs instead after a form of the verb *to be,* the hyphen usually should be retained to avoid confusion: *The man is well-known. The woman is quick-witted. The play is second-rate.*

The principle of using a hyphen to avoid confusion explains why no hyphen is required with *very* and with *-ly* adverbs. Readers can expect them to modify the word that follows. But if a combination such as *little-known man* were not hyphenated, the reader could logically be expecting *little* to be followed by a noun, as in *little man.* Instead, the reader encountering *little known* without the hyphen would have to back up mentally and make the compound connection on his own.

Words such as *more, most, less* and *least* often modify the succeeding word and don't always require the hyphen for clarity: *The most disastrous earthquake in history. The least understood economics book in recent times.* But the hyphen is sometimes required to avoid ambiguity: *We need more-industrious reporters.*

TWO-ELEMEMT COMPOUNDS: *seriocomic, socio-economic.*

DUAL HERITAGE: Use a hyphen to designate dual heritage: *Italian-American, Mexican-American.* Exceptions: *French Canadian* and *Latin American.*

AIRCRAFT: Designations usually, but not always, take a hyphen between the letters and the numbers: *DC-10, F-111, L-1011.*

See **aircraft** entries.

COMPOUND NOUNS: Those that don't appear in Webster's New World Dictionary or this stylebook should be used as two words, without a hyphen.

Don't hyphenate *commander in chief* or *editor in chief,* but do use hyphen in *secretary-treasurer.*

AVOID AMBIGUITY: Use a hyphen to avoid ambiguity in words such as *re-creation,* meaning re-creation of a scene or whatever. Also *co-respondent* in a divorce proceeding.

See **prefixes.**

hypo- Solid: *hypodermic, hypoglycemia, hypothyroid.*

I i

Iberia The Spanish airline's name stands alone.

ICBM, ICBMs The abbreviations are acceptable in first reference for *intercontinental ballistic missile(s),* but the spelled-out version should be included in the article. Avoid the redundancy *ICBM missiles.*

Icelandair It is based in Reykjavik, Iceland.

Idaho Don't abbreviate it. Residents are *Idahoans.*

See **state names.**

illegal Use it only to mean a violation of the law. In labor-management disputes, for example, *unauthorized* is usually appropriate to refer to strikes or other actions that one side in the dispute may call illegal.

Illinois Abbreviate as *Ill.* after city names. Residents are *Illinoisans.*

See **state names.**

illusion *See* **allusion, illusion.**

imam Lowercase it to refer to the leader of a prayer in a Muslim mosque. Capitalize it before a name of a Muslim leader.

See **religious titles.**

immigrate

See **emigrate, immigrate** entry.

impact Avoid using *impact* as a verb.

impel, impelled, impelling

imperial gallon The standard in Britain, the *imperial gallon* is equal to about 1.2 U.S. gallons. The metric equivalent is approximately 4.5 liters.

See **liter.**

implausible

imply, infer

A writer or speaker *implies* in the words he uses.

A listener or reader *infers* something from those words.

impostor

impromptu It means without preparation or advance thought.

-in With noun forms, use a hyphen: *break-in, walk-in, cave-in, write-in.*

in When *in* is used to indicate that something is in vogue, use quotation marks only if followed by a noun: *It was the "in" thing to do.* But: *Short skirts are in again.*

in- Use no hyphen when it means *not:*

inaccurate insufficient

Other uses without hyphens:

inbound	inpatient (n., adj.)
infighting	infield
indoor	

With a hyphen:

in-depth	in-group
in-house	in-law

inasmuch as

Inauguration Day Capitalize when referring to the inauguration of a U.S. president.

Inc.
See **incorporated.**

inch The metric equivalent is exactly 2.54 centimeters.

To convert to centimeters, multiply by 2.54.

See **centimeter** and **foot.**

include

Use *include* to introduce a series when the items that follow are only part of the total: *The price includes tax.*

Use *comprise* or *constitute* when all the elements are given: *The industry comprises 200 companies. The 200 companies constitute the industry.*

See **compose, comprise, constitute.**

incorporated Abbreviate and capitalize as *Inc.* when it is part of a formal corporate name: *PepsiCo Inc.,* without a comma before the *Inc.* But drop the *Inc.* after *Co., Corp.* or *Ltd.* in a company name.

See **company names.**

incorporator

incredible, incredulous

Incredible means unbelievable.

Incredulous means unbelieving or skeptical.

incubator In the sphere of *venture-capital investment organizations,* it is one that uses its internal staff to propose and explore ideas for start-up business investments. Standard venture-capital concerns, by contrast, review outsiders' ideas to invest in.

incur, incurred, incurring

indenture In the securities business, an *indenture* is a legal contract between a borrower and investors, specifying the terms of a bond offering. It typically includes covenants that place restrictions on the borrower.

index, indexes

index arbitrage
See **program trading.**

index fund It is a mutual fund that seeks to produce the same return that investors would get if they owned all the stocks in a particular stock index, such as the Dow Jones Industrial Average.

See **mutual fund.**

index of leading economic indicators It is a composite of 12 economic measurements, developed to help forecast likely changes in the economy as a whole. It is compiled monthly by the Commerce Department.

Indian *See* **American Indian.**

Indiana Abbreviate as *Ind.* after city names. Residents are *Indianians.*

See **state names.**

Indianapolis The capital of Indiana stands alone in datelines.

Indiana University Its name is *Indiana University,* not the University of Indiana.

Indian Ocean
See **oceans.**

indict Use *indict* only in connection with the legal process of bringing charges against an individual or corporation: *indicted on a charge of murder, indicted on a bribery charge.*

For guidelines on related words, *see* **accused** and **allege** entries.

indiscriminate, indiscriminately

indispensable

indium The minor metal is used in the electronics industry, especially in liquid-crystal display screens and laptop computers.

individual retirement accounts *IRA* is acceptable in second reference.

Indo- It usually is hyphenated and capitalized: *Indo-Aryan, Indo-German, Indo-Hittite, Indo-Iranian.* But: *Indochina.*

Indochina Formerly *French Indochina,* it now is divided into Cambodia, Laos and Vietnam.

Indonesia Use *Indonesia* after the name of a community in datelines. Specify an individual island, if needed, in the text.

indoor (adj.), **indoors** (adv.) *Indoor recreation is conducted indoors.*

industrial development bonds These securities are issued by a state or local government or development agency to finance the construction or purchase of industrial or commercial facilities that are to be sold or leased to private companies. The bonds, backed by the credit of the private companies, no longer are tax-exempt to investors.

infant It is applicable to children through 12 months old.

infantile paralysis The preferred term is *polio.*

inflation It is a sustained rise in prices. The two types:

—*Cost-push inflation* occurs when rising costs are the chief reason for the increased prices.

—*Demand-pull inflation* occurs when the amount of money available exceeds the amount of goods and services available for sale.

The type involved at any point is often in dispute, so using the terms to apply to a given time requires attribution.

informant, informer They both provide information, but use *informer* to designate one who informs against others, often for compensation.

I

information highway, the In effect, it is everyone's computer connected to everyone else's computer. Shorter versions such as *infohighway, infobahn, infoway* and *I-way* are acceptable in contexts where their meanings are clear, but use the full *information highway* whenever possible.

information technology *IT* is acceptable in second reference. *Information technology* is the umbrella term for the development and installation of computer systems and applications.

infra- Solid: *infrared, infrastructure.*

initial public offering *IPO* is acceptable in second reference for *initial public offering.* An IPO is used to take a company public, allowing investors to buy the company's stock. Additional offerings of stock by a company after an initial public offering are referred to as *follow-on offerings.* An initial public offering typically occurs when a company's *venture capitalists* no longer provide enough capital needed for expansion. The company finds investment bankers willing to *underwrite* the stock. The underwriters buy the issue's shares from the offering company and then sell them to investors. The underwriters help the company prepare a *prospectus* to provide to potential investors. It contains a detailed financial history of the company and explanations of its products and services, and it identifies management's background and experience. The prospectus also must enumerate any risks the company faces. The underwriters establish the price they will pay for the company's shares. Investors then bid the shares higher or lower, indicating whether they agree with the underwriters' valuation.

See **prospectus** and **venture capitalists.**

initials

Use periods and no space when an individual uses initials instead of a first name: *H.L. Mencken.*

Don't give a name with a single initial *(J. Jones)* unless it is the individual's preference or a first name cannot be learned.

Abbreviations using just the initials of a person's name don't take periods: *JFK, FDR.*

See **middle or first initials.**

in-law

innocent The legal pleading is *not guilty.*

innocuous

innuendo

inoculate

inquire, inquiry Not *enquire, enquiry.*

insolvency It is the declared inability of a business or person to pay debts when due.

See **bankruptcy.**

in spite of *Despite* means the same thing and is shorter.

install, installment

Instinet Corp. It operates the *Instinet*, the largest electronic communications network.

See **ECN.**

insure

See **ensure, insure, assure.**

integrated services digital network *ISDN* is acceptable in second reference to the high-speed telecommunications system.

inter- The prefix means *among* or *between,* whereas *intra-* means *within.* The rules in prefixes apply. Don't hyphenate unless the base word is capitalized:

inter-American
interstate
interracial

intercontinental ballistic missile The abbreviation *ICBM* is acceptable in first reference for *intercontinental ballistic missile,* but the spelled-out version should be included in the article. Avoid the redundancy *ICBM missiles.*

interday, intraday

Interday denotes stock trading or other action that straddles two or more days.

Intraday denotes activity contained within one day.

interest rates *Real* interest rates are adjusted for expected inflation. *Nominal* interest rates are unadjusted.

See **loan terminology.**

Internal Revenue Service *IRS* is acceptable in second reference. Capitalize also *Internal Revenue,* but lowercase *the revenue service.*

International Association of Machinists The shortened form *Machinists union* is acceptable in all references. Headquarters is in Washington.

International Bank for Reconstruction and Development *World Bank* is acceptable in all references.

International Brotherhood of Electrical Workers Use the full name in first reference to avoid confusion with the United Electrical, Radio and Machine Workers of America. *IBEW* is acceptable in second reference. Headquarters is in Washington.

International Brotherhood of Teamsters, Chauffeurs, Warehousemen and Helpers
See **Teamsters union,** which is acceptable in all references.

International Business Machines Corp. *IBM* is acceptable in second reference. Headquarters is in Armonk, N.Y.

International Court of Justice It is the principal judicial organ of the United Nations. The court, unavailable to individuals, has jurisdiction over matters specifically provided for in the U.N. charter or in treaties and conventions. It also has jurisdiction over cases referred to it by U.N. members and by nonmembers that subscribe to the court statutes. In second reference, use *international court* or *world court* in lowercase. Don't abbreviate.

International Criminal Police Organization *Interpol* is acceptable in all references.

international date line It extends north and south through the Pacific Ocean, largely along the 180th meridian.

By international agreement, when it is 12:01 a.m. Sunday just west of the line, it is 12:01 a.m. Saturday just east of it.

See **time zones.**

International Energy Agency Part of the Paris-based Organization for Economic Cooperation and Development, it was formed to help major industrial countries deal with energy needs. It issues a widely followed report at the start of each month on the world oil market, which indicates demand for OPEC oil.

See **Organization for Economic Cooperation and Development.**

International Finance Corp
See **World Bank.**

International Labor Organization A U.N. agency based in Geneva, it monitors employment conditions around the world. *ILO* is acceptable in second reference

International Longshoremen's and Warehousemen's Union *ILWU* is acceptable in second reference.

International Longshoremen's Association *ILA* is acceptable in second reference.

International Monetary Fund *IMF* is acceptable in second reference. Established in 1945 and based in Washington, the IMF supervises a supply of money supported by subscriptions of member nations to help stabilize international exchange and promote orderly and balanced trade. Member nations may obtain foreign currency when needed, making it possible to correct temporary deficits in their balance of payments without currency depreciation. It is sometimes called *G182,* because of the number of its members.

International Telecommunications Satellite Organization *Intelsat* is acceptable on first reference, but the body of the story should identify it as the *shortened* form of the full name.

Internet, the *The Internet,* also called *the Net,* is the global computer network that connects independent networks. *Internet addresses* include e-mail addresses and Web-site designations. In articles, if an Internet address falls at the end of a sentence, use a period. If an address breaks between lines, split it directly before a slash or a dot that is part of the address, without inserting a hyphen.

An *Internet host* is a computer on which Internet-accessible data are stored.

See **intranet,** which is lowercase.

Interpol It is acceptable in all references to *the International Criminal Police Organization.*

Interstate Commerce Commission *ICC* is acceptable in second reference.

intifada Italicize it as a foreign word on first reference. It refers to any uprising, but specifically to the Arab uprising against Israel in the occupied territories of the Gaza Strip and the West Bank of the Jordan River, begun in 1987.

intraday

See **interday, intraday.**

intranet Lowercase the word for a generic internal corporate network.

intrauterine device *IUD* is acceptable on second reference.

Inuit

See **Eskimo, Eskimos.**

IOU, IOUs

Iowa Don't abbreviate. Residents are Iowans.

See **state names.**

IQ *IQ* is acceptable in all references for *intelligence quotient.*

Iran Once called Persia, *Iran* is not an Arab country. The people are *Iranians,* not *Persians* or *Iranis.* The language is usually called *Persian* outside Iran. Inside Iran, the language is called *Farsi.*

Iraq The Arab nation encompasses ancient Mesopotamia. Its people are *Iraqis.* Iraq's dialect of Arabic is *Iraqi.*

Ireland *Ireland* is acceptable in most references to *the Republic of Ireland.* Use *Irish Republic* when a distinction is needed between this nation and *Northern Ireland,* a part of the United Kingdom. In subsequent references: *the republic.*

iridium A platinum-group metal, it is used in electronics.

Irish coffee It is brewed coffee, with Irish whiskey and whipped cream.

Irish International Airlines The preferred name is *Aer Lingus.* Headquarters is in Dublin.

Irish Republican Army The group seeks to wrest Northern Ireland from British rule and unite it with the Irish Republic.

IRA is acceptable in an unambiguous second reference.

Iron Curtain Use it only in quoted matter.

irregardless *Regardless* is correct.

ISDN It stands for *integrated services digital network,* used by telecommunications companies to deliver high-speed services. The abbreviation is acceptable in second reference.

Islam It refers to the Muslim religion, as well as to Muslims in general and their area of dominance. Allah is Islam's deity, and Muhammad is its founder and chief prophet. The adjective is *Islamic.*

See **Muslim.**

Islamite, Islamist *Islamite* is considered archaic usage for Muslim. *Islamist* refers to *someone* or *something involved with the Muslim political cause.* Don't use it to mean *orthodox Muslim.*

island

Capitalize *island* or *islands* as part of a proper name: *the Hawaiian Islands.* But *the Pacific islands.*

it Use this pronoun, rather than *she,* in references to countries and hurricanes.

See **animals** and **boats, ships** entries.

IT It is acceptable in second reference for *information technology,* the umbrella term for the development and installation of computer systems and applications.

italics Use italics for emphasis and for more obscure foreign words and phrases.

See **foreign words.**

ITT Industries Inc. Based in White Plains, N.Y., it makes connectors, switches and other products. It isn't connected with *ITT Educational Services Inc.,* of Indianapolis, which runs tech training schools.

IUD *See* **intrauterine device.**

Ivory Coast Use this English-language version of the country's name, without the article *the.* The people are *Ivoirians.*

Ivy League The members are Dartmouth College; Brown, Columbia, Cornell, Harvard, Princeton and Yale universities; and the University of Pennsylvania (not Pennsylvania State University).

Jj

Jacuzzi It is a trade name for a whirlpool bath or spa.

jail The word isn't interchangeable with *prison.*

See **prison, jail, penitentiary.**

Jamaica rum Not *Jamaican rum.*

January *See* **months.**

Japan Airlines *JAL* is acceptable in second reference.

Japan Current It is warm current flowing from the Philippine Sea east of Taiwan and northeast past Japan.

Java The high-level computer programming language, suitable for use on the Web, was developed by Sun Microsystems Inc.

Jaycees It is the official name of the former Junior Chamber of Commerce. The U.S. Jaycees, the parent domestic organization, is affiliated with the world-wide body, the Jaycees International.

J.C. Penney Co. The retailer is based in Dallas.

jeep, Jeep

Lowercase the military vehicle.

Capitalize references to the trademarked four-wheel-drive civilian vehicle.

Jehovah's Witnesses The denomination was founded in Pittsburgh in 1872 by Charles Taze Russell. Witnesses have no formal titles but these levels of ministry: *publishers* (members who do evangelical work), *regular pioneers* (who devote more time to evangelism) and *special pioneers* (full-time workers).

jell As a verb meaning solidify, it is preferred over *gel.*

Jell-O It is a trademark for a brand of gelatin dessert.

jerry-built It means built cheaply or shoddily, from poor materials. Don't confuse it with *jury-rigged,* which means intended for temporary or emergency use.

Jersey It is an island in the English Channel. Don't use it as a short form for *New Jersey,* except in quotations.

Jerusalem It stands alone in datelines.

Jesus Christianity's central figure is called *Jesus* or *Jesus Christ* or *Christ* by followers. Use lowercase personal pronouns to refer to him.

jet, jetliner, jet plane
See **aircraft terms.**

Jew Because *a Jew* is sometimes considered pejorative when applied to an individual, say instead that he or she is *Jewish.* Don't use *Jewess.*

Jewish congregations Each Jewish synagogue or temple is autonomous, with no hierarchies to control its activities. In the U.S., the Synagogue Council of America in New York coordinates the activities and interrelations of the three basic expressions of Judaism:

Orthodox Judaism. Its national bodies are the Union of Orthodox Jewish Congregations of America and the Rabbinical Council of America.

Conservative Judaism. Its national bodies are the United Synagogue of America and the Rabbinical Assembly.

Reform Judaism. Its national bodies are the Union of American Hebrew Congregations and the Central Conference of American Rabbis.

TITLES: The only formal titles in the U.S. are *rabbi,* for the spiritual leader of a congregation, and *cantor,* for the individual who leads the congregation in song. Use the titles on each reference: *Rabbi Jeffrey Beller of Congregation Beth Shalom, Rabbi Beller, the rabbi, the spiritual leader of the congregation. Cantor Roberta Gardner, Cantor Gardner, the cantor.*

Chief rabbi and *grand rabbi* are used in some countries for the national leaders. Capitalize them when they are used as titles immediately before a name. *See religious titles.*

See **religious titles.**

Jewish holy days
See separate listings for Hanukkah, Passover, Purim, Rosh Hashana, Sukkot and Yom Kippur.

The High Holy Days are *Rosh Hashana* and *Yom Kippur.*

jibe, gibe
See gibe, jibe.

Jidda Use this spelling for the Saudi Arabian port city.

jihad It is a Muslim holy war.

Jockey shorts *Jockey* is a trademark.

John F. Kennedy Space Center Situated at Cape Canaveral, Fla., it is the National Aeronautics and Space Administration's principal launch site. *Kennedy Space Center* is acceptable in all references.

Johns Hopkins University It is in Baltimore.

Joint Chiefs of Staff Also: *the Joint Chiefs.* But lowercase *the chiefs* or *the chiefs of staff.*

Jr. *See* **junior, senior.**

Judaism
See **Jewish congregations.**

judge
Capitalize it in all references before a name when it is the formal title for an individual who presides in a court of law. *Don't* use *Mr., Mrs., Miss* or *Ms.* as an alternative in any reference.

The word *court* should not be used as part of the title unless confusion would result without it: *U.S. District Judge J. Paul Goble, District Judge J. Paul Goble, Judge J. Paul Goble; U.S. Circuit Judge Robert Sack, Juvenile Court Judge David Maj, Criminal Court Judge Eric Martin, Superior Court Judge Gregory Langan, state Supreme Court Judge Martha Ohr, appellate Judge Nicholas Klemmer.*

When the formal title *chief judge* is relevant in context, put the court name after the judge's name: *Chief Judge J. Paul Goble, J. Paul Goble of the U.S. District Court in Washington, D.C.*

Put long court names after the name of a judge: *Judge Amanda Langan of Allegheny County Common Pleas Court.* Not: *Allegheny County Common Pleas Court Judge Amanda Langan.*

Lowercase *judge* as an occupational designation in phrases such as *beauty contest judge David Maj.*

See **administrative law judge; court names; judicial branch; justice.**

judge advocate, judge advocates, judge advocate general, judge advocates general Capitalize these titles as formal titles before names.

See **titles.**

judgment

judicial branch It is always lowercase. The federal court system comprises *the Supreme Court of the U.S., the U.S. Court of Appeals, U.S. district courts, the U.S. Court of Claims,* and *the U.S. Customs Court.* There are also four district judges for U.S. territories. Be sure to provide each court's location, whether or not you use its full formal name.

The U.S. Tax Court and *the U.S. Court of Military Appeals* are not considered part of the judicial branch.

Judicial Conference of the U.S. This rule-making body for the courts meets twice a year. Members are the chief justice, the chief judges of the 11 circuit courts, one district judge from each of the circuits, and the chief judges of the U.S. Court of Claims and the U.S. Court of Customs and Patent Appeals.

jukebox

July

See **months.**

jumbo jet The generic term is applied to very large planes, including the Boeing 747, the DC-10, the L-1011, the C-5A and Airbus Industrie's large jets.

June

See **months.**

Junior Chamber of Commerce It now is officially *the Jaycees.*

junior, senior Abbreviate it as *Jr.* and *Sr.* only with full names of people or animals. Do not precede by a comma: *J. Paul Goble Jr.*

II and *2nd* aren't necessarily the equivalent of *junior.* They often are used by a namesake grandson or nephew.

If necessary to distinguish between father and son in second reference, use *the elder Mr. Goble* and *the younger Mr.* Goble.

junk bonds The jargon term applies to high-yield corporate and municipal bonds that rating agencies consider speculative. The bonds typically offer higher yields and higher risk than bonds with *investment-grade* ratings. If junk bonds are rated at all, they are rated below triple-B by Standard & Poor's and below Baa by Moody's.

See **loan terminology.**

junta *See* **government, junta, regime.**

jury Do not capitalize: a *U.S. district court jury,* a *federal jury,* a *Massachusetts Superior Court jury.*

See **grand jury.**

jury-rigged It means intended for temporary or emergency use. Don't confuse it with *jerry-built,* which means built cheaply or shoddily.

justice Capitalize *Justice* before a name when it is the formal title for a jurist. It is the formal title for members of the U.S. Supreme Court and for some state courts. In these cases, do not use *Judge* in any references.

J

Continue to use *Justice* before the name on subsequent references. (Do *not* use *Mr., Mrs., Miss* or *Ms.* as an alternative.)

See **judge, U.S. Supreme** and **Court titles.**

justice of the peace Capitalize as a formal title before a name: *Justice of the Peace Marion Solomon.* Don't abbreviate.

See **titles.**

juvenile delinquent Juveniles may be declared delinquents in many states for antisocial behavior or for breaking the law.Some states prohibit publishing or broadcasting the names of juvenile delinquents.

juvenile diabetes Because it is found in adults as well as juveniles, call it *Type 1 diabetes* or *insulin-dependent diabetes.*

Kk

Kansas Abbreviate as *Kan.* after city names (despite the dictionary's use of Kans.). Residents are *Kansans. See* **state names.**

karat *See* **carat, caret, karat.**

Kazakhstan Its capital is Almaty.

See **Commonwealth of Independent States.**

Kelvin scale A scale of temperature based on the Celsius scale and used primarily in science to record very high and very low temperatures. Zero on the Kelvin scale is equal to minus 273.16 degrees Celsius and minus 460 degrees Fahrenheit.

See **Celsius** and **Fahrenheit.**

Kennedy Space Center

See **John F. Kennedy Space Center.**

Kentucky Abbreviate as *Ky.* after city names. Residents are *Kentuckians.*

See **state names.**

kerosene Once a trademark, it now is a generic term.

ketchup Not *catchup* or *catsup.*

key Use it sparingly as an adjective.

keynote address, keynote speech

keypad, keypunch

Keystone Kops

KGB It was the Soviet secret police organization.

kibbutz It is an Israeli collective settlement. The plural is *kibbutzim.*

kidnap, kidnapped, kidnapping, kidnapper

kids The use of the word to mean *children* should be limited to informal contexts.

killer

See **assassin, killer, murderer.**

kilobyte It equals a thousand bytes.

See **computer storage capacity.**

kilocycles The correct term is now *kilohertz.*

kilogram It is the metric term for 1,000 grams. A *kilogram* is equal to approximately 2.2 pounds or 35 ounces.

To convert to pounds, multiply by 2.2.

See **gram; metric system; pound.**

kilohertz It equals 1,000 hertz (1,000 cycles per second). It replaces *kilocycles* as the correct term in broadcast frequencies.

See **hertz.**

kilometer It equals 1,000 meters, or 3,281 feet, or five-eighths (0.62) mile.

To convert to miles, multiply by 0.62.

See **meter; metric system; mile.**

kiloton, kilotonnage *Kiloton* is a measure of the power of nuclear explosions. A kiloton has the explosive force of 1,000 tons of TNT.

kilowatt, kilowatt-hour The *watt* and *kilowatt* are measures of power—that is, the effort needed to move an electric current through a wire. *Watt-hour* and *kilowatt-hour* are measures of energy, or the amount of electricity moved during one hour. A *kilowatt-hour* equals the energy needed to run a 100-watt bulb for 10 hours.

The abbreviation *kwh* is acceptable on second reference.

kindergarten

king

Capitalize *king* only when used before the name of royalty: *King Louis XIV, King Louis.* Also capitalize it in plural uses before names: *Kings George and Henry.*

Lowercase it in phrases such as *chess king Garry Kasparov.*

See **titles.**

Kitty Litter It is a trademark for a brand of cat-box filler.

Klan in America *See* **Ku Klux Klan.**

Kleenex It is a brand of facial tissue.

KLM Royal Dutch Airlines *KLM* alone is acceptable in most references.

Kmart Corp. The retailer is based in Troy, Mich.

Knesset It is the name of the Israeli parliament. But *Israel's parliament* is normally preferred.

See **foreign legislative bodies.**

knickknack

knight

See **nobility.**

Knight Ridder Inc. The newspaper company, based in San Jose, Calif., doesn't use a hyphen in its name.

Knights of Columbus *The Knights* may be used on second reference.

See **fraternal organizations and service clubs.**

knot A *knot* is one nautical mile (6,076.12 feet) an hour. *Knots per hour* is a redundancy.

know-how

Kodak *Kodak* is acceptable on second reference and in headlines for *Eastman Kodak Co.,* of Rochester, N.Y.

Koran, Quran *Quran* is the preferred spelling of the Muslim sacred book believed to contain the words of Allah dictated to the Prophet Muhammad through the Angel Gabriel.

Korean War

kosher Always lowercase.

kowtow

KPMG LLP The accounting firm no longer has *Peat Marwick* as part of its name.

Kriss Kringle Not *Kris.*

krona A Swedish or Icelandic monetary unit. The plural is *kronor* for the Swedish money, *kronur* for the Icelandic money.

krone A Danish or Norwegian monetary unit. The plural is *kroner.*

kudos The Greek word of praise for an achievement is best avoided in English. Purists consider the word a singular, so the back-formed *kudo* certainly should be avoided.

Ku Klux Klan It applies to a number of organizations known collectively as the *Klan in America. KKK* is acceptable in second reference.

Capitalize *Imperial Wizard, Grand Dragon* and other titles before a name. Members are *Klansmen.*

Kuomintang It is the Chinese Nationalist political party. *Tang* means party, so don't follow Kuomintang with *party.*

Kuril Islands Use this in datelines after a community name. The Kuril Islands are Russian-occupied islands claimed by Japan.

Kuwait City It stands alone in datelines. Although the name of the capital of Kuwait is often rendered simply as *Kuwait,* use *Kuwait City* to avoid confusion.

Kwanzaa The seven-day festival beginning Dec. 26 is celebrated by some black Americans.

Kyrgyzstan It is also called *Kyrgyz Republic.*

See **Commonwealth of Independent States.**

Ll

L.A.
See **Los Angeles.**

laboratory, laboratories In corporate names, *Lab* and *Labs* are acceptable on second references and in headlines.

Labor Day

Labour Party Use the British spelling.

Labrador The mainland portion of the Canadian province of Newfoundland. Use *Newfoundland* in datelines after the name of a city or town. Specify in the text that the community is in Labrador.

Ladies' Home Journal

lady Generally avoid as a synonym for *woman.*
See **nobility** and **first lady.**

lag The verb is intransitive. The indicator lags *behind* economic developments. It doesn't *lag the developments.*

La Guardia Airport In New York.

laissez-faire

lake Capitalize it as part of a full proper name: *Lake Erie, Lake Sunapee, the Finger Lakes.* Lowercase in plural uses: *lakes, Erie, Ontario and Sunapee.*

lamebrain

lame duck (n.), **lame-duck** (adj.)

LAN The abbreviation is acceptable in second reference for *local-area network.*

Lancet, the The London medical publication isn't to be confused with *the British Medical Journal.*

Land Rover It is a trademark for a brand of all-terrain vehicle.

Lands' End The catalog company is based in Dodgeville, Wis.

languages Capitalize the proper names of languages and dialects: *Aramaic, Cajun, English, Persian, Serbo-Croatian, Yiddish.*

La Nina *La Nina*, meaning little girl, was coined to contrast with *El Nino.* The term is applied to a pattern that turns tropical Pacific Ocean waters unusually cold, affecting weather patterns.
See **El Nino.**

lanolin Formerly a trademark, it now is a generic term.

lanthanides These *rare-earth* chemical elements include the metals lanthanum, neodymium and yttrium.

laptop *See* **computer.**

larceny
See **burglary, larceny, robbery, theft.**

largess Not *largesse.*

laser disc (n.), **laser-disc** (adj.)

last
Avoid the use of *last* as a synonym for the *latest,* to avoid implying finality. *The company's last announcement was made Thursday* is ambiguous, so use *latest* instead.

Use *past* instead of *last* in other contexts to avoid the suggestion of finality: *in the past 10 days*; *in the past 12 months.*

To prevent ambiguity, the word *last* should be avoided in references to earlier days in the current week or earlier months or seasons in the current year: on a Friday, for example, refer to the most recent Tuesday as *this Tuesday,* or use simply *on Tuesday* if the reference to the past is clear in context.

In August, for example, refer to the most recent February as *this February* or use simply *in February* if the allusion to the past is clear in context. And in a December, refer to *this summer* if the allusion to the past is clear in context. Otherwise, use the year involved: *In the summer of 2001.*

See **next.**

last mile In telecommunications, *last mile* refers to the final link into homes and businesses for data services. Traditionally, this link has been a bottleneck because the user's copper phone lines are much slower than the fiber-optic connections between servers and also because cable-television coaxial pipe into homes hasn't allowed for two-way, high-speed services.

See **twisted pair.**

Last Supper

Las Vegas The Nevada city stands alone in datelines.

late In the sense of dead, generally use it only in reference to those who died recently. Don't use *late* when describing an individual's actions while he was alive: *Only Rep. Betty Firm opposed the bill,* not *the late* Rep. Betty Firm. She wasn't deceased at the time. Also note that *widow of the late* is redundant.

latex A resin-based substance used in making elastic materials and paints.

Latin America The term applies to most of the region south of the U.S. Exceptions include Suriname, which is the former Dutch Guiana, and these areas with a British heritage: the Bahamas, Barbados, Belize, Grenada, Guyana, Jamaica, Trinidad and Tobago, and various islands in the West Indies.

Latino (n. and adj.) This synonym for *Hispanic* is widely used in the Southwest and is gaining elsewhere. The feminine noun is *Latina.* With specific groups, use *Latino* or *Hispanic* as they prefer, but continue to use *Hispanic* as a general rule. Both words refer to those of any race descended from a Spanish-speaking land or culture. *Latino* and *Latina,* however, don't apply to *Spaniards.*

latitude and longitude *Latitude,* the distance north or south of the equator, is designated by parallels. *Longitude,* the distance east or west of Greenwich, England, is designated by meridians.

See **meridians.**

Latvia
See **Commonwealth of Independent States.**

Laundromat It is a trademark for a coin-operated laundry.

lawmaker, lawsuit

laws Capitalize legislative acts but not bills: *the Taft-Hartley Act, the Kennedy bill.*

lawyer It is the preferred term for all members of the bar.

An *attorney* is a legally named representative to act for another, not always a lawyer, who is technically an *attorney at law.*

Counselor, in a legal sense, is someone who conducts a case in court, usually a lawyer, or *counselor at law. Counsel* frequently is used collectively for a group of lawyers or counselors.

A *barrister* is a British lawyer who appears exclusively as a trial lawyer in higher courts.

In Britain, a *solicitor* is a lawyer who performs legal services for the public. A solicitor appears in lower courts but does not have the right to appear in higher courts, which are reserved to barristers.

In the U.S., a *solicitor* is a lawyer for a governmental body.

Solicitor general is a title for a chief law officer, equivalent to an attorney general.

Sometimes it refers to the deputy to the attorney general. Capitalize *Solicitor General* before a name.

Do not use *lawyer* as a formal title.

See **attorney, lawyer** and **titles.**

lay, lie

Lay is the transitive verb, taking a direct object. *Laid* is the past tense and past participle. *Laying* is the present participle. *I lay this before you. I laid it before you yesterday. I had laid it before you earlier yesterday. I was laying it before you.*

Lie, indicating a state of reclining, is intransitive and does not take a direct object. Its past tense is *lay.* Its past participle is *lain.* Its present participle is *lying. I lie on the beach, I am lying on the beach. I lay on the beach all day yesterday. I had lain on the beach before going home yesterday.*

When *lie* means to make an untrue statement, the verb forms are *lie, lied, lying.*

lay off (v.), **layoff** (n.) A *layoff* is a temporary or permanent removal from the payroll because of the employer's lack of business (and not because of the employee's job performance or rule infractions).

See **fire.**

leach (v.), **leech** (n.) Liquids *leach* or seep through materials.

Leeches are bloodsuckers or people who act like them.

lead This base metal is traded on the London Metal Exchange. It is used mostly in solder and batteries and for shielding against radiation.

leading indicators

See **index of leading economic indicators.**

lead time The time between when an item is ordered and when it is ready for use.

L

leak In news gathering, a *leak* is an intentional disclosure by someone who wants to remain anonymous. Don't use the term unless you know the circumstance and the term clearly applies.

Leaning Tower of Pisa

leapt The past tense of *leap.*

leatherneck Lowercase this nickname for a member of the U.S. Marine Corps.

lectern, podium A speaker stands *behind* or *at a lectern* and *on a podium* or *rostrum.*

lecturer A formal title in the Christian Science Church. An occupational description in colleges.

LED It stands for *light-emitting diode.* Include the definition when you use the term.

leder This spelling is often used in-house at The Wall Street Journal for *leader,* in reference to articles on page one in column one or column six. Don't use *leder* in the paper.

left hand (n.), **left-handed** (adj.), **left-hander** (n.)

leftist Try to use a more precise term to describe a political philosophy.

left wing (n.), **left-wing** (adj.), **left-winger** (n.)

legal terminology

civil and criminal *Civil* cases are divided into causes of action; *criminal* cases are divided into counts.

Make it clear in articles whether the suit is civil or criminal. If you use the word *charge* in reference to a civil case, be sure to specify the charge is in a *civil complaint.*

verdict Reserve the word for decisions in *criminal* cases. In civil cases, use *judgment, award* or *decision.*

guilty In criminal actions, defendants plead *guilty* or *not guilty.* Be especially careful with copy that mentions a not-guilty pleading to avoid dropping the *not* or inadvertently typing *now.*

In criminal-case verdicts, defendants are either *found guilty* or *acquitted.* Don't use the word *guilty* in civil-case decisions. Judges or juries in civil cases *rule against* or *rule in favor of* defendants.

indictments They come from grand juries, not from prosecutors. They are handed *up* to the court, not down.

sentences Be conservative in calculating *maximum sentences* by adding up the maximums for each of the charges in an action, because such totals can be highly misleading. Sentences usually run concurrently, not consecutively, and defendants rarely receive the maximum sentence. In federal cases, sentencing guidelines establish the likely sentences for particular crimes, and these are far lower than the theoretical maximums. It is often better to generalize than to try to establish the likely range for a crime under the guidelines: *If convicted of the most serious charges, the defendant could face a substantial prison term.* If it is relevant to use a theoretical maximum, make clear how you arrived at it.

class actions The party filing a suit may request *class-action status,* but one doesn't file a *class-action suit.* Class-action status can be granted only by a judge, who may decline to let the named plaintiffs represent anyone but themselves. A solution: *Three shareholders sued XYZ Co. on stock-manipulation charges, asking that the suit become a class action on behalf of all shareholders.*

derivative suit It is a suit brought by a shareholder for the benefit of the company rather than for the shareholder. Any damages awarded go to the company and not to the shareholder.

exaggerated claims Be wary of breathless announcements of the filing of *$100 million lawsuits* or the like. A plaintiff typically may name any sum as his damage demand when he brings a case. The sum doesn't suggest the suit has merit, and it certainly doesn't mean it will cost the defendant the amount claimed. Rather than describe the filing as a *$100 million suit,* say that the plaintiff *seeks $100 million in damages*—and give the defendant's response immediately, if possible.

technicalities Avoid writing that a case was *dismissed on a technicality.* One person's legal technicality is another person's constitutional right, as in cases in which evidence was gathered unlawfully or a jury was given improper instructions.

allegations A claim in a civil suit should be treated with skepticism because the plaintiff doesn't need to present any proof of wrongdoing to file such a suit, as the government must in criminal cases to get an indictment.

company attributions Articles that quote a company as saying, for example, that a judge has dismissed a lawsuit against it are frequently inaccurate because the company has put its own spin on a judicial opinion that may not be nearly so clear-cut. Whenever possible, refer instead to the court opinion and talk to lawyers representing the two sides.

discovery This refers to the pretrial fact-finding stage of civil lawsuits. Depositions, interrogatories and requests for documents are all elements of discovery. Generally use *pretrial fact-finding* instead of *discovery.*

tort A *tort* is a wrongful act, causing damage or injury, done willfully, negligently or in circumstances involving strict liability. Torts, which can lead to civil suits, include libel, personal injury, medical malpractice, product liability, wrongful firing and sexual harassment.

Try to avoid the word *tort* by referring to a case more specifically as a *negligence* or *personal-injury* lawsuit. Note that contract disputes, which have their own category, aren't torts.

Tort reform refers to efforts, mostly by insurance companies and other businesses in state legislatures and Congress, to limit damages in civil cases or to limit the circumstances under which plaintiffs can bring such suits.

punitive damages *Compensatory damages* compensate a plaintiff for injuries or losses caused by the defendant. *Punitive damages* are awarded to the plaintiff, in addition to compensatory damages, to punish or deter a defendant found to have acted recklessly or maliciously.

Punitive damages are also called *exemplary damages.*

summary judgment This refers to a decision by the judge to resolve a civil case before trial, based on the judge's conclusion that there isn't any dispute as to any relevant fact and that the law dictates that one of the parties prevail. Cases are often thrown out as a result of such motions. In such cases, one usually can avoid the term *summary judgment* and say that *"the judge dismissed the case before trial."*

dismissal This is a judge's ruling in a civil case that the facts alleged, even if they are true, don't constitute legal wrong. A motion to dismiss is based solely on the complaint, while a *motion for summary judgment* usually follows some *discovery.*

legerdemain

legion, legionnaire

See **American Legion** and **French Foreign Legion.**

Legionnaires' disease It is so named because it was diagnosed after an outbreak at an American Legion convention at the Bellevue-Stratford Hotel in Philadelphia in July 1976.

L

legislative branch

legislative titles

Use *Rep., Reps., Sen.* and *Sens.* as formal titles before one or more names. Spell out and lowercase *representative* and *senator* in other uses.

Spell out other legislative titles in all uses. Capitalize titles such as *assemblyman, assemblywoman* or *city councilor* when they are used before a name. Lowercase in other uses.

Add *U.S.* or *state* before a title only if necessary to avoid confusion: *U.S. Sen. Hillary Clinton spoke with state Sen. John Marchi.*

In second references, use the legislative titles or *Mr., Miss, Mrs.* or *Ms.* before a name.

CONGRESS: *Rep.* is the preferred first-reference term for use before the name of a member of the U.S. House of Representatives. The word *congressman* or *congresswoman,* in lowercase, may be used in subsequent references that do not use an individual's name.

TITLES: Capitalize titles when they are used before a name: *House Speaker Dennis Hastert, Senate Minority Leader Trent Lott, Democratic Whip David Bonior, Chairman Jesse Helms of the Senate Foreign Relations Committee.*

See **party affiliation** and **titles.**

legislature

The Pennsylvania Legislature, the Legislature, another state legislature.

Although the word *legislature* isn't part of the formal, proper name for the lawmaking bodies in many states, it may be used instead of a formal name. *General Assembly* or *assembly.*

Lowercase *legislature* in plural references: *The Missouri and Michigan legislatures are in session.*

In 49 states the separate bodies are a *senate* and a *house* or *assembly. The Nebraska Legislature* is a unicameral body.

Lent, Lenten

lesbian, lesbianism Lowercase the words in references to homosexual women, except in names of organizations.

-less No hyphen before this suffix:

childless
treeless
tailless

less

See **fewer, less.**

lessee, lessor

A *lessee* is one to whom property is leased.

A *lessor* is one who gives a lease for property.

letter of credit It is traditionally a bank's promise that a shipment of goods will be paid for on arrival. It has been used mostly to facilitate foreign trade but is also used domestically to guarantee payment of securities.

letter of intent In the early stages of a merger or acquisition, the signing of a *letter of intent* represents an agreement in principle to carry out the deal.

let up (v.), **letup** (n. and adj.)

leverage It refers to the use of borrowed assets by a business to enhance the return to the owner's equity. The expectation is that the interest rate charged will be lower than the earnings made on the money.

leveraged buyout The purchase of a company by a small group of investors, financed largely by debt. Ultimately, the group's borrowings are repaid with funds generated by the acquired company's operations or the sale of its assets.

Levi's It is a jeans trademark of Levi Strauss & Co.

liabilities They represent claims against a corporation or other entity, including accounts payable, wages and salaries due to be paid, dividends declared payable, taxes payable and obligations such as bonds, debentures and bank loans.

liaison

libel The best defense against *libel* is accuracy. If a lawyer or individual threatens a libel action, respond courteously and get any details the person complaining is willing to offer. But do not discuss unpublished information. If the person is aggressive, you should refer him or her to the Journal's legal department. In any event, get in touch with your supervisors immediately and be prepared to relate all the facts in the matter.

liberal, liberalism
See **political parties and philosophies.**

licensee, licenser

lie
See **lay, lie.**

lie in state Only people who are entitled to a state funeral service *lie in state,* which in the U.S. occurs in the rotunda in the Capitol in Washington. Those entitled to a state funeral are a president, a former president, a president-elect or any other person designated by the president.

Members of Congress may also lie in state, if the House or Senate decides.

Entitled to an official funeral, but not to lie in state, are the vice president, the chief justice, cabinet members and other government officials, at the request of the president.

lieutenant It is abbreviated *Lt.*
See **military titles.**

lieutenant governor
Capitalize it and abbreviate as *Lt. Gov.* or *Lt. Govs.* when used as a formal title before one or more names in regular text.

Lowercase it and spell it out in other uses.
See **titles.**

lifesaver, lifesaving *Life Saver* is a trademark for a brand of candy.

life-size Not *life-sized.*

lifestyle

lifetime

LIFO For *last-in, first-out* system of inventory accounting. Don't use *LIFO* without including the definition in the text.
See **FIFO.**

light, lighted, lighting Use *lighted,* not *lit,* as the past tense.

lightning The electrical discharge.

light-year The distance that light travels in one year at the rate of 186,282 miles a second. It works out to about 5.88 trillion miles.

likable Not *likeable.*

-like Generally don't precede this suffix by a hyphen. Use a hyphen if the letter *l* would be tripled or if the word is a coinage:

bill-like	shell-like
lifelike	confetti-like
businesslike	

like- Follow with a hyphen when it is used as a prefix meaning similar to:

like-minded
like-natured

like, as Use *like* as a preposition to compare nouns and pronouns. It requires an object: *Mr. Adams talks like this.* The conjunction *as* is the correct word to introduce clauses: *Mr. Adams talks as he should.*

limited Abbreviate it and capitalize as *Ltd.* when used as part of a formal corporate name. Do not set off from the name with commas.

limit orders They are requests by investors that their brokers purchase or sell shares of a stock at a specific price, rather than at the prevailing market price.

limousine

linage, lineage
Linage is the number of lines of type.
Lineage is ancestry or descent.

Lincoln's Birthday

line numbers Use figures and lowercase the word *line* in identifying individual lines of a text: *line 1, line 9.* But: *the first line, the 10th line.*

linoleum Formerly a trademark, it is now a generic term.

liquefied natural gas *LNG* is acceptable in second reference. The natural gas, usually methane, is liquefied for transport on vessels.

liquefied petroleum gas *LPG* is acceptable in second reference. It usually is propane and butane, derived from the refining of crude oil and liquefied under pressure.

liquidation It is the process of converting assets such as shares of stock into cash. When a company is liquidated in a bankruptcy or other action, the cash obtained is used to repay debt, first to holders of bonds and preferred stock. Any remaining cash is distributed to holders of common stock.

See **bankruptcy.**

liquidity An asset's *liquidity* refers to its ability to be bought or sold quickly and in large volume without substantially affecting its price. Checking accounts, money-market mutual funds and Treasury bills are considered liquid assets.

lira Italian money. The plural is *lire.*

Lisbon The capital of Portugal stands alone in datelines.

lit Use *lighted* instead.

liter It is the basic unit of volume in the metric system, defined as the volume occupied by one kilogram of distilled water at four degrees Celsius. A *liter* is 1,000 cubic centimeters or one cubic decimeter.

A liter is equal to approximately 34 fluid ounces or 1.06 liquid quarts. A liter also equals 0.91 dry quart.

To convert to liquid quarts, multiply by 1.06. To convert to dry quarts, multiply by 0.91.

See **bushel; gallon; kilogram; metric system; quart (dry); quart (liquid).**

literally

See **figuratively, literally.**

literature

See **composition titles.**

Lithuania

See **Commonwealth of Independent States.**

livable Not *liveable.*

livid If a person turns *livid* with rage, his face becomes ashen or pale, not crimson.

Lloyd's of London A prominent London insurance operation.

Lloyds Bank PLC A prominent London-based bank.

LNG

See **liquefied natural gas.**

load factor On an airline, the percentage of available seats that are occupied.

loan Avoid as a verb. Use *lend, lent.*

loan loss provision It refers to the amount a bank puts aside in a given period to offset potential losses from delinquent or nonperforming loans. It is subtracted from a bank's net interest income. Don't confuse *loan loss provision* with *loan loss reserve* or *allowance,* the total pool of funds a bank has set aside to cover delinquent loans. The *provision* is the bank's contribution to the *reserve* for one period.

loan terminology Note the meanings of these terms in describing loans by governments and corporations:

bond This may be used as a general term for debt instruments. But in the U.S. it also refers specifically to a certificate issued by a corporation or government stating the amount of a loan, the interest to be paid, the time for repayment and the collateral pledged if payment cannot be made. Repayment generally is not due for a long period, usually seven years or more.

collateral Stock or other property that a borrower is obligated to turn over to a lender if unable to repay a loan.

commercial paper A document describing the details of a short-term loan between corporations.

convertible bond A bond carrying the stipulation that it may be exchanged for a specific amount of stock in the company that issued it.

coupon A slip of paper attached to a bond that the bondholder clips at specified times and returns to the issuer for payment of the interest due.

debenture A certificate stating the amount of a loan, the interest to be paid and the time for repayment, but not providing collateral. It is backed only by the corporation's reputation and promises to pay.

default A person, corporation or government is in default if it fails to meet the terms for repayment.

full-faith-and-credit bond An alternative term for a *general-obligation bond,* often used to contrast such a bond with a *moral-obligation bond* or *revenue bond.*

general-obligation bond A bond that has had the formal approval of either the voters or their legislature. The government's promise to repay the principal and pay the interest is constitutionally guaranteed on the strength of its taxing power.

maturity The date on which a bond, debenture or note must be repaid.

moral-obligation bond A government bond that has not had the formal approval of either the voters or their legislature. It is backed only by the government's "moral obligation" to repay the principal and interest on time.

municipal bond A general-obligation bond issued by a state, county, city, town, village, possession or territory, or a bond issued by an agency or authority set up by one of these governmental units. In general, interest paid on municipal bonds is exempt from federal income taxes. It also usually is exempt from state and local income taxes if held by someone living within the state of issue.

note A certificate issued by a corporation or government stating the amount of a loan, the interest to be paid and the collateral pledged in the event payment cannot be made. The date for repayment is generally more than a year after issue but not more than seven or eight years later. The shorter interval for repayment is the principal difference between a note and a bond.

revenue bond A bond backed only by the revenue of the airport, turnpike or other facility that was built with the money it raised.

Treasury borrowings A *Treasury bill* is a certificate representing a short-term loan to the federal government, usually maturing in three, six or 12 months. A *Treasury note* may mature in one to 10 years. A *Treasury bond* matures in 10 years or more.

See **bond ratings**.

loath (adj.), **loathe** (v.) *We are loath (reluctant) to loathe our competitors.*

local of a union Use a numeral and capitalize *local* when giving the name of a union subdivision: *Local 222 of the Teamsters union.*

Otherwise: *The local will vote, as will locals 2 and 4.*

local-area network A group of computers, such as in an office, connected with coaxial cables, optical fibers or standard telephone lines.

locker room

Lockheed Martin Corp. It is based in Bethesda, Md.

lock out (v.), **lockout** (n.)

lodges

See **fraternal organizations and service clubs.**

Lombard rate In Germany, the interest rate charged for supplemental borrowings from the central bank that use securities as collateral. The *Lombard rate* is closely watched by the credit markets because it serves as a ceiling for short-term money-market rates.

L

London The capital of England stands alone in datelines. The *City of London* section, which encompasses London's financial district, should be called *the City* in second reference, not London.

London Club The informal group of commercial bank creditors meets in London with the governments of debtor countries to negotiate terms of refinancings.

London interbank offered rate It is the rate that the most credit-worthy international banks dealing in Eurodollars charge each other for large loans. It is usually the base for other large Eurodollar loans to less credit-worthy corporate and government borrowers.

London Metal Exchange The world's leading base-metals exchange, it trades rolling three-month-forward contracts rather than futures contracts fixed to certain calendar months. Trading pits and sessions at the exchange are called *rings.*

long distance, long-distance Use a hyphen in reference to telephone calls: *We keep in touch by long-distance. He called long-distance.*

In other uses, hyphenate only when used before the word it modifies: *She traveled a long distance. She made a long-distance trip.*

longitude *See* **latitude and longitude.**

longshoreman Capitalize *longshoreman* only in reference to a member of the International Longshoremen's and Warehousemen's Union or the International Longshoremen's Association.

longstanding

long term, long-term *The contract covers the long term. He has a long-term contract.*

long time, longtime *They have known each other a long time. They are longtime partners.*

long ton Equal to 2,240 pounds.

See **ton.**

Loop, the It refers to Chicago's downtown area.

Los Angeles The city in California stands alone in datelines. Generally confine *L.A.* to quoted matter and informal contexts.

loss A loss or deficit *widens* or *narrows.* Don't use *increase* or *decline* or the like to describe a loss.

See **profit terminology.**

Louisiana Abbreviate as *La.* after city names. Residents are *Louisianians.*

See **state names.**

Louisiana Light Sweet crude It is a main U.S. grade of oil, deliverable at St. James, La.

Louisiana Offshore Oil Port It is the only deep-water oil-tanker terminal in the U.S. Most of the crude oil passing through the port comes from the Middle East.

low- Hyphenate when used to form a compound adjective: *low-flying, low-grade, low-income, low-priced.*

Low Countries Belgium, Luxembourg and the Netherlands.

lowercase One word (n., v., adj.) to refer to the absence of capital letters.

LPG
See **liquefied petroleum gas.**

LSD The abbreviation is acceptable in all references for *lysergic acid diethylamide.*

Lt. This abbreviation for *lieutenant* is used before names in military and police ranks.
See **military titles.**

Ltd.
See **limited.**

Lt. Gov.
See **lieutenant governor.**

Lucite A trademark for acrylic plastic.

Lufthansa The name of the German airline stands alone.

Lutheran churches The Evangelical Lutheran Church in America is the principal body in the U.S.

CLERGY: Members of the clergy are known as *ministers* or, in congregations, *pastors.* Use *the Rev.* before a name in first reference. In subsequent references, use *Mr., Mrs., Miss or Ms.*

See **religious titles.**

OTHER OFFICIALS: Elected officials include *elders, deacons* and *trustees*, which are capitalized only if used before a name.

Luxembourg Stands alone in datelines.

Luxembourg franc Technically, it is a separate currency from the *Belgian franc*, but the two are convertible to third currencies at the same rate.

-ly Don't use a hyphen between adverbs ending in *-ly* and the words they modify: *a rapidly rising rate.*

See the compound-modifiers section of the **hyphen** entry.

Lyndon B. Johnson Space Center Formerly the Manned Spacecraft Center. Situated in Houston, it is the National Aeronautics and Space Administration's principal control and training center for manned spaceflight. *Johnson Space Center* is acceptable in all references.

See **John F. Kennedy Space Center.**

Mm

Maastricht Treaty The *Treaty on Monetary and Political Union,* known as the *Maastricht Treaty,* was issued at a European Community summit in Maastricht, the Netherlands, in 1991. The treaty called for the creation of a common European currency and gave the European Union far-reaching responsibility in defense and foreign affairs.

See **European economic and monetary union.**

Macau It stands alone in datelines. The spelling formerly was *Macao.*

Mace *Chemical Mace* is a trademark for a tear gas in aerosol canisters.

Macedonia The country was once a republic in Yugoslavia. The name also applies to districts in Greece and Bulgaria. Always make clear which Macedonia is being referred to.

machine gun (n.), **machine-gun** (adj. and v.), **machine-gunner**

See **weapons.**

machine tools They are metalworking machines: *Cutting* tools include lathes and milling machines. *Forming* tools are used to press materials into shape.

Mach number It represents the ratio of the speed of an object to the speed of sound in the air the object is moving through. The speed of sound is 750 miles an hour at sea level, and lower numbers above sea level.

Traveling at Mach 1 is equal to the speed of sound. Mach 2 is equal to twice the speed of sound. Mach is named for Austrian physicist Ernst Mach.

Madagascar Its capital is Antananarivo. Its people are *Malagasy.*

Madison, Dolley Note the *e* is usually used in the name of President James Madison's wife. *Dolly Madison* is an ice-cream and baked-products trade name.

Madrid The capital of Spain stands alone in datelines.

Mafia, Mafioso, Mafiosi The terms apply to a secret society of criminals and its members. Lowercase, it refers in general to those in *organized crime* or *the underworld.*

magazine names Capitalize the name but don't place it in quotes. Lowercase the word *magazine* unless it is part of the publication's formal title: *Smart Money magazine, Newsweek magazine, Time magazine.*

Check the masthead if in doubt.

magistrate Capitalize it when it is a formal title before a name. *See* **titles.**

magistrate judge In the federal court system, *magistrate judges* formerly were called magistrates. They are lawyers appointed by district judges to handle pretrial motions and other duties. *Gregory Langan, a federal magistrate judge* or *Magistrate Judge Gregory Langan;* in subsequent refernces, *Magistrate Langan,* not *Judge Langan.*

See **judge** and **administrative law judge.**

Magna Carta, the The charter the English barons forced King John of England to grant at Runnymede in June 1215 guaranteed certain political and civil liberties.

magnesium The minor metal is used in pharmaceuticals, electrical devices, structural alloys and fireworks. It is obtained mostly from seawater.

Mailgram A trademark for a telegram sent to a post office near the recipient's address and delivered there by letter carrier.

M

mailman The term *letter carrier* is more descriptive because many women hold this job.

Maine Don't abbreviate. Residents are *Mainers.*

See **state names.**

mainframe Centrally located and connected to numerous terminals, a *mainframe* contains all the programs and most of the memory for a computing system. *See* **computer.**

mainland China *See* **China.**

major *See* **military titles.**

Majorca Don't use this spelling.

See **Mallorca.**

majority leader Capitalize it as a formal title before a name: *Majority Leader Robert Byrd.* Lowercase elsewhere.

See **legislative titles** and **titles.**

majority, plurality A *majority* is more than half. A *plurality* is the excess over the next-highest number. To describe the size of a majority, use the excess over half of the total. To describe the size of a plurality, use the highest number and subtract the next-highest number. When *majority* and *plurality* are used alone, they take singular verbs and pronouns: *The majority has made its decision.* If a plural word follows an *of* construction, the number of the verb depends on the sense of the sentence: *A majority of the absentee votes was calculated. The majority of the people on the plane were killed.*

major leagues, major leaguer Lowercase the terms in informal references to baseball's American League and National League. But uppercase references to the formal entity *Major League Baseball.*

make up (v.), **makeup** (n. and adj.)

Malay, Malaya, Malaysia

Malay refers to those in the Polynesian ethnic group on the Malay Peninsula and their language.

Malayan refers to inhabitants of Malaya, which includes the peninsula and the nearby area.

Malaysia is the larger territory, and *Malaysian* refers to its people. For *Malaysian names*, check to determine which part of the name the individual uses with courtesy titles in second reference.

Maldives Use *the Maldives,* not *the Maldive Islands.*

malfeasance, misfeasance, nonfeasance

Malfeasance is illegal wrongdoing or misconduct, particularly by a public official.

Misfeasance is doing a lawful act in an improper way so it infringes on others' rights.

Nonfeasance is failure to do what duty requires.

malice The term used in libel law is not *malice* but *actual malice.*

See **actual malice.**

Mallorca Use this spelling, not *Majorca.* Use *Mallorca,* not Spain, in datelines of articles from communities on this island.

manageable

manager Capitalize it when used as a formal title before a name: *Manager Joe Torre.* Don't capitalize in job descriptions such as *plant manager Brodie Martin.*

See **titles.**

managing editor Capitalize it when used as a formal title before a name. *See* **titles.**

manganese The minor metal is used in making steel and alloys.

man-hour It is a unit of time equal to one hour of work done by one person.

manic-depressive illness In psychiatry, the term *bipolar disorder* now is preferred.

Manitoba Do not abbreviate the name of the province in central Canada.

See **datelines.**

manslaughter

See **homicide, murder, manslaughter.**

mantel, mantle

A *mantel* is a shelf.

A *mantle* is a cloak.

manufacturing In an article, use the abbreviation *Mfg.* only if a company uses the abbreviation in its corporate name. The abbreviation may be used in tabular matter and in a corporate name in a headline.

Maoism, Maoist The terms refer to the Communist philosophy and policies of Mao Tse-tung and to adherents of the philosophy.

See **political parties and philosophies.**

March *See* **months.**

Mardi Gras

margin

In general, *margin* represents the degree of difference between two numbers, not the ratio of the numbers. Thus, Al Gore won the popular vote in 2000 by a *300,000-vote margin,* not by a *margin of 0.3%.*

In securities trading, it is the amount of cash that a buyer must put up in borrowing from a broker. If the *margin requirement* set by the Federal Reserve Board is 50%, that is the percentage of the purchase price the buyer must put up; he can borrow the rest. A *margin call* for additional margin results if the value of the securities declines.

In corporate finance, *margin,* or *gross profit margin,* is the difference between a company's cost of producing products and the price it receives for them.

marijuana

Marines

Capitalize it when referring to U.S. forces: *the U.S. Marines, the Marines, a Marine, the Marine Corps, Marine regulations, the Corps. See* **corps.** Do not use the abbreviation *USMC.*

Use lowercase for the forces of other nations: *South Vietnamese marines.*

mark Use *mark* instead of *deutsche mark* or *D-mark* for the German currency, except in quotes.

marketbasket, marketer, marketplace

markup In the retailing industry, the *markup* or *gross profit* is figured by dividing the difference by the *selling price* rather than dividing the difference by the *acquisition cost.* Thus, an item bought for $100 and sold for $200 is said to have a *50% markup,* not a 100% markup.

When the markup is a significant part of the story, wording should be included to explain the aberration: ... *That is a 50% markup as retailers figure it, based on the selling price.*

Marshall Islands Named for John Marshall, a British explorer. In datelines, use a city and *Marshall Islands.*

marshal, marshaled, marshaling, Marshall
Marshal is the spelling for both the verb and the noun.

Marshall is a proper name: *George C. Marshall.*

Martin Luther King's Birthday The observance is the third Monday in January.

M

Marxism (Marxist) The system of thought was developed by Karl Marx and Friedrich Engels.

See **political parties and philosophies.**

Maryland Abbreviate as *Md.* after city names. Residents are *Marylanders.*

See **state names.**

Mason-Dixon Line

Masonite It is a trademark for a brand of hardboard.

Mass A *low Mass* is *celebrated, offered* or *said.* A *high Mass* is *sung.* A *funeral Mass* is a *requiem Mass.*

See **Roman Catholic Church.**

Massachusetts Abbreviate as *Mass.* after city names. Residents are *Massachusettsans.*

See **state names.**

MasterCard

masterful, masterly
A *masterful* person is domineering and imperious.

A *masterly* person is skillfully efficient.

master of arts, master of science The term *master's degree* is acceptable in any reference.

See **academic degrees** for guidelines on when the abbreviations *M.A.* and *M.S.* are acceptable.

masthead The listing of officers and editors of a publication usually appears on the editorial page of a newspaper and a contents page of a magazine. It is not the *nameplate* or *flag,* which appears at the top of page one.

matched sale-purchase transactions They occur when the Federal Reserve borrows money from dealers and lends them its securities, generally Treasury bills. The *matched sales* temporarily drain reserves from the banking system, since dealer money leaves banks and goes to the Fed.

See **repurchase agreement.**

match trading
See **composite trading.**

maturity In the securities market, *maturity* refers to the time at which a debt instrument is due and payable. A bond due to *mature* July 1, 2020, will return the holder's principal and final interest payment on that date.

See **duration** and **yield** entries.

maxi- Use the rules in **prefixes.** Don't hyphenate unless the base word begins with an *i: maxiskirt, maxi-intelligence.*

May
See **months.**

May Day, mayday
May Day is May 1, often observed as a festive or political holiday.

Mayday is the international distress signal, from the French *m'aidez,* meaning *help me.*

mayors' conference
See **U.S. Conference of Mayors.**

MC For *master of ceremonies,* the abbreviation is preferred over *emcee.*

McDonald's Corp. The fast-food company is based in Oak Brook, Ill.

M.D. A term such as *physician* or *surgeon* is preferred in reference to individuals.
See **doctor** and **academic titles.**

meager

mean
See **average, mean, median, mode, norm.**

Medal of Honor The nation's highest military honor, it is given by Congress for risk of life in combat beyond the call of duty. There is no *Congressional Medal of Honor.*

meddle, mettle
Meddle is a verb meaning interfere.
Mettle is a noun meaning courage or strength of character.

media The term is plural referring to mass-communication instruments, such as magazines, newspapers, the news services, radio and television: *The news media are opposed to the legislation.* But use the overworked term sparingly.

median
See **average, mean, median, mode, norm.**

mediate
See **arbitrate, mediate.**

Medicaid The federal-state program helps pay for health care for the needy, aged, blind and disabled and for low-income families with children.

The states decide eligibility, and the federal government reimburses them for a percentage of the expenditures.

Medicare The federal health-care insurance program applies to people aged 65 and over and the disabled. It helps pay for hospitalization, physicians' charges and some other costs.

medicine
See **drugs.**

medieval

mega- The prefix denotes a million units. The rules in **prefixes** apply. A hyphen is used only if the word that follows begins with an *a.*

megabyte It equals a million bytes.
See **computer storage capacity.**

megahertz Representing a million operating cycles per second, *megahertz* is typically used in reference to a computer's *clock rate,* which is a measure of its power and speed.

megawatt Equals 1,000 kilowatts.

melee

memento, mementos

memorandum, memorandums

Memorial Day

Mennonite The evangelical Christian group favors plain clothes and opposes military service. *Amish* is an offshoot.

menswear Not *men's wear.*

Mercedes-Benz The plural for the Daimler-

Chrysler auto is either Mercedeses or Mercedes-Benzes.

merchant marine The U.S. merchant marine is staffed by *merchant seamen.*

Mercosur The South American trade bloc is formally the *Southern Cone Common Market.* Argentina, Brazil, Paraguay and Uruguay established it in 1995, eliminating tariffs on most goods traded among the countries and levying a common external tariff on goods from outside the bloc. Chile and Bolivia became associate members.

Mercurochrome Trademark for an antiseptic for wounds.

mercury The highly toxic minor metal is used in barometers, thermometers and batteries.

meridians Use numerals and lowercase to identify the imaginary locator lines that ring the globe from north to south through the poles. They are measured in units of 0 to 180 degrees east and west of the prime meridian, which runs through Greenwich, England.

Merrill Lynch & Co. The brokerage firm is based in New York.

messiah Capitalize it only in religious contexts.

meter It is the basic unit of length in the metric system, equal to 1,650,763.73 wavelengths of the orange-red radiation of an isotope of krypton. It is equal to approximately 39.37 inches.

It takes 100 centimeters to make a meter. It takes 1,000 meters to make a kilometer.

To convert to inches, multiply by 39.37. To convert to yards, multiply by 1.1.

See **inch; metric system; yard.**

metaphor It is a figure of speech in which a word or phrase usually used in one context is used in another: *He is a lion of industry. His walk was a marathon. All the world is a stage.*

methane It is the lightest hydrocarbon and principal component of natural gas.

Methodist churches The principal Methodist body in the U.S. is the United Methodist Church, formed in 1968 by the merger of the Methodist Church and the Evangelical United Brethren Church.

CLERGY: Ordained spiritual leaders are known as *bishops* and *ministers.* The term *pastor* applies if a minister leads a congregation.

For bishops: *Bishop Nicholas Klemmer of Rosemont, Pa.* On subsequent references: *Bishop Klemmer or Mr. Klemmer.*

For pastors and ministers: *the Rev. Nicholas Klemmer, Pastor Klemmer* or *Mr. Klemmer.* (The designations *Most Rev.* or *Rt. Rev.* don't apply.)

See **religious titles.**

methyl tertiary butyl ether An additive, or oxygenate, it is added to gasoline to make it burn cleaner.

See **ethyl tertiary butyl ether.**

metric system Metric terms are often relevant to include in articles; for example, when the source of the information uses the metric terms. In those cases, follow the metric units with equivalents in parentheses for the terms more widely known in the U.S. A general statement (such as: *A kilometer is 0.625 mile*) is acceptable to avoid repeated use of the parenthetical equivalents.

ABBREVIATIONS: The abbreviation *mm* for millimeter is acceptable in references to film widths (*8mm film*) and weapons (*a 105mm cannon*). Do not otherwise use metric abbreviations in body copy.

In charts and tabular matter, these abbreviations may be used for singulars or plurals, without periods: *g* (gram), *kg* (kilogram), *t* (metric ton), *m* (meter), *cm*

METRIC CONVERSION CHART

INTO METRIC			OUT OF METRIC		
If You Know	*Multiply By*	*To Get*	*If You Know*	*Multiply By*	*To Get*
	LENGTH			**LENGTH**	
inches	2.54	centimeters	millimeters	0.04	inches
feet	30	centimeters	centimeters	0.4	inches
yards	0.9144	meters	meters	3.3	feet
miles	1.6	kilometers	kilometers	0.62	miles
	AREA			**AREA**	
sq. inches	6.5	sq. centimeters	sq. centimeters	0.16	sq. inches
sq. feet	0.09	sq. meters	sq. meters	1.2	sq. yards
sq. yards	0.8	sq. meters	sq. kilometers	0.4	sq. miles
sq. miles	2.6	sq. kilometers	hectares	2.47	acres
acres	0.4	hectares			
	MASS (Weight)			**MASS** (Weight)	
ounces	28	grams	grams	0.035	ounces
pounds	0.45	kilograms	kilograms	2.2	pounds
short ton	0.9	metric ton	metric tons	1.1	short tons
	VOLUME			**VOLUME**	
teaspoons	5	milliliters	milliliters	0.03381497	fluid ounces
tablespoons	15	milliliters	liters	2.1	pints
fluid ounces	30	milliliters	liters	1.06	quarts
cups	0.24	liters	liters	0.26	gallons
pints	0.47	liters	cubic meters	35	cubic feet
quarts	0.95	liters	cubic meters	1.3	cubic yards
gallons	3.8	liters			
cubic feet	0.03	cubic meters			
cubic yards	0.76	cubic meters			
	TEMPERATURE			**TEMPERATURE**	
Fahrenheit	Subtract 32, then multiply by 5/9 ths	Celsius	Celsius	Multiply by 9/5 ths, then add 32	Fahrenheit

But don't use this formula to convert incremental changes in temperature.

M

(centimeter), *km* (kilometer), *mm* (millimeter), *L* (liter, capital *L* to avoid confusion with the figure *1*), and *mL* (milliliter).

Separate listings for metric terms provide definitions of them and formulas to convert them to equivalents in the terminology generally used in the U.S.

Separate listings such as **pound**, **inch** and **quart**, contain formulas for converting these terms to metric equivalents.

See also the conversion chart on page 153.

metric ton It is equal to 2,204.62 pounds.
See **ton.**

Mexicana The short form is acceptable for the Mexican airline *Mexicana de Aviacion.*

Mexico City The capital of Mexico stands alone in datelines.

Miami The city in Florida stands alone in datelines.

M

Michigan Abbreviate as *Mich.* after city names. Residents are *Michiganders.*
See **state names.**

micro- The rules under **prefixes** apply. Hyphenate only if the following word begins with an *o: micro-organism.*

micron It is a unit of linear measure equal to one-millionth of a meter, or about 1/100th the width of a human hair.

microcomputer It is a very small computer, primarily used as a personal computer.

Microsoft Corp. It is based in Redmond, Wash.

microwave (n. and v.), **microwavable.**

mid- No hyphen unless a capitalized word or numeral follows:

mid-America	midday
midcontinent	mid-40s
mid-Atlantic	midsize

middle age It is usually considered to be the age range of about 40 to 65.

Middle Ages A.D. 476 to A.D. 1450.
See **Dark Ages.**

Middle Atlantic states New Jersey, New York and Pennsylvania. Informally, Delaware is often considered part of the group.

middle class (n.), **middle-class** (adj.) *He is a member of the middle class, with middle-class values.*

Middle East or Mideast It comprises Cyprus, Egypt, Iran, Iraq, Israel, Jordan, Kuwait, Lebanon, Libya, Oman, Qatar, Saudi Arabia, South Yemen, Sudan, Syria, Turkey, United Arab Emirates and Yemen.

middle income There is no universally accepted definition of *middle income,* but the Census Bureau says that families in the middle 20% of the income spectrum had gross incomes in 1999 between $39,600 and $59,400. The middle 60% had gross incomes between $22,826 and $88,082. Families with incomes above $155,000 are in the top 5% of all American families and are not middle income.

middleman

middle or first initials Initials may be used if available in the first mention of individuals: *W. Michael Blumenthal, Thomas A. Edison, J. Paul Goble.* The initial is omitted if a person doesn't use it or is publicly known without it.

midnight Don't put a 12 in front of it. It is the part of the day that is ending, not the one that is beginning. To avoid confusion, particularly in labor-contract stories, put the deadline at 12:01 a.m., not midnight.

midshipman
See **military academies.**

midsize Not *midsized.*

Midwest The term generally applies to the 12 states that the U.S. Census Bureau includes in the North Central region: North Dakota, South Dakota, Kansas, Missouri, Iowa, Nebraska, Illinois, Indiana, Minnesota, Wisconsin, Michigan and Ohio.

The adjective form is *Midwestern.*

See **directions and regions.**

MiG The *i* refers to the Russian word for *and.* The initials are from the last names of the fighter plane's designers, Arten Mikoyan and Mikhail Gurevich.

mile It is equal to 5,280 feet.

To convert to kilometers, multiply by 1.6.

Use figures in dimensions, formulas and speeds: *The plot is 5 miles by 4.5 miles.*

But in distances, spell out numbers below 10: *He drove six miles.*

miles per gallon The abbreviation *mpg* is acceptable in second reference. In headlines, *MPG* is uppercase.

miles per hour The abbreviation *mph* is acceptable in second reference. In headlines, *MPH* is uppercase. *Miles an hour* is preferable if the abbreviation *mph* isn't used subsequently.

military academies Referring to the U.S. academies, capitalize *Air Force Academy, Coast Guard Academy, U.S. Military Academy, Naval Academy.* Lowercase *academy* whenever it stands alone. Lowercase *academies* in plural constructions: *the Army, Navy and Air Force academies. Cadet* refers to students at the Army and Air Force academies. *Midshipman* refers to students at the Navy and Coast Guard academies.

military titles A military rank is capitalized when it is used before an individual's name. A title should appear before the full name of any member of the military on first reference: *Maj. Gen. James Goble, Staff Sgt. Greg Langan.* On subsequent references, use short forms of the titles: *Gen. Goble, Sgt. Langan.*

Spell out and lowercase all titles when they are used on second reference as substitutes for the individual's name: *Gen. Rory Langan arrived today. The general plans to review the troops.*

Explain the significance of unusual titles in the text: *Army Sgt. Maj. Graham Goble holds the Army's highest rank for enlisted men.*

In addition to the ranks listed below, each service has ratings such as *machinist* and *torpedoman* that are primarily job descriptions and aren't capitalized.

The abbreviations:

RANK	USAGE BEFORE A FULL NAME
ARMY	
Commissioned Officers:	
general	Gen.
lieutenant general	Lt. Gen.
major general	Maj. Gen.
brigadier general	Brig. Gen.
colonel	Col.
lieutenant colonel	Lt. Col.
major	Maj.
captain	Capt.
first lieutenant	First Lt.
second lieutenant	Second Lt.
Warrant Officers:	
chief warrant officer	Chief Warrant Officer
warrant officer	Warrant Officer
Enlisted Personnel:	
sergeant major of the Army	Army Sgt. Maj.

M

command sergeant major	Command Sgt. Maj.
staff sergeant major	Staff Sgt. Maj.
first sergeant	First Sgt.
master sergeant	Master Sgt.
platoon sergeant	Platoon Sgt.
sergeant first class	Sgt. First Class
staff sergeant	Staff Sgt.
sergeant	Sgt.
corporal	Cpl.
specialist	Spc.
private first class	Pfc.
private	Pvt.

NAVY, COAST GUARD

Commissioned Officers:

admiral	Adm.
vice admiral	Vice Adm.
rear admiral	Rear Adm.
captain	Capt.
commander	Cmdr.
lieutenant commander	Lt. Cmdr.
lieutenant	Lt.
lieutenant junior grade	Lt. j.g.
ensign	Ensign

Warrant Officers:

chief warrant officer	Chief Warrant Officer
warrant officer	Warrant Officer

Enlisted Personnel:

master chief petty officer	Master Chief Petty Officer
senior chief petty officer	Senior Chief Petty Officer
chief petty officer	Chief Petty Officer
petty officer first class	Petty Officer First Class
petty officer second class	Petty Officer Second Class
petty officer third class	Petty Officer Third Class
seaman	Seaman
seaman apprentice	Seaman Apprentice
seaman recruit	Seaman Recruit

MARINE CORPS

Ranks and abbreviations for commissioned officers are the same as those in the Army. Warrant-officer ratings follow the same system used in the Navy. There are no specialist ratings.

Others:

sergeant major	Sgt. Maj.
master gunnery sergeant	Master Gunnery Sgt.
master sergeant	Master Sgt.
first sergeant	First Sgt.
gunnery sergeant	Gunnery Sgt.
staff sergeant	Staff Sgt.
sergeant	Sgt.
corporal	Cpl.
lance corporal	Lance Cpl.
private first class	Pfc.
private	Pvt.

AIR FORCE

Ranks and abbreviations for commissioned officers are the same as those in the Army.

Enlisted designations:

chief master sergeant of the Air Force	Chief Master Sgt. of the Air Force
senior master sergeant	Senior Master Sgt.
master sergeant	Master Sgt.
technical sergeant	Tech. Sgt.
staff sergeant	Staff Sgt.
sergeant	Sgt.
senior airman	Senior Airman
airman first class	Airman First Class
airman	Airman
airman basic	Airman

PLURALS: Add *s* to the principal element in the title: *Majs. James Goble and Greg Langan; Sgts. Fred Saez and Eric Martin.*

M

RETIRED OFFICERS: A military rank may be used with the name of a retired officer if it is relevant: *They invited retired Army Gen. Graham Goble.*

See **titles.**

FIREFIGHTERS, POLICE OFFICERS: Use the abbreviations listed here when a military-style title appears before the name of a police officer or firefighter. Add *police* or *fire* before the title if necessary in the context: *police Sgt. Eric Martin, fire Capt. David Maj.*

military units *First Infantry Division, 395th Field Artillery, Seventh Fleet.* But: *the division, the artillery, the fleet.*

militate, mitigate

To militate against means to work against.

To mitigate means to soften.

Milky Way

millennium, millennia

milliliter It is one-thousandth of a liter, equal to approximately one-fifth of a teaspoon.

To convert to teaspoons, multiply by 0.2. Thirty milliliters equal one fluid ounce.

See **liter** and **metric system.**

millimeter It is one-thousandth of a meter. Ten millimeters equal a centimeter.

To convert to inches, multiply by 0.04.

Millimeter may be abbreviated as *mm* when used with a numeral in first or subsequent references to film or weapons: *35mm film, 105mm artillery piece.*

See **meter; metric system; inch.**

millions, billions, trillions *Seven million people, 15 million tons.* For dollar figures, whenever possible, round off to one decimal place for million, two places for billions, three places for trillions: *$12.1 million, $12.10 billion, $12.103 trillion.* Don't drop the word *million* or *billion* in the first figure of a range: *earnings of $30 million to $35 million.* Note that a hyphen is not used between the figures and the words.

See **dollars and cents.**

milquetoast It refers to a timid person.

Milwaukee The city in Wisconsin stands alone in datelines.

mimeograph Formerly a trademark, it is now a generic term.

minefield

mini- The rules in **prefixes** apply. Don't hyphenate unless the base word begins with an *i* or a capital letter:

minibus	miniseries
mini-Olympics	mini-invasion
minicomputer	miniskirt

minister Don't use as a capitalized title before the name of a member of the clergy.

See **religious titles** and the entry for an individual's denomination.

ministry *See* **foreign governmental bodies.**

Ministry of International Trade and Industry The Japanese governmental trade body is based in Tokyo. *MITI* is acceptable in second reference.

Minneapolis The city in Minnesota stands alone in datelines.

Minnesota Abbreviate as *Minn.* after city names. Residents are *Minnesotans.*

See **state names.**

Minnesota Mining & Manufacturing Co. Its name has been changed to *3M Co.*

See **3M Co.**

minority *Minority-group member* is more

appropriate and less jargonistic for an individual. Use *minority* as a modifier: *minority applicant.*

minority leader Capitalize it before a name: *Minority Leader Richard Gephardt; the minority leader.*

See **legislative titles.**

minuscule Not *miniscule.*

minus sign Spell out *minus* except in tables and charts.

misdemeanor

See **felony, misdemeanor.**

misfeasance

See **malfeasance, misfeasance, nonfeasance.**

mishap It refers to a minor misfortune. *Accident* is usually the better word.

M

mishmash

Miss *See* **Mr., Mrs., Miss, Ms.**

missile names Use Arabic numerals and capitalize the proper name, but not the word *missile: Titan 2 missile.*

See **ABM; ICBM; SAM.**

Mississippi Abbreviate as *Miss.* after city names. Residents are *Mississippians.*

See **state names.**

Missouri Abbreviate as *Mo.* after city names. Residents are *Missourians.*

See **state names.**

MITI

See **Ministry of International Trade and Industry.**

mitigate, militate

To mitigate is to soften.

To militate against means to work against.

mix up (v.), **mix-up** (n. and adj.)

MOB spread *MOB* stands for *municipal over bond.* It is the difference, in 32nds of a dollar, between the prices of two similarly dated futures contracts, one on U.S. Treasury bonds and one on municipal bonds. It always is a negative number: *The March MOB spread was –435,* meaning minus 435/32.

mobile home, motor home

A *mobile home* is mobile only when it is en route to its foundation.

A *motor home* is a van-type motor vehicle used as a traveling home.

mock-up (n.)

model *Model A, Model 14, the Chevelle model.*

modem It comes from *modulate, demodulate* and refers to a device that allows a computer to link by phone line to a central database.

molybdenum The minor metal is used mainly as an alloy to produce toughened steel.

Monaco The *Monaco* section stands alone in datelines. The other two sections, *La Condamine* and *Monte Carlo,* are followed by *Monaco:*

MONTE CARLO, Monaco—

Monday

See **days of the week.**

monetary It applies to the money supply.

See **fiscal policy, monetary policy.**

monetary policy

See **fiscal policy, monetary policy.**

monetary units
See **dollars and cents.**

moneymaker

money, moneys The plural is generally used only in referring to the mediums of exchange of two or more countries. Sums of money generally take singular verbs: *About $10 million is still unpaid, and $50 million of that is overdue.*
See **dollars and cents.**

money market It is the market in which short-term debt instruments are issued and traded. This includes Treasury bills, commercial paper and bankers' acceptances.

money supply The term applies to the total stock of money in the economy, consisting primarily of currency in circulation and deposits in savings and checking accounts. Too much money in relation to the output of goods tends to push interest rates down and push prices and inflation up; too little money tends to push interest rates up, lower prices and output and cause unemployment and excess plant capacity.

money-supply measures The basic money-supply gauge is *M1,* which consists of funds that are readily available for spending, including checking accounts that pay interest and those that don't, and currency.

M1 is sometimes broken down into *M1-A* and *M1-B.*

M1-A is the total of private checking-account deposits at commercial banks plus cash in the public hands.

M1-B is cash plus checking-type deposits at all financial institutions, including credit unions and savings-and-loan associations.

M2 consists of cash and all private deposits except very large ones left for a specified period of time. It also includes certain short-term assets such as the amounts held in money-market mutual funds.

M3 is the total of cash plus all private deposits and certain financial assets, such as money-market funds.

L is a broad liquidity measure and consists of cash, deposits and short-term securities readily convertible to cash.

monsignor
See **Roman Catholic Church.**

Montana Abbreviate as *Mont.* after city names. Residents are *Montanans.*
See **state names.**

Montessori (method or system) Named after Maria Montessori, it is a system of teaching that emphasizes self-education.

monthlong

months Capitalize the names of months in all uses. When a month is used with a specific date, abbreviate only *Jan., Feb., Aug., Sept., Oct., Nov.* and *Dec.* Spell them out when using alone or with a year alone.

When a phrase lists only a month and a year, don't separate the year with commas. When a phrase refers to a month, day and year, set off the year with commas.

EXAMPLES: *January 2001 was a cold month. Jan. 14 was the coldest day of the month. His birthday is March 15. June 5, 2001, was the scheduled date.*

See **dates** and **years.**

Montreal The city in Canada stands alone in datelines.

Moody's Corp *Moody's Investors Service* now is a subsidiary of *Moody's Corp.,* which split off from its former parent, Dun & Bradstreet, the business-information and credit-reports company. Moody's, based in New York, is a leading ratings agency, along with McGraw Hill Cos.' Standard & Poor's Corp. Moody's rates bonds, commercial paper, common and preferred stock and short-term municipal issues.

moon It is lowercase.

mop up (v.), **mop-up** (n. and adj.)

moral-obligation bond
See **loan terminology.**

more than *See* **over.**

Moravian Church

Morgan Chase & Co., J.P. *J.P. Morgan Chase & Co.* resulted from the merger of J.P. Morgan & Co. and Chase Manhattan bank in New York.

Morgan Stanley The brokerage firm is based in New York. It is incorporated as Morgan Stanley Dean Witter & Co., but uses just *Morgan Stanley* in its business.

Mormon *Mormon* is a nickname for members of the *Church of Jesus Christ of Latter-day Saints,* and *Mormon Church* is an acceptable alternative name for the church. But don't refer to splinter organizations or polygamous groups as *Mormon. See* the entry under the church's formal name for further guidance.

mortgage bank A business that channels funds to builders and home buyers from large investors such as insurance companies and banks. Builders normally visit *mortgage bankers* to line up construction loans and mortgage money for the buildings they expect to build in the next year. The mortgage banks then approach investors to seek commitments to supply the funds.

Moscow The capital of Russia stands alone in datelines.

Moslem Use *Muslim* instead. *See* **Muslim.**

mosquito, mosquitoes

"most favored nation" status Use the quotes, as it refers to the trading privileges and tariff levels that the U.S. grants most of its trading partners.

Mother's Day

mother-in-law, mothers-in-law

Mother Nature

mount Spell out in all uses, including the names of cities and of mountains: *Mount Everest, Mount Vernon, Mount Holyoke.*

mountains Capitalize as part of a proper name: *Appalachian Mountains, Ozark Mountains, Rocky Mountains.* Or simply: *the Appalachians, the Ozarks, the Rockies.*

Mountain Standard Time (MST), Mountain Daylight Time (MDT)
See **time zones.**

Mountain States Arizona, Colorado, Idaho, Montana, Nevada, New Mexico, Utah and Wyoming.

mouse The plural for the computer mouse is *mouses.*

movie ratings The rankings used by the Motion Picture Association of America Inc. follow:

G: General Audiences. All ages admitted.
PG: Parental Guidance. All ages admitted.

PG-13: Parental guidance advised. Some material may not be suitable for children under 13 years old.

R: Restricted. People under 17 must be accompanied by a parent or adult guardian.

NC-17: No one under 17 admitted.

(The *X* rating is used informally for pornographic films that aren't submitted to the MPAA for a rating.)

Capitalize as shown here. Hyphenate adjectival forms: *an R-rated film.*

movie titles *See* **composition titles.**

MP The abbreviation for *member of parliament* is used in Britain. Avoid it except in quotations.

mpg It is acceptable in second reference for *miles per gallon.* Capitalize in headlines.

mph Acceptable in second references for *miles per hour.* Capitalize in headlines.

Mr., Mrs., Miss, Ms. In general, don't use these courtesy titles in first reference or in headlines, although they are permitted with surnames in feature headlines.

In stories, use the first and second names in first reference, without the courtesy titles. An exception is made when couples are named together: *Mr. and Mrs. Drew Martin.*

MEN: In subsequent references to men, use *Mr.* except with famous men of history: *Washington, Brahms.* For young boys, use the construction *the young Mr. Martin* or repeat the full name.

The plural *Messrs.* may be used in a listing of two or more names.

MARRIED WOMEN: The preferred form in first reference is to identify a woman by her own first name and her husband's last name: *Monica Goble.* Use *Mrs.* in first reference only if a woman requests that her husband's first name be used or her own first name cannot be determined: *Mrs. Drew Martin.*

In second reference, use *Mrs.* unless a woman initially identified by her own first name prefers *Ms.: Elaine Martin, Ms. Martin.*

If a married woman is known by her maiden last name, precede it by *Miss* in second reference unless she prefers *Ms.: Jane Fonda, Miss Fonda.*

UNMARRIED WOMEN: For women who have never been married, use *Miss* or *Ms.* in second reference, according to the woman's preference.

For divorced women and widows, the normal practice is to use *Mrs.* in second reference. Use *Miss* if the woman returns to the use of her maiden name. Use *Ms.* if she prefers it.

MARITAL STATUS: If a woman prefers *Ms.*, do not include her marital status in a story unless it is clearly pertinent.

As with *Mrs.*, there is no plural for *Ms.* If several women who prefer *Ms.* must be listed in a series, repeat *Ms.* before each name.

Muhammad This spelling is preferred over *Mohammed* for the founder of the Muslim religion.

M

mull The verb is overused in headlines. Try to avoid it in favor of *study* or the like.

multi- The rules in **prefixes** apply, but in general, no hyphen. Some examples:

multicolored	multilateral
multimillion	multimillionaire

Multigraph It is a trademark for a brand of dictating machine.

multiple *See* **price/earnings ratio.**

municipal bond
See **loan terminology.**

municipal defeasance In a *municipal defeasance* program, a state or local government issues new debt to refund older debt with higher interest costs. Until the outstanding debt can be called, the government invests proceeds from the new issuance, frequently in Treasury securities.

murder
See **homicide, murder, manslaughter.**

murderer
See **assassin, killer, murderer.**

Murphy's Law It states: *If something can go wrong, it will.*

music The basic guidelines for capitalizing and using quotation marks with the titles of musical works are described in **composition titles.**

Symphony No. 8 of Mahler, the "Symphony of a Thousand"; Symphony No. 3 of Beethoven, the "Eroica" Symphony.

musket
See **weapons.**

Muslim(s) The preferred term to describe adherents of Islam.

mutual funds They are securities portfolios managed by an investment company to provide investors diversification. Also called *open-end investment funds,* they continually sell and redeem shares at prices based on the asset value of the funds' portfolios. So-called *load funds* are offered through brokers, with their fees added. *No-load funds* are offered directly to individual investors.

See **index fund; sector fund.**

Muzak It is a trademark for a type of recorded background music.

Myanmar It formerly was Burma. Its capital is *Yangon,* formerly Rangoon. The language is *Burmese,* and the people are informally called *Burmese.*

Nn

NAACP

See **National Association for the Advancement of Colored People.**

Nafta

See **North American Free Trade Agreement.**

namesake A person is the *namesake* of the person he is named after. Although the person whose name is taken by another is sometimes also called the namesake, avoid that usage.

Namibia It formerly was South-West Africa.

naphtha This petroleum product is used mainly as a feedstock for the production of gasoline and other light, finished oil products and petrochemicals.

See **gasoline.**

narrow-minded

NASD

See **National Association of Securities Dealers** and **over-the-counter stock.**

Nasdaq Stock Market Inc.

In mid-2001, it was considering breaking off from its parent NASD and becoming an independent operation.

See **National Association of Securities Dealers.**

national

See **citizen, resident, subject, national, native.**

National Aeronautics and Space Administration *NASA* is acceptable on second reference.

National Association for the Advancement of Colored People *NAACP* is acceptable on first reference, but provide the full name later unless the reference is an offhand one. *The NAACP Legal Defense and Educational Fund* is a separate entity, and in this name the *NAACP* isn't spelled out.

National Association of Securities Dealers *The NASD* is acceptable in second reference. Based in Washington, D.C., the self-regulatory organization is responsible for the operation and regulation of the Nasdaq securities market.

The *Nasdaq Stock Market Inc.* is to cease being an NASD subsidiary if the Securities and Exchange Commission grants it stock-market status in 2003 or later. As an automated-quotation system, Nasdaq uses computers and telecommunications for the trading and surveillance of thousands of securities, which are colloquially called *over-the-counter stocks.*

The *NASD Regulation Inc.* subsidiary of the NASD regulates the activities of broker-dealers who trade Nasdaq stocks. *NASDR* also regulates the sale of mutual funds, direct-participation programs and variable annuities. NASDR will continue to regulate the Nasdaq Stock Market even after its planned separation from the NASD.

national chairman Capitalize it before the name of the head of a political party: *Republican National Chairman Jim Nicholson.* Also, *the Republican national chairman, Jim Nicholson.*

National Conference of Catholic Bishops
See **Roman Catholic Church.**

National Council of the Churches of Christ in the U.S.A. *National Council of Churches* is acceptable in all references.

National Education Association *NEA* is acceptable on second reference. Based in Washington, it is a teachers-union organization.

National Governors' Association Note the apostrophe.

N

National Guard, the Guard For individuals: *National Guardsman; guardsman.*
See **military titles.**

National Institutes of Health It is part of the Department of Health and Human Services. Treat it as a singular despite the plural *Institutes.*

Individual institutes, based in Bethesda, Md., include the National Cancer Institute; National Eye Institute; National Heart, Lung, and Blood Institute; National Institute of Allergy and Infectious Diseases; National Institute of Arthritis and Musculo-Skeletal Diseases; National Institute of Child Health and Human Development; National Institute of Dental Research; National Institute of Environmental Health Sciences; National Institute of General Medical Sciences; National Institute of Neurological and Communicative Disorders and Stroke; National Institute on Aging.

nationalist
Capitalize it only when referring to a political party for which this is the proper name.
See **political parties and philosophies.**

Nationalist China
See **China.**

nationalities and races Capitalize the proper names of nationalities, peoples, and races: *Arab, Arabic, African, American, Caucasian, Cherokee, Chinese, Eskimo* (plural *Eskimos*), *French Canadian, Gypsy (Gypsies), Japanese, Jew, Jewish, Nordic, Sioux, Swede.*
Lowercase *black, white, red, mulatto.*

National Labor Relations Board *NLRB* is acceptable on second reference.

National League of Cities Cities with 30,000 or more residents are members.

National Organization for Women *NOW* is acceptable on second reference. Headquarters is in Washington.

National Rifle Association *NRA* is acceptable on second reference. Headquarters is in Washington.

National Weather Service It is no longer the U.S. Weather Bureau, although *the weather bureau* may be used.
See **weather terms.**

nationwide

native
See **citizen, resident, subject, national, native.**

Native American
See **American Indian.**

NATO
See **North Atlantic Treaty Organization.**

natural gas *Gas* is acceptable in headlines and after references to natural gas in articles.
See **gas.**

natural gas liquids They comprise all liquid products separated from crude oil or natural gas at the wellhead, including *ethane, propane, butane* and *condensate.*

Naugahyde It is a trademark for a brand of simulated leather.

nauseous, nauseated *Nauseous* means causing nausea. *Nauseated* means victimized by nausea. The rough sea is *nauseous;* the novice sailor is *nauseated* by it.

nautical mile It equals 6,076 feet, or 1,852 meters. To convert to miles of 5,280 feet, multiply number of nautical miles by 1.15.
See **knots.**

naval, navel
Naval pertains to any navy.
A *navel* is a type of orange or the remnant of a person's umbilical cord.

navy
Capitalize it when referring to U.S. forces: *the U.S. Navy, the Navy, Navy policy.*
Lowercase it when referring informally to the naval forces of other nations: *the French navy.*
See **military academies** and **military titles.**

Nazi, Nazism
The terms refer to the National Socialist German Workers' Party, the fascist political party that controlled Germany 1933-45.
See **political parties and philosophies.**

NBC The television network is owned by General Electric Co. Its divisions include *NBC News, NBC Entertainment, NBC Sports* and *CNBC. MSNBC* is a joint venture with Microsoft Corp. The former name, National Broadcasting Co., is no longer used.

NC-17 Rating for "no one under 17 admitted."
See **movie ratings.**

Near East An outdated description; don't use it.
See **Middle East.**

nearsighted In medical terminology, it means an individual can see well at close range but has difficulty seeing objects at a distance.

Nebraska Abbreviate as *Neb.* after city names. Residents are *Nebraskans.*
See **state names.**

negotiated sale In the bond market, it refers to a municipality's sale of a new issue through an exclusive agreement with underwriters. A *competitive sale* requires bidding by underwriters.

N

Neiman Marcus Group Inc. No hyphen is used in the name. It is based in Chestnut Hill, Mass., and includes Bergdorf Goodman stores.

neither . . . nor
See **either . . . or, neither . . . nor.**

nerve-racking

net, the Net Don't use *net* as a verb meaning *attain profit.* As a noun, *net* may be used as a short form for *net income* on second references and in headlines.
See **profit terminology.**
The Net is an acceptable short form for *the Internet* when the meaning is clear.

Netherlands
In datelines, use *Netherlands: HAARLEM, Netherlands—*

In articles, use *the Netherlands* or *Netherlands* as sentence construction dictates. Don't capitalize *the* unless it starts a sentence.

Holland is used loosely to refer to the Netherlands, as North Holland and South Holland are major provinces.

See **Hague, The.**

Netherlands Antilles In datelines, the city name is followed by *Netherlands Antilles.* Don't abbreviate. Specify an individual island, if needed, in the text.

neutron weapon It is a small warhead, not a bomb, designed to be mounted on a missile or fired from a large gun and produce much radiation but little explosive power. The warhead theoretically would kill people while causing little damage to buildings. It is officially known as an *enhanced radiation weapon.*

Nevada Abbreviate as *Nev.* after city names. Residents are *Nevadans.*

See **state names.**

N

New Age It refers to a cultural movement in the 1980s characterized by a concern with spiritual consciousness and combining belief in reincarnation and astrology with such practices as meditation, vegetarianism and holistic medicine. It also refers to a repetitive style of music intended to create a serene mood.

New Brunswick It is a Maritime Province of Canada. Don't abbreviate it.

See **datelines.**

New Delhi The capital of India stands alone in datelines.

New Economy It is notable for the *increased productivity* caused by new technology, or the higher value of the goods and services produced per hour of work because of technology. Companies' operations often include elements of both the New and Old economies.

New England It comprises Connecticut, Maine, Massachusetts, New Hampshire, Rhode Island and Vermont.

newfound

Newfoundland This Canadian province comprises the island of Newfoundland and the mainland section known as Labrador. Don't abbreviate. Don't use the term *Newfie* to identify residents; it is considered derogatory.

In datelines, use *Newfoundland* after the names of all cities and towns. Specify in the text whether the community is on the island or in Labrador.

See **datelines.**

New Hampshire Abbreviate as *N.H.* after city names. Residents are *New Hampshirites.*

See **state names.**

New Jersey Abbreviate as *N.J.* after city names. Don't use the short form *Jersey,* except in quotes. Residents are *New Jerseyites.*

See **state names.**

New Mexico Abbreviate as *N.M.* after city names. Residents are *New Mexicans.*

See **state names.**

New Orleans The city in Louisiana stands alone in datelines.

newspaper names Don't capitalize *the* in any newspaper name except *The Wall Street Journal* and its sister papers.

See **Wall Street Journal, The.**

Where location is needed but is not part of the official name, use parentheses: *the Huntsville (Ala.) Times.*

Consult the International Year Book published by Editor & Publisher to determine whether a two-name combination is hyphenated.

newsstand

New Testament *See* **Bible.**

New World It refers to the Western Hemisphere.

New Year's, New Year's Day, New Year's Eve

New York Abbreviate the state as *N.Y.* after city names. Use *New York state* when a distinction must be made between the state and city. Residents are *New Yorkers.*

See **state names.**

New York Board of Trade It was formed in 1998 by the merger of the Coffee, Sugar & Cocoa Exchange and the New York Cotton Exchange.

New York City Use *NEW YORK* in datelines of articles involving the city in general or the borough of Manhattan.

Datelines of *Brooklyn, Queens, the Bronx* and *Staten Island, N.Y.,* are acceptable. Neighborhoods in Queens may also be used: *Jackson Heights, N.Y.; Long Island City, N.Y.*

In articles that are substantially about the individual boroughs or neighborhoods, mention the relationship to the city prominently.

New York Mercantile Exchange *Nymex* is acceptable on second reference. It is a center for trading of oil, gas, electricity, platinum and palladium futures and options. Among its contracts are heating oil, gasoline, light sweet crude, natural gas and two electricity contracts. *Commodity Exchange Inc.* is a division of Nymex.

See **Comex.**

New York Stock Exchange *NYSE* or *Big Board* is acceptable on second reference. It is the oldest stock exchange in the U.S., founded in 1792.

See **circuit breakers; program trading.**

next To avoid ambiguity, don't use the word *next* in references to the days later in the current week or months or seasons later in the current year.

On a Tuesday, for example, refer to the approaching Friday as *this Friday,* or use simply *on Friday* if the allusion to the future is clear in context.

In February, refer to the approaching May as *this May* or use simply *in May* if the allusion to the future is clear in context. In summer, refer to the approaching winter as *this winter* if the allusion to the future is clear in context.

See **last.**

nickel The base metal, traded on the London Metal Exchange, is used primarily to make stainless steel and batteries.

nicknames A nickname should be used in place of a person's given name in news articles only when it is the way the individual prefers to be known: *Jimmy Carter, Dan Quayle.* If in doubt about the individual's preference, use his or her formal name rather than a short form or a nickname.

When a nickname is inserted into the identification of an individual, use quotation marks: *Averell "Ace" Smith, Edwin Eugene "Buzz" Aldren.* Also: *Astronaut Aldren was known as "Buzz."*

Capitalize without quotation marks such terms as *Keystone State, Motown* and *Old Glory.*

Nielsen, AC The television-ratings company *AC Nielsen Corp.* is based in Stamford, Conn.

nightclub

nighttime

Nihon Keizai Shimbun Inc. Japan's leading financial news provider, it is also a partner of Dow Jones & Co. in Japan. It publishes Japan's largest financial newspaper, the Nihon Keizai Shimbun, and maintains the Nikkei Stock Average, sometimes called the Nikkei 225, the benchmark stock index of the Tokyo Stock Exchange.

nisei It refers to the children born of Japanese immigrants in the U.S. or Canada.

nitpicking

nitty-gritty

No. Use *No.* as the abbreviation for *number* in conjunction with a numeral to indicate position or rank: *No. 1 man, No. 3 choice, No. 2 auto maker.*

Don't use it in addresses or in the names of schools: *Public School 19.*

Nobel Prize, Nobel Prizes The five Nobel Prizes established under the will of Alfred Nobel are: *Nobel Peace Prize, Nobel Prize in chemistry, Nobel Prize in literature, Nobel Prize in physics, Nobel Prize in physiology or medicine.*

The separate Nobel Memorial Prize in Economic Science was established in 1968 as a memorial to Alfred Nobel.

A *Nobel Prize winner,* a *Nobel Prize–winning poet,* a *Nobel laureate.*

nobility Some guidelines, using British nobility as examples:

royalty Capitalize *king, queen, prince* and *princess* when they are used directly before one or more names; lowercase when they stand alone: *Queen Elizabeth II, Queen Elizabeth,* and in later references, *the queen. Kings George and Edward. Queen Elizabeth, the queen mother.*

Also capitalize a longer form: *Her Majesty Queen Elizabeth.*

Use *Prince* or *Princess* before the names of a sovereign's children: *Prince Edward, the prince.* Queen Elizabeth's daughter, Anne, has the title of the *Princess Royal* (or, in full, *Her Royal Highness, the Princess Royal*). *Princess Anne,* as she was formerly titled, remains in informal usage.

The male heir to the throne normally is designated *Prince of Wales,* and the title becomes an alternative name. The queen's eldest son is *Charles, Prince of Wales; the Prince of Wales; the prince. Prince Charles* remains in informal usage.

Charles, Prince of Wales, married Lady Diana Spencer, who became *the Princess of Wales.* Their two children are *Prince William and Prince Harry.*

duke The full title—*Duke of Wellington,* for example—is an alternative name, capitalized in all uses. Lowercase *duke* when it stands alone.

The designation *Arthur, Duke of Wellington,* is appropriate in some cases, but never *Duke Arthur* or *Lord Arthur.*

The wife of a duke is a *duchess: the Duchess of Wellington, the duchess,* but never *Duchess Diana.*

A duke normally also has a lesser title. It is commonly used for his eldest son if he has one. Use the courtesy titles *Lord* or *Lady* before the names of a duke's children.

Some examples:

Lady Jane Wellesley, only daughter of the eighth Duke of Wellington, had been linked romantically with Prince Charles, heir to the British throne. The eldest of Lady Jane's four brothers is Arthur Charles, the Marquess Douro.

marquess, earl, viscount, baron The full titles serve as alternative names and should be capitalized. Frequently, however, the holder of such a title is identified as *Lord: The Marquess of Bath,* for example, more commonly is known as *Lord Bath.*

Use *Lady* before the name of a woman

married to a man who holds one of these titles. The wife of a marquess is a *marchioness,* the wife of an earl is a *countess* (earl is the British equivalent of count), the wife of a viscount is a *viscountess,* the wife of a baron is a *baroness.*

Following her resignation as prime minister and leader of the Conservative Party, Margaret Thatcher was dubbed *Baroness Thatcher.* Her husband was given a knighthood and is now *Sir Denis Thatcher.* In second reference, use *Lady Thatcher* and *Sir Denis.* (If Sir Denis had not been given a knighthood, he would have remained plain Mr. Thatcher, even though his wife became a baroness.)

Use *Lord* or *Lady* before the names of the children of a marquess.

Use *Lady* before the name of an earl's daughter.

Some examples:

Princess Margaret's former husband, Antony Armstrong-Jones, remains the *Earl of Snowdon,* or *Lord Snowdon* in second reference. Their son, David, is *Viscount Linley.* They also have a married daughter, *Lady Sarah Chatto.* Her husband is Daniel Chatto, who in second reference is *Mr. Chatto.*

baronet, knight Men with these titles are not peers. Use *Sir* before their names: *Harold Wilson* on first reference, *Sir Harold* (not *Sir Wilson* or *Mr. Wilson*) on second.

Use *Lady* before the surname of the wife of a baronet or knight.

The chairman of HSBC Holdings PLC, Willie Purves, was knighted by Queen Elizabeth in 1993, becoming *Sir William Purves.* His wife, Rebecca, became *Lady Purves* (not *Lady Rebecca Purves*). *Sir William and Lady Purves live in London.*

For a woman who has received an honor in her own right, use *Dame* before her name if it is the way she is known or if it is appropriate in the context: *Dame Judi Dench* in first reference, *Dame Judi* in second.

nobody, no one

nod The expression *gives nod to,* meaning *approves* or *clears,* is overworked in headlines. Try to avoid it.

noisome, noisy

Noisome means offensive, noxious.

Noisy means clamorous.

nolo contendere The literal meaning is "I do not wish to contend." The term *no contest* or *no-contest plea* is preferred in all references.

When a defendant in a criminal case enters this plea, it means that he is not admitting guilt but is stating that he will offer no defense. The person is then subject to being judged guilty and punished just as if he had pleaded guilty or been convicted. The principal difference is that the defendant retains the option of denying the same charge in another legal proceeding.

no man's land

nominee In the securities industry, a partnership or other entity in whose name securities are recorded for a beneficial owner, to simplify transfer of the certificates.

non- The rules in **prefixes** apply. Use a hyphen if the base word begins with a capital letter: *non-Asian, non-Jewish, non-Catholic.*

Otherwise, in general, do not use a hyphen: *noncollectible, nonessential, noninductive, nonnuclear, nonnutritive, nonprofit, nonsmoker.*

Use two words in certain Latin idioms: *non prosequitur, non sequitur.*

none It usually takes a plural verb or pronoun: *None of the companies pay taxes. None of them pay taxes.* But it takes a singular verb or pronoun if it is followed by a singular noun: *None of the work was done on time.* It also can take a singular verb or pronoun to stress the idea of *not one: None of the com-*

panies has ever paid a penny of tax. But in that case, it would be better to supply the emphasis by changing the *none* to *not one.*

nonfeasance *See* **malfeasance, misfeasance, nonfeasance.**

noon Don't put a *12* in front of it.

no one

Nordic Council Based in Copenhagen, the council promotes cooperation among members: Denmark, Finland, Iceland, Norway and Sweden.

norm *See* **average, mean, median, mode, norm.**

Norscan It stands for *North America and Scandinavia*, and it comprises the U.S., Canada, Finland, Sweden and Norway. The Norscan pulp-stocks figure, released monthly, is a pulp-market indicator.

N

North American Electric Reliability Council Based in Princeton, N.J., it is a voluntary group of utilities and energy companies that oversees power-grid reliability.

North American Free Trade Agreement *Nafta* is acceptable in second reference and in headlines. It involves the U.S., Mexico and Canada.

North Atlantic Treaty Organization *NATO* is acceptable on second reference. Based in Brussels, it is a multilateral organization the U.S. and Western Europe formed after World War II.

North Carolina Abbreviate as *N.C.* after city names. Residents are *North Carolinians.*

See **state names.**

North Dakota Abbreviate as *N.D.* after city names. Residents are *North Dakotans.*

See **state names.**

Northeast The U.S. region encompasses the New England states (Connecticut, Maine, Massachusetts, New Hampshire, Rhode Island and Vermont) and the Middle Atlantic states (New Jersey, New York and Pennsylvania), plus Delaware.

Northern Hemisphere But *the hemisphere.*

Northern Ireland Use *Northern Ireland* after the names of all communities in datelines.

See **datelines, United Kingdom** and **Ulster.**

north, northern, northeast, northwest

See **directions and regions.**

North Slope It refers to Alaska north of Brooks Range.

Northwest Airlines

Northwest Territories Don't abbreviate the territorial section of Canada. Spell out in datelines after the names of all cities and towns. If appropriate, specify in the text the territorial subdivision: *Franklin, Keewatin* or *Mackenzie.*

See **Canada.**

nose-dive (v.), **nose dive** (n.)

not Avoid the word whenever possible, or rearrange its position in the sentence so any inadvertent dropping of the *not* or mistyping as *now* wouldn't reverse the intended meaning. Make contractions out of negative verbs whenever possible (*See* **contractions**) or revise sentence: Instead of *He decided not to run again,* make it, *He decided against running again.*

See **now.**

notes

See **loan terminology.**

not only . . . but also The construction following the *not only* should parallel the construction after the *but also.* The *also* is required except when another word is used in its place or the expression following the *but* is intensified: *He not only sent her but even paid for her trip. He not only passed but got an "A."*

notoriety, notorious They denote *unfavorable* fame.

Nova Scotia It is a Maritime Province of Canada. Don't abbreviate it.

See **datelines.**

November

See **months.**

Novocain It is a trademark for a drug used as a local anesthetic. It may also be called *procaine.*

now Use the word carefully, to prevent a reversal of intended meanings when it is mistyped as *not.*

NOW It stands for *the National Organization for Women.*

nowadays

Nuclear Regulatory Commission *NRC* is acceptable in second reference. As overseer of the nuclear-power industry, it inspects nuclear and can penalize or close those it deems unsafe.

nuclear terminology

core The part of a nuclear reactor where the atoms of uranium or another fuel are split. This *fission* releases heat that is used to boil water to power a steam generator.

meltdown A serious nuclear accident causing the reactor core to overheat. If the overheated fuel penetrates the protective housing of the core, radioactive materials may be released into the environment.

plutonium A radioactive element. Its *plutonium-230* isotope is used in reactors and in nuclear weapons.

rem The standard unit of measurement of radiation from radioactive material that is absorbed in living tissue.

roentgen The standard measure of X-ray exposure.

uranium A radioactive element used as fuel in nuclear reactors.

number of It takes a plural verb when preceded by *a: A number of companies were bankrupt.* It takes a singular verb when preceded by *the: The number of companies was unknown.*

numbers Generally, spell out *one* through *nine* and *first* through *ninth*, and use numerals for higher numbers.

EXCEPTIONS: Spell out numbers that start sentences (or rearrange the sentence to avoid starting with a number).

Use numerals in scores, court decisions, legislative votes and similar constructions: *a 6–3 decision; a 4–2 victory; a Senate vote of 42–8; the House voted 210–17.* (But for numbers over 1,000, don't use the hyphens: *A popular vote of 40,000 to 15,000.*) *A ratio of 2 to 1. A stock split of 2 for 1. A 2-for-1 stock split. The Red Sox won, 6–4.*

Use numerals with percentage sign: *1%, 90%, 2.3%.*

Also: *No. 3 choice, No. 10 insurance company.*

For ordinal numbers, spell out *first* through *ninth.* Starting with *10th,* use the figures.

See **fractions, decimals** and **headlines.**

nylon It is not a trademark.

Nymex

See **New York Mercantile Exchange.**

NYSE

See **New York Stock Exchange.**

Oo

O, oh

The exclamation *O*, always uppercase, is used mostly in poetic and religious contexts: *"O Canada" is the national anthem.*

The interjection *oh* is lowercase except starting a sentence, usually with an exclamation mark: *Oh, the pain!*

oasis, oases

objet(s) d'art

obscenities, profanities, vulgarities Don't include them in stories unless they are part of direct quotations and the editors agree there is a compelling reason for including them. Generally, we paraphrase instead, or use just the first letter followed by a dash to indicate the word used.

Occident, Occidental Capitalize the words when they refer to Europe, the Western Hemisphere or the inhabitants.

Occupational Safety and Health Administration *OSHA* is acceptable in second reference and in headlines.

occupational titles Lowercase.

See **titles.**

occur, occurred, occurring, occurrence

oceangoing

oceans In order of size, they are Pacific Ocean, Atlantic Ocean, Indian Ocean, Antarctic Ocean, Arctic Ocean. *The ocean, the Atlantic and Pacific oceans.*

o'clock Capitalize *O'Clock* in headlines.

octane number It is a measure, on a scale 1 to 100, of the resistance of a fuel, usually gasoline, to preignition or knocking in an internal combustion engine.

See also **cetane number.**

October

See **months.**

odd- Hyphenate: *odd-looking, odd-numbered, 40-odd.* But: *oddball.*

odd lot In stock trading, it refers to any purchase or sale of fewer than 100 shares.

See also **round lot.**

OECD

See **Organization for Economic Cooperation and Development.**

OEM

See **original-equipment manufacturer.**

off-Broadway, off-off-Broadway Theatrical terms, defined by union contracts, describe conditions under which plays may be produced. They do not indicate a location.

offer
See **bid and asked.**

offering circular It is a document giving the terms of a tender offer and certain information about the maker of the offer.

offering price It refers to the price at which new issues of stock are marketed to the public.

office
Capitalize *office* when it is part of an agency's formal name: *Office of Management and Budget.*
Lowercase other uses: *the office of the attorney general, the U.S. attorney's office.*
See **Oval Office.**

officeholder

Office National Interprofessionnel des Cereales It is the name of the French cereal regulatory board, based in Paris.

offline, online
See **online, offline.**

O

offload Avoid the word, except in quoted matter. Use *unload* instead.

off of Use the substandard expression only in quotes. Otherwise, either delete the superfluous *of (she went* off *the medicine)* or change the *off of* to *from (he borrowed $100* from *her).*

off-, -off Follow Webster's New World Dictionary, but for *offline.*

off-color	off-site
charge-off (n.)	stop-off (n.)
off-peak	off-white
send-off (n.)	write-off (n.)

Without a hyphen:

cutoff (n.)	offline
offside	playoff (n.)
liftoff (n.)	standoff (n.)
offstage	offshore
offhand	takeoff (n.)
offset	

offshore banking units The term refers to shell branches owned by nonresident banks in an international financial center that, by accepting deposits from foreign banks and other offshore banking units, makes loans in the Eurocurrency market, unrestricted by local monetary authorities or governments. An *offshore banking unit* cannot, however, take domestic deposits. Since the 1970s, these financial units have sprung up in major European cities, the Mideast, Asia and the Caribbean. Major offshore banking centers for U.S. banks are the Bahamas, the Cayman Islands, Hong Kong, Panama and Singapore, which offer favorable political, regulatory and tax treatment.

offshore dollars
See **Eurodollars.**

offshore waters They extend from the coast to a distance of about 250 miles.

Ohio Don't abbreviate. Residents are *Ohioans.*
See **state names.**

oil field, oil man

oil production The *upstream* part of the oil industry involves oil exploration and production activities. *Downstream* refers to all the subsequent activities, including the refining and marketing of oil products. The major oil companies are *integrated,* meaning they have extensive upstream and downstream operations.

oil-production payment It involves the contractual paying of a percentage of the proceeds from oil production until a specified dollar sum has been received.

OK, OK'd, OK'ing, OK's Use the terms only in informal contexts. Don't use *okay.*

Oklahoma Abbreviate as *Okla*. Residents are *Oklahomans.*
See **state names.**

Oklahoma City The capital of Oklahoma stands alone in datelines.

Old City of Jerusalem It refers to the walled part of that city.

Old Testament

old-time, old-timer, old times

Old World It refers to the Eastern Hemisphere: *Asia, Europe, Africa.*

olein
See **palm oil.**

Olympic Airways

Olympic Games Use also *the Olympics, the Summer Olympics, the Winter Olympics, the Summer Games, the Games.* But: *an arm-wrestling olympics.*

Olympic-size swimming pool It must be 50 meters long, or about 164 feet, by 25 meters, or about 82 feet.

on Don't use the word *on* routinely before a date or day of the week.

on- Hyphens aren't used in *onrush, onshore, onside, onstage. See* **ongoing.**

one- Hyphenate *one-* when it is used in writing fractions: *one-half, one-third, one-fourth. A half, a third* and the like are also acceptable.

one another, each other Two people correspond with *each other*; three or more correspond with *one another.*
See **each other, one another** entry.

one man, one vote (n.); **one-man, one-vote** (adj.)

one-sided

onetime, one-time No hyphen is used when it means *former.* Use a hyphen when it refers to something done just once: *The onetime chairman said the dividend omission was a one-time event.*

ongoing Avoid except in quoted matter. Instead use words such as *continuing* or *progressing.*

ONIC
See **Office National Interprofessionnel des Cereales.**

online, offline They are one word in all uses relating to computer connections or factory operations: *She went online to find the answer, then went offline again.* And: *The plant's manufacturing went offline for repairs in August but is scheduled to go back online next year.*

For standing in a queue, avoid the New York regionalism *on line: He stood in line two hours for show tickets.*

only Generally, place *only* before the word it modifies: *She only goes to the store* means she doesn't go elsewhere. *Only she goes to the store* means she is the sole shopper. It's only natural that there are idiomatic exceptions: *She was only trying to help. I only have eyes for you.*

Ontario This Canadian province is the largest in total population. Do not abbreviate.
See **datelines.**

OPEC

See **Organization of Petroleum Exporting Countries.**

OPEC basket OPEC's so-called *basket of crude* was designed in 1986 as an indicator of the price for OPEC oil against the group's *minimum reference price,* or target price. The basket contains Algerian Saharan Blend, Indonesian Minas, Nigerian Bonny Light, Saudi Arabian Arab Light, Dubai Fateh, Venezuelan Tia Juana Light and non-OPEC Mexican Isthmus.

op-ed page It is the page in a newspaper opposite the editorial page.

open access In the world of broadband Internet services, *open access* potentially gives multiple Internet service providers, or *ISPs,* access to a cable-television company's lines, allowing the providers to deliver high-speed Internet access directly to consumers. Cable companies typically offer their own Internet service to customers; implementing *open access* gives their Internet competitors the right to use the cable company's line as well.

open-end investment fund

See **mutual funds.**

open interest A measure of liquidity in futures contracts, *open interest* refers to the total number of futures contracts that have been opened, with either a purchase or a sale, and not yet closed by an offsetting purchase or sale. A liquidation closing an open contract position is thus called an *offset.*

open shop The term applies to a workplace where workers aren't required to be union members.

See **closed shop.**

operas

See **composition titles.**

operating profit Analysts and companies often refer to *operating profit* or *operating income,* to exclude income from sources other than the company's regular activities and before charges and other deductions. But the term is ill-defined, so explain references to it in earnings articles and also include *net income,* the figure required by the SEC and accountants.

operating system In the computer world, it is the software connecting other software to the hardware.

ophthalmology, ophthamalogist

opposition Don't capitalize it when referring to a political faction: *the Labour opposition, the opposition.*

opprobrium

See **approbation, opprobrium.**

options In the securities business, they are contracts that give the holders the right, but not the obligation, to buy or sell a set amount of securities or commodities at a set level.

See **call; exercise; put; strike price.**

oral, verbal, written Use *oral* to refer to spoken words, *written* to refer to words on paper, and *verbal* to encompass both.

Oregon Abbreviate as *Ore.* after city names. Residents are *Oregonians. See* **state names.**

organisms

See **taxonomic names.**

Organization for Economic Cooperation and Development *OECD* is acceptable in headlines and second references in text. Based in Paris, it was founded in 1961 to replace the Organization for European Economic Cooperation. The OECD is a forum for discussing and coordinating members' economic policies. Its 29 members are Australia, Austria, Belgium, Canada, Czech Republic, Denmark, Finland, France, Germany, Greece, Hungary, Iceland, Ireland, Italy, Japan, Luxembourg, Mexico, Netherlands, New Zealand, Norway, Poland, Portugal, South Korea, Spain, Sweden, Switzerland, Turkey, the U.K. and the U.S.

Organization of American States *OAS* is acceptable on second reference.

Organization of Arab Petroleum Exporting Countries *OAPEC* is acceptable in second reference, but *the organization* is better. Established in 1968 to safeguard interests and further cooperation among members, it is based in Kuwait. Its 10 members are Algeria, Bahrain, Egypt, Iraq, Kuwait, Libya, Qatar, Saudi Arabia, Syria and United Arab Emirates.

Organization of Petroleum Exporting Countries *OPEC* is acceptable in headlines and second reference. Established in 1960, it is based in Vienna. Its 11 members are Algeria, Indonesia, Iran, Iraq, Kuwait, Libya, Nigeria, Qatar, Saudi Arabia, United Arab Emirates and Venezuela. Ecuador quit the group in 1992. Founder members are Iran, Iraq, Kuwait, Saudi Arabia and Venezuela.

The secretary-general, the organization's main official, participates in meetings but is meant to be a facilitator, not a political official as national oil ministers are. OPEC is required by its statutes to meet twice yearly but meets more often when oil-market issues arise. At each required meeting, OPEC names from among the ministers a conference president, who is assigned to run the meeting. He may be referred to as *OPEC president.*

See also **OPEC basket.**

organizations and institutions

Capitalize the full names of organizations and institutions: *the American Medical Association, the First Presbyterian Church, the association, the church.* Use lowercase for segments of an organization when they have names that are widely used generic terms: *the board of trustees of Columbia University, the history department of Dartmouth College.*

ABBREVIATIONS AND ACRONYMS: Some organizations and institutions are widely recognized by their shorter forms: *GOP, NATO.*

For proper-name acronyms of more than four letters, arbitrarily capitalize only the first letter: *Ascap, Awacs, Nafta, Swapo, Unicef.* But unpronounceable abbreviations are uppercase: *NAACP, SPEBSQSA.* For guidelines on when such abbreviations may be used, see the individual listings and the entries under **abbreviations and acronymns; company names; second reference.**

Orient, Oriental Capitalize when referring to the nations of Asia and nearby islands. *Asian* is the preferred term for the people. Also: *an Oriental rug.*

original-equipment manufacturer In the computer industry, it is a manufacturer that provides a product used by another manufacturer in the production of its hardware or software. Intel Corp., which makes chips for Compaq Computer Corp.'s personal computers, is an *original-equipment manufacturer* for Compaq.

Orlon It is a trademark for a form of acrylic fiber similar to nylon.

orthodox Capitalize it when referring to membership in or the activities of an Eastern Orthodox church. The church is *Christian*, but not Protestant.

See **Eastern Orthodox churches.**

Capitalize also in phrases such as *Orthodox Judaism* or *Orthodox Jew.*

See **Jewish congregations.**

Orthodox Church in America
See **Eastern Orthodox churches.**

Osaka Mercantile Exchange It was formed by the merger of the Kobe Rubber Exchange and the Osaka Textile Exchange.

Oscar, Oscars
See **Academy Awards.**

oscillator In the securities industry, it refers to a mathematical construction plotted on a chart and used by technicians to judge whether a market trend is gaining or slowing. The gauge typically oscillates around a zero line that is the midpoint of a negative-to-positive scale. A *positive and rising oscillator* confirms an upward trend, and a *falling and negative oscillator* confirms a downtrend.

See **overbought or oversold; resistance level; support level.**

Oslo The capital of Norway stands alone in datelines.

Ottawa The capital of Canada stands alone in datelines.

O

Ottaway Newspapers Inc. A subsidiary of Dow Jones & Co., it publishes community newspapers.

Ouija It is a trademark.

ounce (liquid)
See **fluid ounce.**

ounce (troy) It is 480 grains, or about 31 grams. It is used in measuring precious metals. There are 32,150.7 troy ounces in a metric ton.

ounce (weight) It is 437.5 grains. The metric equivalent is approximately 28 grams.

To convert to grams, multiply by 28.

See **grain** and **gram.**

out- Follow Webster's New World. Hyphenate if not listed there.

outdo	outscore
outpost	outfield
outbox	outstrip
output	outfox
outdated	outtalk
outrun	outpatient (n., adj.)

-out Follow Webster's New World. Hyphenate nouns and adjectives not listed there.

The following nouns would be used as two words for the verb forms:

bailout	fade-out
flameout	walkout
buyout	fallout
cop-out	washout
pullout	

Outer Banks The name applies to the sandy islands along the North Carolina coast.

outgoing To avoid ambiguity, generally use the word only to refer to a personality trait. Use *departing* to apply to someone leaving office or leaving town.

out of court (adv.), **out-of-court** (adj.) *They settled out of court. He accepted an out-of-court settlement.*

outright purchase or sale At the Federal Reserve, the terms refer to its dealings in Treasury securities with its primary dealers, known as dealings for its *system account.* A purchase adds permanent reserves to the banking system, while a sale drains reserves from the banking system. Although it isn't permitted to buy securities directly from the Treasury, it does roll over its holding of maturing securities at auctions.

See **Federal Reserve terminology** and **federal funds.**

out-turn In the petroleum industry, this involves delivery of crude oil or oil products to shore tanks from a tanker. Use the term only in contexts where the meaning is clear. *Out-turn loss* is crude oil or products lost in the delivery. *Out-turn quality and quantity* refers to oil delivered to the shore tanks, as opposed to *bill of lading quantity and quality* measured at the loading terminal.

Oval Office In the White House, it is the office of the president.

over It generally refers to spatial relationships: *The plane flew over the city.*

Over can, at times, be used with numbers: *She is over 30.* But *more than* usually is called for: *Their salaries rose more than $20.*

over- Follow Webster's New World. A hyphen is seldom used.

overbuy	overexert
overrate	override

See the **overall** entry.

-over Follow Webster's New World. Hyphenate if not listed there.

Some nouns or adjectives:

carry-over	walkover
stopover	takeover
holdover	

Use two words when any of these occurs as a verb. *See* **suffixes.**

overall, over all, overalls *It was the overall policy of the farmers to wear overalls, but over all, their wives didn't.*

overbought or oversold

In the securities business, *overbought* refers to a security or market that has had an unexpected price spurt and is therefore considered vulnerable to a price drop.

Oversold describes a stock or market that has had an unexpectedly sharp price decline and is deemed ready for a rebound.

See **technical analysis.**

overcollateralization It describes a technique used to enhance yield or provide additional credit support in asset-backed securities.

See **asset-backed securities.**

over-the-counter stock A stock not listed and traded on an organized exchange or on Nasdaq. *OTC* is acceptable in second reference.

See also **pink sheets.**

owner Lowercase: *Atlanta Braves owner Ted Turner.*

owner's trust It is used to issue asset-backed certificates. Senior certificates issued from the trust are classified as senior notes, so interest payments are treated as debt expense and thus can be deducted from corporate income and not taxed. Subordinated classes are issued as certificates that effectively represent ownership interests in the trust, making it look more like a partnership.

See **asset-backed securities.**

oxygenated gasoline

See **gasoline.**

Ozark Mountains Or *the Ozarks.*

Pp

Pacific Basin or Pacific Rim *See* **Asian geographic terms.**

Pacific Exchange It is no longer called the Pacific *Stock* Exchange.

Pacific Ocean *See* **oceans.**

Pacific Standard Time (PST), Pacific Daylight Time (PDT) *See* **time zones.**

page numbers Jump lines use the format: *Please Turn to Page A8, Column 5.* In referral boxes and lines in articles calling attention to related stories, use these forms: . . . *text (see article on page A3).* Or: . . . *text (see story on page one).* Note that *page* is lowercase (except in jump lines), and that only *page one* is written out; numerals are used for all other pages, including the first pages of the second and third sections (*page B1, C1*).

PaineWebber Inc. It is the money-management unit of UBS Ag, of Zurich.

paintings Capitalize and use quotation marks for their formal titles as described in **composition titles.**

palate, palette, pallet

The palate is the roof of the mouth.

A *palette* is an artist's paint board.

A *pallet* is a bed or a low, portable platform.

Palestine Liberation Organization *PLO* is acceptable in second reference.

palladium The platinum-group metal is used in electronics, engineering and dentistry.

Palm Inc. Based in Santa Clara, Calif., it makes handheld computing devices. An early brand name, *Palm Pilot,* is no longer used.

palmtop It is a classification for a tiny computer. *See* **computer.**

pan- No hyphen when combined with a common noun:

panchromatic

pantheism

Most combinations with *pan-* are proper nouns, however, and both *pan-* and the proper name it is combined with are capitalized:

Pan-African

Pan-Asiatic

Pan-American

Panama Canal Zone It no longer exists.

Panama City Use *PANAMA CITY, Fla.,* or *PANAMA CITY, Panama,* in datelines to avoid confusion between the two.

Pandora's box

pantsuit Not *pants suit.*

paperback

paperwork

par It is the stated amount, or *face value,* of a security. For a debt security, it is the amount at which the issuer of the security agrees to redeem it at maturity.

parallel, paralleled, paralleling

parallels They are the imaginary east-west locator lines that ring the globe. They are measured in units of 0 to 90 degrees north or south of the equator:

28th parallel (if location north or south of the equator is obvious), or *fourth parallel north, 89th parallel south.*

See **latitude and longitude** and **meridians.**

pardon, parole, probation The terms are often confused, but each has a specific meaning.

A *pardon* forgives and releases a person. It is granted by a chief of state or a governor.

A *general pardon,* usually for political offenses, is called *amnesty.*

Parole refers to the release of a prisoner before his sentence has been served, on condition of good behavior.

Probation is the suspension of sentence for a person convicted but not yet imprisoned, on condition of good behavior. It is imposed by a judge and may be revoked by the judge.

parentheses ( )

Place a period outside a closing parenthesis if the material inside is not a sentence. (*But a complete parenthetical sentence takes a period before the closing parenthesis.*) Use parentheses if a state name or similar information is inserted within a proper name: *the Lancaster (Pa.) New Era.* But use commas if no proper name is involved: *The Lancaster, Pa., assemblyman.*

POLITICAL AFFILIATIONS: Parentheses may be used to denote a political figure's party and jurisdiction: *Rep. Averell Smith (D., Calif.).* But in page-one and other feature stories, it is almost always preferable to say: *Rep. Averell Smith, a Democrat from California. See* **party affiliation.**

See **brackets.**

parent-teacher association *PTA* is acceptable in second reference. Capitalize it as part of a proper name: *the Beller School Parent-Teacher Association* or *the Parent-Teacher Association of the Beller School.*

Paris The French capital stands alone in datelines.

Paris Club The informal group of government representatives meets irregularly in the French capital to consider debt reschedulings for debtor nations, covering government-to-government debt and officially guaranteed export credits. Reschedulings usually are limited to debtors who have an economic adjustment plan in place with the International Monetary Fund.

Paris Stock Exchange

See **Euronext.**

parish

Capitalize it as part of the formal name for an individual congregation or governmental jurisdiction: *St. Peter's Parish, the parish.* In Louisiana, *parish* is the equivalent of a county: *Vernon Parish, Union Parish, the parish.*

Lowercase it in plural combinations: *the parish, St. John's and St. Mary's parishes.*

See **county** for additional guidelines on governmental jurisdictions.

Parkinson's disease It is named after James

P

Parkinson, the English physician who first described this degenerative disease.

Parkinson's law Named after C. Northcote Parkinson, the British economist, it states: Work expands to fill the time allotted to it.

parliament
See **foreign legislative bodies.**

parliamentary Lowercase it except when it is part of a proper name.

parochial school It is a school supported by a church, a parish or a diocese.

parole *See* **pardon, parole, probation.**

partner Avoid using it as a verb in business and similar contexts, although *partnering* is traditional in ballet.

part time (adv.), **part-time** (adj.), **part-timer** (n.)

party *See* **political parties and philosophies.**

party affiliation When party designations are needed, use any of these constructions:
—*Republican Sen. Arlen Specter of Pennsylvania said . . .*
—*Sen. Arlen Specter (R., Pa.) said . . .* (But generally avoid this form in page-one and other feature stories.)
—*Sen. Arlen Specter also spoke. The Pennsylvania Republican said . . .*
—*Sen. Arlen Specter of Pennsylvania may seek the Republican presidential nomination.*
See **legislative titles.**

pass *See* **adopt, approve, enact, pass.**

passenger mile It represents one passenger carried one mile.

passerby, passersby

Passover The weeklong Jewish holiday commemorating the deliverance of the ancient Hebrews from slavery in Egypt. Occurs in March or April.

past
See **last** and **next.**

pasteurize

pastor
See **religious titles** and the entry for the individual's denomination.

Patriots' Day In Massachusetts, it is April 19, a legal holiday.

patrolman, patrolwoman Capitalize before a name only if the word is a formal title.
See **titles.**

patrol, patrolled, patrolling

payload

pay out (v.), **payout** (n. and adj.)

payout event Also called *early amortization,* it occurs when the principal payments in securities backed by revolving loans are used to retire the securities. The *event* is triggered when the portfolio yield in a pool backing the security reaches a specified base rate. The mechanism ensures that investors are repaid principal should there be a marked deterioration in the credit quality of a pool of receivables.
See **asset-backed securities.**

peacekeeping

peacemaker, peacemaking

peace offering

peacetime

peak A high point, followed by a decline. Not a synonym for *record.*

Peat Marwick The accounting firm was succeeded by KPMG LLP.

See **accounting firms.**

peck It is a unit of dry measure equal to eight dry quarts or one-fourth of a bushel.

The metric equivalent is approximately 8.8 liters.

To convert to liters, multiply by 8.8.

See **liter.**

pedal, peddle

You *pedal* a bicycle.

You *peddle* wares.

peddler

pell-mell

peninsula Capitalize it as part of proper name: *the Upper Peninsula of Michigan.*

penitentiary *See* **prison, jail, penitentiary.**

Pennsylvania Abbreviate as *Pa.* Residents are *Pennsylvanians.*

See **state names.**

P

Pennsylvania Dutch The people are of German or Swiss descent. The word *Dutch* came from *Deutsch,* the German word for *German.*

penny-wise *See* **-wise.**

Pentecost

people, persons *People* is preferred in all plural uses: *Only 20 people attended the annual meeting. Some people pay no income tax. The company employs 50 people.*

People takes a plural verb when used to refer to a single race or nation: *The Argentine people are united on the issue.*

people's Use this possessive form in general and when the word occurs in the formal name of a nation: *the People's Republic of China.*

PepsiCo Inc. It is based in Purchase, N.Y. *Pepsi* and *Pepsi-Cola* are its trademarks.

per Generally *a* is preferable in constructions such as *a gallon, a mile, a share, a hundred bushels.* But: *per 100 bushels.*

percent (%), percentages, percentage points The symbol % is generally used with figures: *a 1% rise, a 25% rise.* Corporate-earnings articles and other such articles should include percentage increases or declines for all the major dollar figures except in the cases listed below. To calculate the percentages, use figures that haven't been rounded off, from earnings tables, for example. To calculate the rise or fall of earnings, use the total earnings, not the per-share figure.

EXCEPTIONS:

—Don't attempt to calculate year-to-year percentage gains or declines when a company's fortunes have swung from a loss for one year to profit for the next year, or vice versa.

—Don't use a percentage figure if the company is in the red both years: Simply say the loss or deficit *widened* or *narrowed.*

For figures below 10, generally round off to one digit past the decimal point: *4.87%* becomes *4.9%; 3.42%* becomes *3.4%.*

For 10 and above (except in formal statistics such as economic indicators), don't use a decimal: *11.3%* becomes *11%, 15.5%* becomes *16%.* (But: *a rise to 15.8% from 15.3%.*) Don't use *percent* or % when *percentage point* is meant. An increase in a rate from 10% to 11% is a rise of one percentage point, but it is an increase of 10%.

Repeat the % in a series: *Profit rose 10% or 15%.*

Percentages take singular verbs when standing alone or when a singular word follows an *of* construction: *The company said 60% is the limit. It said 40% of the staff was laid off.* But percentages take plural verbs when a plural word follows an *of* construction: *He said 40% of the workers are present.*

OTHER HINTS:

Note that positive figures don't fall more than 100%, as a 100% decline drops the figure to zero.

With percentage gains of over 100%, generally provide figures without the percentage change: *Sales rose to $315.5 million in the latest quarter, from $146.7 million a year earlier.* Or say sales *more than doubled.*

A 100% increase, say, to 60 from 30, represents a *doubling.* A 200% increase, to 90 from 30, represents a tripling (not a *trebling*).

See also **basis point.**

periods (.)

END OF SOME RHETORICAL QUESTIONS: The period is preferable to a question mark if a question is intended primarily as a suggestion: *Why don't we go.*

ABBREVIATIONS: For the forms, see **abbreviations and acronyms** and individual alphabetized listings under the full name or term.

INITIALS: Abbreviations using just the initials of an individual's name don't take periods: *JFK, LBJ.*

ELLIPSES: *See* **ellipses.**

PLACEMENT WITH QUOTATION MARKS: Periods always go inside quotation marks. *See* **quotation marks.**

Perl It is a computer-programming language used for applications running on the Web and for other tasks. It is not an acronym.

permissible

per-share earnings, earnings per share Don't shorten to *share earnings.* Use *a share* in most constructions: *Earnings were $2.15 a share.* When a company has preferred stock outstanding, the per-share earnings are after preferred dividends.

Persian Gulf Use this long-established name for the body of water off the southern coast of Iran. Some Arab nations call it *the Arabian Gulf.* Use *Arabian Gulf* only in direct quotations and explain in the text that the body of water is more commonly known as *the Persian Gulf.*

Persian Gulf War, Gulf War

person

See **people, persons.**

-person Don't use *chairperson* or *spokesperson, except in direct quotations.* Instead, use *chairman* or *spokesman* if referring to a man or the office in general. Use *chairwoman* or *spokeswoman* if referring to a woman. Or, if applicable, use a neutral word such as *leader* or *representative.*

personifications Capitalize personifications such as *Grim Reaper* and *Mother Nature.*

persuade

See **convince, persuade.**

Peter Principle It holds that each employee is promoted until he reaches his level of incompetence.

petty officer

See **military titles.**

PG For the parental-guidance rating.

See **movie ratings.**

pharaoh

phase

See **faze, phase.**

Ph.D., Ph.D.s The preferred form is to say a person holds a doctorate and name the individual's area of specialty. *See* **academic degrees** and **doctor.**

phenomenon, phenomena

Philadelphia The city in Pennsylvania stands alone in datelines.

Philip Morris Cos. The parent company now is Altria Group Inc., which encompasses Kraft Foods, Philip Morris USA, Philip Morris International and Philip Morris Capital Corp.

Philippine (adj.), **Philippines** (n., always singular) In datelines, give the name of a city or town followed by *Philippines: MANILA, Philippines—*

In stories: *the Philippines, the Philippine Islands.*

The people are *Filipinos.* The language is called *Pilipino.*

Phnom Penh It is the capital of Cambodia.

Phoenix The capital of Arizona stands alone in datelines.

P

PhoneMail It is a trademark of Rolm Co. Generally use *voice mail* instead.

phony

Photostat A trademark for a type of photocopy.

physician assistant Those licensed to practice under a physician are *physician assistants,* with no apostrophe.

piano, pianos

pica A unit of measure in printing, equal to about one-sixth of an inch. A pica contains 12 points.

picket, pickets, picketed, picket line *Picket* is both the verb and the noun. Don't use *picketer.*

pick up (v.), **pickup** (n. and adj.) *Pickup* may be used alone to mean *pickup truck.*

picnic, picnicked, picnicking, picnicker

pigeonhole (n. and v.)

pig iron Produced in a blast furnace, it takes its name from channels leading from the furnace called *sows* and *pigs.*

Pikes Peak

pile up (v.), **pileup** (n., adj.)

PIN It stands for *personal identification number.* Don't use the redundancy *PIN number.*

ping pong A synonym for *table tennis. Ping-Pong* is the trademark name.

Pink Sheets Capitalize the over-the-counter stock-quotation sheets issued by Pink Sheets LLC, formerly the National Quotation Bureau.

See **over-the-counter stock.**

pint (dry) It is equal to 33.6 cubic inches, or one-half of a dry quart. The metric equivalent is approximately 0.55 liter.

To convert to liters, multiply by 0.55.

See **liter** and **quart (dry).**

pint (liquid) It is equal to 16 fluid ounces, or two cups. The metric equivalents are about 470 milliliters and 0.47 liter.

To convert to liters, multiply by 0.47.

See **liter.**

pipeline One word except in some company names.

pistol A *pistol* can be either an automatic or

a revolver. A *revolver* has a revolving cylinder that holds cartridges.

See **weapons.**

Pittsburgh The city in Pennsylvania stands alone in datelines.

The spelling is *Pittsburg* for cities in California, Illinois, Kansas, New Hampshire, Oklahoma and Texas.

plains *See* **Great Plains.**

planets Capitalize the names of the nine planets of the solar system. In order of their mean distance from the sun, they are Mercury, Venus, Earth, Mars, Jupiter, Saturn, Uranus, Neptune and Pluto.

Capitalize *earth* as the name of our planet.

See **heavenly bodies** and **earth.**

planning Avoid the redundancy *future planning.*

plants Lowercase the names of plants, but capitalize proper nouns: *fir, white fir, Douglas fir.* If a botanical name is used, capitalize the first word, lowercase others: *blue azalea (Callicarpa americana).*

Plastic Wood It is a trademark for a brand of wood filler.

platform In the computer world, a *platform* is equipment or software used as a basis for building something else. Microsoft Windows, for example, is a *desktop platform* for application software. The Internet and various cellular technologies also are *platforms.*

platinum The precious metal is used mostly in jewelry, electronics and auto-catalysts.

play titles *See* **composition titles.**

PLC The letters, used after the names of some European companies, mean *public limited company. See* **foreign companies.**

plead The past tense is *pleaded.* Don't use the colloquial *pled.*

plead not guilty

See **guilty.**

Plexiglas Note the single s. A trademark for a synthetic glass, also generically called *plexiglass.*

PLO It stands for *Palestine Liberation Organization.*

plow Not plough.

plurality *See* **majority, plurality.**

plurals

Many Latin-root words ending in *us* are changed to *i* for the plural: *alumnus, alumni.* Most ending in *a* change to *ae: alumna, alumnae.* Those ending in *on* change to *a: phenomenon, phenomena.*

Most ending in *um* add *s: memorandums, referendums, stadiums.* Among those that still use the Latin ending: *addenda, curricula, data, media.*

—Compound words written solid add *s* at the end for the plural: *cupfuls, handfuls, tablespoonfuls.* Separate words or words linked by a hyphen, in general, add an *s* to the most significant word to form the plural: *adjutants general, aides-de-camp, assistant attorneys general, courts-martial, sons-in-law, postmasters general, secretaries general, sergeants major, assistant corporation counsels, deputy sheriffs, major generals.*

Proper names ending in *s, sh, ch* or *z* add *es* for the plural: *Joneses, Charleses, Bushes, Hatches, Gonzalezes.* Most names ending in *y* add *s* for the plural even if preceded by a consonant: *the Duffys, the Kennedys, the two Kansas Citys, Treasurys.* For other proper names simply add *s: the Martins, the McCoys.*

NUMERALS: Add *s: The custom began in the 1920s. The airline has two 727s. Temperatures will be in the low 20s.*

SINGLE LETTERS: Use *'s: Mind your p's* and *q's. The three R's, the Oakland A's.*

SEVERAL LETTERS: Add *s: She knows her ABCs. Many VIPs attended.*

See **collective nouns** and **possessives.**

plus (conj.) As a substitute for *and, plus* is considered informal usage.

p.m., a.m. In copy and headlines. Avoid the redundant *10 p.m. tonight.*

pocketbook, pocket book

A *pocketbook* is a purse.

A *pocket book* is a book small enough to be carried in a pocket.

pocketknife, pocket phone, pocket-size

pocket veto After Congress adjourns, a bill that is unsigned by the president for 10 days automatically receives a *pocket veto*—it is effectively vetoed without any presidential action. If Congress remains in session, however, a bill that remains on the president's desk for 10 days becomes law without his signature.

podium

See **lectern, podium.**

poetry Capitalize the first word in a line of poetry, unless the author has deliberately used lowercase for a special effect.

See **composition titles.**

point Don't abbreviate. In stock and bond prices, a *point* is $1. In printing, a *point* is a unit of measure equaling a 72nd of an inch; 12 points make a *pica.* In other contexts, it is short for *percentage point.* In real estate, a *point* is equal to a percentage point of the face amount of the mortgage; the points represent a one-time payment to the lender.

See **percent (%), percentages, percentage points** and **basis points.**

point-blank

poison pill The term is commonly applied to so-called *shareholder-rights plans,* defense tactics designed to make hostile takeovers prohibitively expensive.

Explain the term: *A shareholder-rights plan, commonly known as a poison pill, is designed to make a threatened takeover more expensive through the issuance of huge amounts of stock.*

Poland Poland's government has been led in recent years by activists in the Solidarity labor union. Solidarity members in the parliament represent parties in the Solidarity Election Action coalition, or AWS. Use *Solidarity Election Action (AWS) coalition* for the first reference and *AWS* in second reference. The largest party in the coalition is *the Christian National Union.* The leading opposition party is *the Democratic Left Alliance (SLD).*

Polaroid Corp. The Cambridge, Mass., company holds the *Polaroid* trademarks for instant-picture cameras and other photographic materials.

police department

Capitalize it with or without the name of the community: *the Los Angeles Police Department, the Police Department.*

Lowercase it in plural uses: *the Los Angeles and San Francisco police departments.*

police titles *See* **military titles** and **titles.**

policyholder

policy making (n.), **policy-making** (adj.), **policy maker**

polio The preferred term for *poliomyelitis* and *infantile paralysis.*

political divisions *First Ward, 10th Precinct, Third Ward, the ward, the precinct, the 102nd Congressional District, the district.*

political parties and philosophies

The Democratic Party, the Republican Party. In subsequent references, however: *the party.*

Capitalize *Communist, Conservative, Democrat, Liberal, Republican, Socialist* when they refer to a specific party or its members.

Lowercase philosophies unless they derive from a proper name: *communism, democracy, socialism, Marxism, Marxist Nazism, Nazi.* Also: *liberal Republican, conservative Democrat, Communist dictator.*

See **convention** and **party affiliation.**

politicking

politics It can take a singular or plural verb. But as an art or science, it is singular: *All politics is local.*

pompom, pompon

Pompoms or *pompons* are flower-like fluffs of crepe paper, like the ones used by cheerleaders.

Chrsanthemum flowers are also called *pompoms.*

pontiff Not a formal title. Always lowercase.

See **pope.**

Ponzi scheme Named for Charles Ponzi, who set up such a scheme in the 1920s, it is a fraudulent technique using money paid by later investors to provide inflated returns to the original investors. The scheme collapses when redemptions exceed new investments.

See **scheme.**

pooh-pooh

pooling of interests An accounting method used in the combining or merging of companies after an acquisition, in which the assets and liabilities on the two companies' balance sheets are added together, item by item. Reported earnings are higher under this method than under the *purchase method,* so most companies prefer it.

pope Capitalize when used as a formal title before a name; lowercase in all other uses: *Pope Paul VI, Pope Paul, the pope.*

See **Roman Catholic Church** and **titles.**

Popsicle A trademark for a brand of flavored ice on a stick.

pore, pour One *pours* tea but *pores over* (i.e., studies carefully) a book.

portland cement

possessives

PLURAL NOUNS NOT ENDING IN *S*: Add *'s*: *the alumni's donations, the children's games.*

PLURAL NOUNS ENDING IN *S*: Add only an apostrophe: *states' rights, VIPs' entrance.* The same is true when a generically plural word occurs in the name of a singular entity: *General Motors' profits.* But: *the Times's story.*

SINGULAR NOUNS: Add *'s*, even with words ending in sibilant sounds: *Xerox's earnings, the fox's trail.*

SINGULAR NOUNS ENDING IN *S*: Add an apostrophe: *the boss's orders, measles' symptoms.*

NOUNS SINGULAR AND PLURAL: *One deer's tail, two deer's tails.*

SINGULAR NAMES ENDING IN *S*: Ordinarily, add *'s* whether the name's final *s* is sounded or not: *Jules's computer, Mr. Jones's neighborhood, Dickens's novels, Illinois's capital, Arkansas's governor.*

Use only an apostrophe in these cases: ancient classical names: *Euripides' dramas, Socrates' life, Achilles' heel;* names of more than one syllable when the last syllable starts as well as ends with an *s or s* sound and when that last syllable is unaccented: *Kansas' law, Moses' journey, Jesus' teachings, Texas' cowboys.*

EXPRESSIONS FOLLOWED BY *S*: Common possessive expressions ending with an *s* sound and followed by a word that begins with *s* take an apostrophe without an *s: appearance' sake, conscience' sake, goodness' sake.* Use *'s* otherwise: *the appearance's cost, my conscience's voice.*

COMPOUNDS: Add an apostrophe or *'s* to the word closest to the object possessed: *the major general's decision, the attorneys general's request.* Also: *anyone else's job, Paul Martin Jr.'s father.* Use a possessive form after only the last word if ownership is joint: *Jim and Monica's house.* Use a possessive form after both words if the objects are individually owned: *Jim's and Monica's books.*

DESCRIPTIVE TERMS: Don't add an apostrophe to a word ending in *s* when it is primarily descriptive: *a teachers college, a Teamsters strike, a writers guide.*

FORMAL NAMES: Use the entity's practice: *the Ladies' Home Journal, the Veterans Administration.*

DOUBLE POSSESSIVES: The double possession shown in a phrase such as *a friend of Martha's* is acceptable and sometimes necessary. Note the difference between *a picture of Martha* and *a picture of Martha's.*

post- The rules in **prefixes** generally apply. Do not use a hyphen unless the base word begins with a capital letter:

postdate	postscript
post-Columbian	postgraduate
postdoctoral	postmortem
postoperative	postwar

postings Sometimes known as *official selling prices* or *government selling prices,* they apply to crude-oil and other prices issued, or *posted* by national oil companies or refiners, often for their sales in the term or contract business.

post office It isn't capitalized because the agency is the *U.S. Postal Service.* Use lowercase in referring to an individual office: *I went to the post office.*

potato, potatoes

pothole

pound (monetary) The British pound sign (£) occasionally is used with numerals to designate amounts in spot-news articles along with the dollar conversions, at least on first reference. *The cost was £60 million ($115.3 million) in cash and the assumption of £50 million in debt.* In feature articles, convert all figures to dollars unless a special effect is sought.

Pounds technically are the components of British *sterling,* but the words are usually used interchangeably.

For the Irish currency use: *punt* or *Irish currency.*

See **foreign money** and **World Currencies** appendix.

pound (weight)

It is equal to 16 ounces (avoirdupois). The metric equivalent is approximately 454 grams, or 0.45 kilogram.

To convert to kilograms, multiply the number of pounds by 0.45

See **gram; kilogram; ounce.**

power pool It is a group of utilities and other energy companies within a region that have joined to coordinate power-plant and electric-grid operations to maintain reliable delivery.

See **electric power grid.**

Prague The capital of the Czech Republic stands alone in datelines.

pre- These exceptions to first-listed spellings in Webster's New World are based on the general rule that a hyphen is used if a prefix ends in a vowel and the word that follows begins with the same vowel or a capitalized word:

pre-election	pre-exist
pre-establish	pre-empt
pre-eminent	
pre-Columbian	

Unhyphenated examples:

prearrange	predecease
prehistoric	prenatal
precondition	preset
precook	preflight
prejudge	pretax
predate	preheat
premarital	prewar

predominate (v.), **predominant** (adj.), **predominantly** (adv.)

Predominate means to hold sway or have a dominating influence. There isn't a corresponding adverb.

Predominant means prevailing or most frequent.

Predominantly means most frequently.

pre-emptive rights They allow stockholders to purchase additional shares in a new issue before it is offered to the public.

preference stock, preferred stock

See **common stock.**

prefixes The following rules take precedence over listings in Webster's New World Dictionary:

USE A HYPHEN:

—If the word that follows the prefix is capitalized: *anti-Semitic, un-American, de-Stalinize, pre-Roman, post-Columbian.*

—With the exception of *coordinate* and *cooperate*, hyphenate if the prefix ends in a vowel and the word that follows begins with the same vowel: *pre-election, pre-empt, anti-inflation, anti-intellectual, re-emphasize, de-emphasize.*

DON'T USE A HYPHEN:

—If the prefix ends in a consonant: *post-operative, postwar, postindustrial, archenemy, downscale, nonnuclear.*

—If a prefix ends in a vowel and is combined with a word that starts with a different vowel or with a consonant: *antiaircraft, antibias, antiwar, predawn, preconvention.*

MISCELLANEOUS:

—Sometimes a hyphen is used with an unfamiliar compound for clarity: *anti-miscegenation.* Words such as *miniseries*, originally hyphenated, became solid as they became familiar.

—Hyphenate to avoid confusion over the meaning of a word. Thus, *recreation* (meaning play) but *re-creation* (meaning the act of creating again).

See **extra; post-;** and **pro-** for some additional exceptions. *See also* **hyphen.**

premier, premiere

Premier means first or earliest.

Premiere means a first public appearance or performance. Don't use *premiere* as an adjective or verb, except in quoted matter.

premier, prime minister These titles are often used interchangeably in translating to English the title of the first ministers in national government with councils of ministers. Generally, follow the practice in the individual nation, including *chancellor* for the leaders in Germany and Austria.

Prime minister is the correct title in Britain and the Commonwealth nations. It is also used by most of the rest of the world (though *premier* is an acceptable headline substitute).

Use *premier* for leaders of the provincial governments in Canada and the state governments in Australia.

Presbyterian churches The northern and southern branches of Presbyterianism merged in 1983 to become the Presbyterian Church (U.S.A.).

CLERGY: *Minister* is appropriate for all Presbyterian clergymen. *Pastor* may be substituted if an individual leads a congregation. On first reference, use *the Rev.* On subsequent references, use *Mr., Mrs., Miss* or *Ms.*

See **religious titles.**

presently Because its meaning is ambiguous, use it only in quoted material.

presidency Always lowercase.

president

Capitalize president only as a formal title before one or more surnames of U.S. presidents: *President Bush, Presidents Clinton and Carter, President Jeffrey Beller of Acme Corp.*

Lowercase in all other uses: *The president acted today. He is running for president. Acme Corp.'s president, Jeffrey Beller.* Exception: On the editorial page, capitalize *President* in all references to a President of the U.S.

See **titles.**

FORMER U.S. PRESIDENTS: In most cases, the first name of a present or former U.S. president isn't necessary on first reference. Use first names when necessary to avoid confusion: *President Andrew Johnson, President Lyndon Johnson, President George Bush.*

presidential Lowercase unless part of a proper name.

Presidential Medal of Freedom The nation's highest civilian honor is given by the president, on the recommendation of the Distinguished Civilian Service Board, for "exceptionally meritorious contribution to the security of the U.S. or other significant public or private endeavors."

Presidents Day Although not adopted by the federal government as the official name of the Washington's Birthday holiday, most federal agencies, states and local governments use the term *Presidents Day* (no apostrophe), and some states designate it as honoring President Lincoln as well as Washington. It falls on the third Monday of February.

presiding officer Lowercase.

press conference Use *news conference* unless part of a direct quotation.

press secretary Seldom a formal title. For consistency, always use lowercase, even when used before an individual's name. *See* **titles.**

preventative, preventive Always use *preventive.*

price/earnings ratio *P/E ratio* is acceptable on second reference. It is calculated by dividing the price of a stock by its annual earnings per share. The *trailing P/E ratio* uses the reported earnings for the previous 12 months, and the *forward P/E ratio* uses analysts' forecasts for earnings over the next 12 months. The P/E ratio also is known as a stock's *multiple.*

For example, a company whose stock is trading at $50 and whose previous 12-month earnings were $4 a share has a *trailing P/E* or *multiple* of 12.5. If analysts expect the company to earn $5 a share in the coming 12 months, its *forward P/E* is 10.

Stocks with high multiples typically are those of fast-growing, dynamic companies in newer industries. Stocks with lower multiples are typically those in mature industries, or companies with stable earnings and regular dividends.

price fixing

price tag

P

PricewaterhouseCoopers LLP

primary Do not capitalize: *the New Hampshire primary, the Democratic primary, the primary, primary day.*

prime meridian
See **meridians.**

prime minister
See **premier, prime minister.**

prime rate The *prime rate,* also known as the *base rate* of interest, is used by banks as a reference point for a wide range of loans to medium-size and small businesses, as well as for some types of loans to individuals. A borrower might be charged the prime rate plus half a percentage point, for example. (The prime rate is *not* the rate banks charge their biggest and best corporate customers, the way bankers once defined it.) Fluctuations in the prime rate usually affect consumer-loan rates in general, sooner or later.

Prince Edward Island One of the three Maritime Provinces of Canada. Do not abbreviate. *See* **datelines.**

prince, princess Capitalize when used as a royal title before a name; lowercase when it stands alone: *Prince Charles, the prince.*

principal, principle
Principal is a noun and adjective denoting someone or something first in rank or a sum of money drawing interest: *the school principal, the principal of the firm, the principal on the mortgage.*

Principle is a noun relating to a fundamental truth, doctrine or force: *the principles in the corporate charter.*

print out (v.), **printout** (n.)

prior to *Before* is preferred.

prison, jail, penitentiary *Prison* may be applied to the maximum-security institutions often known as *penitentiaries* and to the medium-security facilities often called *correctional institutions* or *reformatories.* Such facilities confine people serving sentences for felonies—generally crimes that carry a penalty of more than a year in confinement.

Jail normally applies to facilities that confine people serving sentences for misdemeanors—crimes that carry a penalty of no more than a year in confinement. Jails also house people awaiting trial or sentencing on either felony or misdemeanor charges or on civil matters such as contempt of court.

Commonly used shortened forms are acceptable for prisons: *Massachusetts Correctional Institution-Walpole* is shortened to *Walpole State Prison; the state prison, the prison. The U.S. Penitentiary at Lewisburg, Pa.,* or *Lewisburg Penitentiary; the federal penitentiary, the penitentiary. Los Angeles County Jail, the county jail.*

private
See **military titles.**

privately held Generally use *closely held* instead. *See* **closely held.**

P

private placement It is the sale of stocks or other investments directly to an institutional investor, such as an insurance company. The securities in private placements don't have to be registered with the Securities and Exchange Commission.

privilege, privileged

pro- Use a hyphen when coining words that denote support for something. Some examples:

pro-business	pro-labor
pro-democracy	pro-war

But: *pro football.*

probation *See* **pardon, parole, probation.**

pro-choice *See* **abortion rights** and **antiabortion.**

Procter & Gamble Co. *P&G* is acceptable on second reference and in headlines. It is based in Cincinnati.

producer-price index Actually, there are three of them, compiled by the Labor Department's Bureau of Labor Statistics. Generally, we emphasize the *index for finished goods,* which are "commodities that will not undergo further processing and are ready for sale to the ultimate user." The other two indexes are for *intermediate materials* and for *crude materials.* The three indexes replaced the *wholesale-price index,* which wholesalers claimed was misleading.

profanity *See* **obscenities, profanities, vulgarities.**

professor *David Maj, a professor of history at Dartmouth College; the professor; Prof. Maj,* or *Mr. Maj* (or *Dr. Maj,* where appropriate).

See **academic titles; titles; doctor.**

P

profit Don't use the plural when referring to a single company's earnings.

profit-taking (n. and adj.) Used loosely, it refers to the selling of securities after a recent rapid rise in price. But such selling often is done to offset losses rather than to take profits, so use the term carefully.

profit terminology Note the meanings of the following terms in reporting a company's financial status. Be careful to specify whether the figures given apply to quarterly, semiannual, nine-month or annual results and note the date the period ends if it is a fiscal rather than a calendar period. The terms are listed in the order in which they might occur in analyzing a company's financial condition:

revenue The amount of money a company took in, including receipts from sales, services provided, rents and royalties. The terms *gross earnings* and *gross income* are best-avoided as synonyms for *revenue.* Generally use the singular *revenue,* even if the company uses the plural *revenues.*

sales The money a company received for the goods and services it sold. In some cases the figure includes receipts from rents and royalties. In others, particularly when rentals and royalties make up a large portion of a company's income, figures for these activities are listed separately. Generally avoid the term *net sales,* even if the company uses it to factor in such things as returns and cash discounts. In our usage, the *net* is assumed.

gross profit The term, which isn't routinely referred to in earnings articles, represents the difference between the sales price of an item or service and the expenses directly attributed to it, such as the cost of raw materials, labor and overhead linked to the production effort.

income before taxes It is gross profit minus companywide expenses not directly attributed to specific products or services. These expenses typically include interest costs, advertising and sales costs, and general administrative overhead. *See* **Ebitda.**

net income, profit, earnings These all refer to the amount left after taxes and all other expenses have been paid. *Net* may be used alone on second reference and in headlines. A portion of net income may be committed to pay preferred dividends. What is then left is called *net income available to common shareholders,* and this is the amount used to calculate *earnings per share.* Earnings tables and articles focus on net income before preferred dividends because this is the bottom-line overall profit. But the per-share figure refers to the earnings on *common* shares.

To avoid confusion, do not use the word *income* alone in reference to an earnings report. *Earnings* may be used as a short for *earnings per share* if the context makes the meaning clear.

operating profit (or loss) Many companies use *operating profit* as a shortcut term to describe *net income excluding income derived from sources other than the company's regular activities and before income deductions.* Avoid using *net operating income (or loss)* because there is no standard definition of what should be included. Instead, refer to *income, excluding one-time items and income taxes,* or whatever the company excludes from its figure.

loss, net loss, deficit These refer to the excess of expenses over revenue. Although the terms are often used interchangeably, generally use *net loss* on first reference for the bottom-line figure. In comparing losses, use the term *widen* or *narrow* rather than *increase* or *decrease.*

earnings per share The figure is obtained by dividing the number of common shares outstanding into the amount left after dividends have been paid on any preferred stock. Companies now are required to report a figure for earnings per share on a *basic* basis as well as on a *diluted* basis. The diluted basis is calculated on the highest number of common shares that would be outstanding if certain convertible issues were converted into common. Use the *diluted* figure in articles, as it is the more-conservative measure of earnings. When a company reports a loss, the *diluted* and *basic* per-share figures should normally be the same.

dividend The amount paid per share per year to holders of common stock. Payments generally are made in quarterly installments. *Payout,* which ordinarily means the overall amount of profits paid out in dividends, may be used in headlines to refer to a per-share dividend rate or rate change.

The dividend usually is a portion of the earnings per share. However, if a company shows no profit during a given period, it may be able to use earnings retained from profitable periods to pay its dividend on schedule.

return on investment A percentage figure obtained by dividing the company's assets into its net income.

extraordinary loss or charge, extraordinary gain An expense or source of revenue that does not occur on a regular basis, such as a loss caused by a major fire or the revenue from the sale of a subsidiary. Extraordinary items should be identified in any report on the company's financial status to avoid creating the false impression that its overall profit trend has changed significantly

charges Normally, *charges* are broken out in the income statement as separate after-tax line items with a corresponding earnings-per-share line. These charges typically refer to accounting charges such as discontinued operations and early retirement of debt, for example. Be aware that many companies label a wide variety of items as *charges* although they actually may be *one-time* or *nonrecurring items.* A *noncash charge* is a one-time expense against earnings that didn't require a cash outlay during the reporting period. Depreciation of real estate is one of the commonest noncash expenses that companies incur.

pro forma In corporate financial statements, *pro forma* results represent what the companies would have achieved had changes in circumstances existed throughout an entire period covered by the report. In a merger, for instance, pro forma figures report what the surviving company would have earned in the previous financial period, had the two companies been merged at the beginning of that period.

However, some companies have in effect broadened the meaning and scope of *pro forma profit* to exclude from their public announcements many cash and noncash expenses, ranging from interest payments and intangible-asset amortization to stock compensation and even marketing costs.

programmed, programmer, programming

program trading It is the large-block trading of groups of stocks via computer, often triggered automatically when prices hit predetermined levels.

Ever since program trading helped worsen the stock-market plunge of Oct. 19, 1987, a so-called *collar* is imposed on program trading whenever the Dow Jones Industrial Average rises or falls by a certain amount from the previous close. The original amount was 50 points, but the trigger points have been revised at intervals since then.

The collar constrains use of the program trading called *index arbitrage* to sell stocks in a falling market or to buy stocks in a rising market. Index arbitrage involves traders, assisted by computers, finding discrepancies between stock prices in the cash and futures markets. When stocks appear expensive relative to futures, the arbitrager sells stocks and buys futures, or vice versa, attempting to lock in a risk-free profit. The collar limits the arbitrager to selling a stock in a down market only when the stock is above or equal to its last trade, and to buying a stock in a rising market only when the stock is below or equal to its last trade. If the DJIA rises by the target amount, the collar is called the *downtick rule.* If the DJIA falls by the target amount, the collar is called the *uptick rule.*

See **circuit breakers.**

Prohibition Capitalize it when referring to the period after the 18th Amendment to the Constitution prohibited the manufacture, sale or transportation of alcoholic beverages. The amendment took effect Jan. 16, 1920. It was repealed by the 21st Amendment, which took effect on Dec. 5, 1933.

propane The light hydrocarbon is a major component of liquefied petroleum gas.

See **liquefied petroleum gas.**

propeller

proper nouns

See **capitalization.**

prophecy (n.), **prophesy** (v.)

proposition Don't abbreviate. Capitalize when used with a number in describing a ballot question: *Proposition 22.*

pro rata, pro rata results Distributed proportionately; for example, according to the number of shares held.

prosecutor Capitalize it before a name when it is the formal title. In most cases, however, the formal title is a term such as *attorney general, state's attorney* or *U.S. attorney.* If so, use the formal title on first reference. Prosecutors normally litigate *criminal* cases, not civil cases.

See **titles.**

prospectus It is a formal document outlining the financial and other information necessary for investors to consider purchasing a new security. The prospectus details the issuing company's financial statements, business history, description of its officers and the current status of outstanding litigation.

See **initial public offering.**

protective tariff It is a duty that is high enough to insure domestic producers against any effective competition from foreign producers.

Protestant Episcopal Church

See **Episcopal Church.**

Protestant, Protestantism Among church

P

groups covered by the term are the Anglican, Baptist, Methodist, Lutheran and Presbyterian denominations. *See* separate entries for each.

The term *Protestant* isn't generally applied to Christian Scientists, Jehovah's Witnesses or Mormons.

Don't use *Protestant* to describe a member of an Eastern Orthodox church. Use a phrase such as *Orthodox Christian* instead.

protester

protocol In the computer world, *protocol* refers to a set of codes and formats for retrieving data.

prove, proved, proving Use *proven* only as an adjective before a noun: *a proven remedy, proven reserves.*

province Don't capitalize: *Quebec province, the province.* But: *Maritime Provinces.*

proviso, provisos

provost marshal, provost marshals

proxy It is an authorization for someone else to vote on behalf of a shareholder.

proxy fight A *proxy fight* is a contest for control of a company in which two or more companies or groups of individuals seek proxies from a company's shareholders to back the takeover attempt. If a holder gives proxies to more than one group, the latest-dated proxy applies.

proxy statement A document distributed with a proxy solicitation giving information about the company or group seeking the proxy votes.

Prudential Securities Inc. The brokerage unit of Prudential Insurance Co. of American in Newark, N.J., is *not* connected with Prudential PLC.

PSA Bond Market Trade Association. *The PSA* was formerly *the Public Securities Association.*

PTA *See* **parent-teacher association.**

PT boat

Public Broadcasting Service It is not a network but an association of public-television stations organized to buy and distribute programs selected by a vote of the members. *PBS* is acceptable on second reference.

public schools For schools known by a numeral, use a figure: *Public School 3, Public School 33.*

publisher Capitalize it when used as a formal title before an individual's name: *Publisher Julia Martin of the New Jersey Eagle.*

See **titles.**

Puerto Rico Do not abbreviate.

See **datelines.**

Pulitzer Prizes Capitalize *Pulitzer Prize,* but lowercase the categories: *Pulitzer Prize for public service, Pulitzer Prize for fiction.* Also: *Pulitzer Prize winner; Pulitzer Prize–winning author.*

pull back (v.), **pullback** (n.)

pull out (v.), **pullout** (n.)

punctuation

See separate entries under **apostrophe; colon; comma; dash; ellipses; exclamation point; hyphen; parentheses; period; question mark; quotation mark; semicolon.**

punt This is the preferred name for the *Irish pound.* But use both names within articles: the *punt,* or *Irish pound.*

pupil, student
Use *pupil* for children in kindergarten through eighth grade.
Student or *pupil* is applicable for grades nine through 12.
Use *student* for college and beyond.

Purim The Jewish Feast of Lots, occurs in February or March.

push-button (n., adj.)

pushover

push up (v.), **push-up** (n., adj.)

put It is an option to sell a security at a specified price, usually within a limited period.

putsch It is a political rebellion.

Pyrex It is a trademark for a brand of oven glassware.

Q q

Q-and-A format
See **question mark.**

Qantas Airways

Q-Tips It is a trademark for a brand of cotton swabs and cotton balls.

Quakers This informal name may be used in all references to members of *the Religious Society of Friends.* The largest congregational, or *weekly meeting,* organization is the Friends United Meeting.

CLERGY: They aren't formally ranked above lay people, but *elders* or *ministers* preside over meetings. Many Quaker ministers use *the Rev.* before their names and call themselves *pastors.*

Capitalize *elder, minister* or *pastor* when used as a formal title immediately before a name. Use *the Rev.* on first reference if it is a minister's practice. Use *Mr., Mrs., Miss* or*Ms.* in subsequent references.

See **religious titles.**

quart (dry) It is equal in volume to 67.2 cubic inches. The metric equivalent is approximately 1.1 liters.

To convert to liters, multiply by 1.1.

See **liter.**

quart (liquid) It is equal in volume to 57.75 cubic inches, or 32 fluid ounces. The approximate metric equivalents are 950 milliliters or 0.95 liter.

To convert to liters, multiply by 0.95.

See **liter.**

quarter *Earnings in the first quarter, first-quarter earnings.*

quasar It is acceptable in all references for *quasi-stellar astronomical object,* considered the farthest objects observable in the heavens.

quasi- The rules in **prefixes** apply, but in general, no hyphen. Some examples:

quasiformal	quasi-invalid
quasiofficial	quasitropical

Quebec The city in Canada stands alone in datelines.

Use *Quebec City* in the body of an article if the city must be distinguished from the province.

Do not abbreviate any reference to the province of Quebec, Canada's largest in area and second-largest in population.

See **datelines.**

queen *Queen Elizabeth II, the queen; Queens Mary and Elizabeth.*

question mark (?)

USAGES: *Who attended the dinner? Did*

you ask who attended the dinner? You attended the dinner?

Did he attend the dinner, take along the cake and say grace? Or: *Did he attend the dinner? Take along the cake? Say grace?*

QUESTION-AND-ANSWER FORMAT: Use separate paragraphs for each speaker, without quotation marks:

Q: Where did you go to attend the dinner?

A: To the 21 Club in New York City.

WITH QUOTATION MARKS: The question marks go inside or outside the quote marks, *depending on the meaning:*

"Who wrote 'Meely LaBauve'?" she asked.

Did you ask who wrote "Meely LaBauve"?

questionnaire

quick-witted

quotation marks (" ")

Use double quotation marks in the body of articles and single marks for quotes within quotations. *"I know who wrote 'Meely LaBauve,'" he said.*

Use single quotation marks in headlines, subheads and graphics such as blurbs, charts and captions. But use double quotation marks in the boldface headings of individual items in columns such as the World-Wide column.

Avoid a fragmented series of quotations in a sentence or paragraph.

If a full paragraph of quoted material is followed by a paragraph that continues the quotation, don't put close-quote marks at the end of the first paragraph, but put open-quote marks at the start of the second paragraph.

If a partial-paragraph quote ends a paragraph, use open-quotation marks and attribution for any continuing quote or new quote starting the following paragraph.

Quotation marks may be used in first reference when introducing an unusual word or phrase to readers: *The company considers him a "white knight" for helping to fend off the hostile takeover. But this isn't an ordinary white knight.*

WITH OTHER PUNCTUATION: Follow these rules:

—The period and the comma always go inside the quotation marks.

—The semicolon, dash and colon always go outside.

—The question mark and exclamation point go inside or out, depending on the meaning.

See **composition titles** and **nicknames** for more guidance in using quotation marks.

quotations in the news Quotations normally should be corrected to avoid the errors in grammar and word usage that can occur unnoticed when someone is speaking but are embarrassing in print. Don't routinely use abnormal spellings such as *gonna* in attempts to convey regional dialects or mispronunciations. Such spellings may be appropriate, however, when the usage is relevant or helps to convey a desired impression in a feature.

Quran This spelling is preferred over *Koran.* The *Quran* is the sacred text of Islam, considered by Muslims to contain God's revelations to the Prophet Muhammad through the Angel Gabriel.

Rr

R The restricted rating.

See **movie ratings.**

rabbi

See **Jewish congregations.**

raccoon

race Identification by race should be made only if it is clearly pertinent; for example, if it helps provide important insights into social or political issues or motivations.

See **nationalities and races.**

racket Use this spelling, not *racquet,* for the instrument used in tennis and similar games, including racquetball.

rack, wrack A *rack* is a shelving or a framework. *To rack* means to arrange on a rack or to torture or trouble. *Inflation racked the economy.* As a modifier: *the inflation-racked economy.*

Wrack as a noun generally is confined to the phrase *wrack and ruin. To wrack* means the same as to *to rack,* but *rack* is preferred.

racquetball The game is played with a short-handled racket.

radio

Capitalize it and use before a name to indicate an official voice of the government: *Radio Havana.*

Lowercase and place it after the name when indicating only that the information was obtained from broadcasts in a city: *Baghdad radio.*

radio stations The call letters alone are usually adequate, but this form is acceptable: *radio station WCBS-AM.*

railroads Most railroads and railways now have corporate names such as *Union Pacific Corp., Norfolk Southern Corp.* and *CSX Corp.*

Don't abbreviate railroad as *RR,* even in headlines. *Road* is an acceptable short form.

See **Amtrak.**

raised, reared Only humans are said to be *reared.* Any living thing, including humans, may be said to be *raised.*

random-access memory It refers to computer memory that can be tapped directly, without following a sequence of storage locations. *RAM* is acceptable in second reference.

ranges *$12 million to $14 million.* Not: *$12 to $14 million.*

Rangoon The name of the capital of Myanmar, formerly Burma, is *Yangon,* not Rangoon.

rank and file (n.), **rank-and-file** (adj.)

Rank Group PLC The company, based in London, is in the film, video and tourism businesses.

rapeseed It is an oilseed used for making cooking oil and animal feed. Canadian rapeseed is called *canola.*

ratio *The ratio was 2 to 1*; *a 10-to-1 ratio.*

Avoid confusion with actual numbers by using the word *ratio* or a phrase such as *a 2-to-1 majority,* rather than *a 2-to-1 vote in the Senate* or the like.

See **margin.**

rayon It is not a trademark.

razzle-dazzle

re- The rules in prefixes apply. The following examples of exceptions to first-listed spellings in Webster's New World are based on the general rule that a hyphen is used if a prefix ends in a vowel and the word that follows begins with the same vowel:

re-elect	re-employ
re-enlist	re-equip
re-election	re-enact
re-enter	re-establish
re-emerge	re-examine

For many other words, the sense is the governing factor:

recover (regain)	re-form (form again)
re-cover (cover again)	resign (quit)
reform (improve)	re-sign (sign again)

Reader's Digest It is published by Reader's Digest Association Inc., Pleasantville, N.Y.

read-only memory It is computer memory that cannot be altered. Use *ROM* on second reference.

ready (adj.) Don't use it as a verb.

ready-made

real estate (n.), **real-estate** (adj.)

real-estate mortgage-investment conduit *Remic* is acceptable on first reference, but *real-estate mortgage-investment conduit* should be spelled out in articles on the subject. Freddie Mac, Fannie Mae and Ginnie Mae create *Remics* as a way to repackage 30-year mortgages and other mortgages into bonds with other maturities that are more attractive to investors. The *Remics* are distributed by investment bankers.

Realtor *Real-estate agent* is the generic term. Use *Realtor* only to indicate that the individual is a member of the National Association of Realtors.

reared

See **raised, reared.**

rebut, refute Rebut means to argue against. Generally avoid *refute,* which implies a judgment of success in an argument. Instead, use *rebut* or *respond to.*

receiver, receivership A *receiver* is a court-appointed person who takes temporary possession of, but not title to, the assets and affairs of a business or estate that is in bankruptcy *receivership* or ensnared in a legal dispute. The receiver collects rents and other income and generally manages the affairs of the entity for the benefit of its owners and creditors until a disposition is made by a court.

See **bankruptcy.**

recession It is a downturn in economic activity. Informally, the rule of thumb is that a *recession* begins after two consecutive quarters of decline in a nation's gross domestic product. Formally, a U.S. recession is *an extended but temporary decline in real gross do-*

mestic product during a period in which the GDP has generally been growing. The National Bureau of Economic Research makes the formal declaration. Until such a declaration is made, always attribute or hedge any references to the arrival of a recession.

See **recovery.**

recision Avoid this spelling in favor of *rescission.*

reconnaissance

record Avoid such constructions as *new record, all-time record* and *record high.* They are redundancies (and some people feel *all-time* implicitly includes the unknowable future). *Record low* is sometimes needed, for clarity.

record-breaking, record-holder, record-setting

record date

See **dividend.**

recovery In a business cycle, it is the period after a downturn or recession when economic activity picks up and the gross domestic product grows, leading into the expansion phase of the cycle, or levels above those prevailing before the recession. Declaration of the end of a recession should usually be attributed or hedged, because opinions often vary.

See **recession.**

rector

See **religious titles.**

recur, recurred, recurring

Not *reoccur.*

Red Capitalize it in references to the one-time Soviet political or military term: *the history of the Red army.*

Redbook survey The report on retail sales is issued by the LJR Redbook Research unit of Lynch Jones & Ryan Inc. each Tuesday.

Red China Avoid the polemic term except in quotes.

redemption In bond trading, it is a transaction in which the issuer *calls* in the bond issue and returns the principal amount to the investor. In some cases, the issuer must pay a premium for calling a bond before its maturity date.

red-haired, redhead, redheaded All are acceptable for a person with red hair.

red-handed (adj. and adv.)

red herring In the investment world, the term is applied to a preliminary prospectus used by underwriters to circulate information among dealers about a securities issue while the issue is awaiting SEC clearance for a public offering. The term in this context derives from the legend printed at the top in red stating that the prospectus is preliminary and isn't an offer to sell.

Otherwise, it is any device designed to divert attention.

red-hot

reefer lines Journalspeak for the referral lines used in articles to direct readers to related articles elsewhere in the paper. For the correct format, *see* **page numbers**.

re-elect, re-election, re-entry

refer

See **allude.**

reference works Capitalize their proper names, but don't place in quotation marks.

See **composition titles.**

referendum, referendums

reflation Stimulation of the economy by monetary means. Avoid the term unless it is in a direct quote, and then define it.

reform Use the word with care, for one person's reform is often another person's exploitation. *Overhaul* and *revision* are more-neutral synonyms. Put *reform* in quotes if there is any question about the word's appropriateness in a given context.

reformatory
See **prison, jail, penitentiary.**

Reform Judaism
See **Jewish congregations.**

refractories They are ceramic materials such as *fireclay, dolomite, magnesite* and *silica,* used to line furnaces. *Refractory metals* include *columbium* and *tantalum.*

refunding In the securities business, it is the redemption of securities using funds raised through the sale of new securities.

refute
See **rebut, refute.**

regime
See **the government, junta, regime.**

regions
See **directions and regions.**

registered bond A *registered bond* is recorded in the name of the holder on the books of the issuer or the issuer's registrar and can be transferred to another owner only when endorsed by the registered owner.
See **loan terminology.**

Regulation FD This rule of the Securities and Exchange Commission, effective in 2000, mandates a full and timely disclosure of "material" corporate information. It requires certain top employees or representatives of publicly traded companies to make public any such information they give to securities analysts and investors.

rein, reign
The leather strap for a horse is a *rein,* hence figuratively: *seize the reins, give free rein to, put a rein on.*
Reign is a period of rule, especially of a sovereign.

reinsurance Companies in this field assume part of an insurer's risk in large policies in return for part of the premium fees the insured pay. This allows an individual insurer to take on clients whose coverage would be too risky for it to carry alone.

REIT This is the acceptable second-reference form for a *real-estate investment trust,* a company that buys, sells and operates land properties.

relative A family member is a *relative,* not a *relation.*

religious references
Capitalize all proper names used to refer to a specific monotheistic deity: *God, Allah, Buddha, the Father, the Son, Jesus Christ, the Son of God, the Holy Spirit.* Lowercase all pronouns: *he, him, his, thee, thou, who, whose, thy, thine.* Lowercase the word *gods* in references to the deities of polytheistic religions. Capitalize the proper names of pagan and mythological gods and goddesses: *Neptune, Thor, Venus.*
Lowercase words such as *god-awful, godlike, godliness, godsend.*
See **Bible; holidays and holy days.**

Religious Society of Friends
See **Quakers.**

religious titles The first reference to a clergyman, clergywoman or nun normally should have a capitalized title before the name: *the Rev. Gregory Langan;* in second reference, *Mr. Langan* for most Protestant clergymen.

CARDINALS, ARCHBISHOPS, MONSIGNORS, BISHOPS: Generally use those titles with the name: *Cardinal Timothy Manning, archbishop of Los Angeles.* Also acceptable if applicable: *the Most Rev. Gregory Langan, archbishop of Cincinnati; the archbishop;* or *Archbishop Langan.*

MINISTERS: *See* listings under denomination names, but generally use *the Rev.* before the full name on first reference and *Mr., Miss, Ms.* or *Mrs.* before the surname on subsequent references.

PRIESTS: Generally use *the Rev.* before the full name and *Father* before the surname in subsequent references.

NUNS: Always use *Sister,* or *Mother* if appropriate, before the name: *Sister Julia* in all references if the nun uses only a religious name; *Sister Julia Martin* on first reference if she uses a surname and *Sister Martin* in second reference.

reluctant, reticent

Reluctant means hesitant to act.

Reticent means silent or taciturn.

Remic

See **real-estate mortgage-investment conduit.**

Reorganized Church of Jesus Christ of Latter Day Saints It is a splinter group formed after Joseph Smith's death, and isn't properly described as a Mormon church, or part of the Church of Jesus Christ of Latter-day Saints.

See **Mormon Church.**

rep *Rep* or *reps* shouldn't be used as a short form for *representative(s)* such as salespeople and telephone troubleshooters. Avoid the short form except in quotes.

representative, Rep.

See **legislative titles** and **party affiliation.**

republic Capitalize *republic* when used as part of a nation's full, formal name: *the Republic of Argentina.*

See **datelines.**

republican

See **political parties and philosophies.**

Republican Governors Association

Republican National Committee In second reference: *the national committee, the committee.*

Similarly: *Republican State Committee, Republican County Committee, Republican City Committee, the state committee, the county committee, the city committee, the committee.*

Republican Party, the party

repurchase agreement In the securities industry, it involves a loan in which one party borrows money in exchange for the temporary use of the other party's securities and agrees to sell them back at a fixed price on a fixed date. Dealers use the agreements extensively to finance their positions. *The Federal Reserve* uses such agreements in implementing monetary policy. It lends money to the primary dealers, adding reserves to the banking system, since the money is deposited into the dealers' checking accounts.

research and development *R&D* is acceptable on second reference.

rescission Use instead of *recision.*

Reserve Officers' Training Corps *ROTC* is acceptable in all references.

reserve requirement The proportion of their customers' deposits that commercial banks must keep in cash or on deposit with the Reserve System, by order of the Federal Reserve Board, to protect the deposits.

resident

See **citizen, resident, subject, national, native.**

resistance level In securities trading, it is a price level at which a rising market is turned back downward. Resistance levels usually are seen as selling opportunities. If a rising market passes a resistance level, the level often becomes a *support level.*

See **breakout, support level** and **oscillator.**

resistible

restaurant, restaurateur

restructure, restructuring In the financial world, *restructuring* refers to changing the terms of corporate or public debt.

reticent, reluctant

Reticent means silent or taciturn.

Reluctant means hesitant to act.

retired *See* **military titles.**

R

return on investment A percentage obtained by dividing the company's assets into its net income.

Reuters Group PLC Based in London, it is co-owner with Dow Jones & Co. of Factiva, an information database. The news agency is *Reuters.*

Rev., the *The Rev. Gregory Langan.* On subsequent references for most Protestants, *Mr., Mrs., Miss* or *Ms.* is used. On second reference for Roman Catholics and some Episcopalians, *Father* is used with the name.

revaluation of currency *Revaluation* technically refers to the *raising* of a currency's value. But use the terminology *raising the value,* rather than *revaluing,* for clarity.

See **devaluation/revaluation** vs. **depreciation/appreciation.**

revenue The amount of money a company takes in, including sales, rents, royalties and interest earned. The figure doesn't normally include excise taxes and sales taxes collected for the government. Avoid the plural *revenues* whenever the singular will do.

See **profit terminology.**

revenue-anticipation notes Issued by states and municipalities, they finance current spending, in anticipation of the future receipt of nontax revenue.

revenue bond A municipal bond payable from a specific source of revenue, it isn't backed by the full faith and credit of the issuer. Pledged revenues come from operation of the financed project, grants, excise or other specified taxes. Voter approval usually isn't required.

revenue passenger mile Define it as one paying passenger carried one mile.

reverse merger It provides a way for a private company to become a publicly traded one, without the requirement of filing stock with the Securities and Exchange Commission. A private company's owners take over a majority of the public company's stock, often through a large issuance of new shares.

reverse repurchase agreement It is used by dealers to borrow securities they previously sold short. The Federal Reserve uses reverse repurchase agreements to drain reserves from the banking system. In the Fed sense, they also are called *matched sales.*

See **matched sale-purchase transactions.**

reverse stock split By reducing the number of shares held by the public, a company making a *reverse stock split* increases the per-share price of the stock. Companies frequently use reverse splits to enable their stock price to meet minimum regulatory listing requirements for the stock price.

See **stock split.**

revise upward or downward Use *raise* or *increase* an estimate, for example, rather than *revise upward.* Use *cut* or *reduce* rather than *revise downward.*

revolutions per minute The abbreviation *rpm* is acceptable on second reference. Uppercase in headlines.

revolver

See **pistol** and **weapons.**

revolving credit It is a line of credit that may be used repeatedly up to a specified total, with periodic full or partial repayments.

Rh factor

Rhode Island Abbreviate as *R.I.* after city names. Residents are *Rhode Islanders.*

See **state names.**

rhodium The platinum-group metal is used in the engineering industry.

Richter scale It is no longer widely used by seismologists as an earthquake measure.

See **earthquakes.**

RICO It refers to *the Racketeer Influenced and Corrupt Organizations law.* Include the full name in articles.

rifle *See* **weapons.**

rifle, riffle

To rifle means to plunder.

To riffle means to leaf rapidly through a book or to shuffle cards.

right hand, right-hander (n.), **right-handed** (adj.)

right of way, rights of way

right, rightist, right wing Don't capitalize them unless they are formal party designations in a country. Also: *right-wing party, right-winger.* But try to avoid these terms in favor of more-precise descriptions, such as *conservative.*

right to work (n.), **right-to-work** (adj.) Laws prohibiting labor contracts that require workers to be union members.

See **closed shop.**

Rio de Janeiro The city in Brazil stands alone in datelines.

Rio Grande Not *Rio Grande River.*

risk arbitrage *See* **arbitrage.**

river

Capitalize it only as part of a proper name: *the Mississippi River.*

Lowercase it in other uses: *the river, the Mississippi and Missouri rivers.*

road *See* **addresses.**

Roaring '20s

See **decades.**

robbery

See **burglary, larceny, robbery, theft.**

Robert's Rules of Order

robusta This type of coffee bean is grown primarily in Brazil, Indonesia and Vietnam. Coming from a hardier plant than *arabica* beans, it has a stronger, more bitter flavor. It is used mostly in blending and in instant coffees.

See **arabica.**

rock 'n' roll

Rocky Mountains Or *the Rockies.*

roll call (n.), **roll-call** (adj.)

Rollerblade It is a trademark for in-line skates.

roll over (v.), **rollover** (n. and adj.) Selling of new securities to pay off old ones coming due, or the refinancing of an existing loan.

Rolls-Royce *Rolls-Royce PLC* is an engine maker. *Rolls-Royce Motor Cars Ltd.* is a unit of Vickers PLC.

Rolodex It is a trademark for a rotary card file.

ROM

See **read-only memory.**

Roman Catholic Church The clergy under the pope are cardinals, archbishops, bishops, monsignors, priests and deacons. In religious orders, besides nuns or sisters, some men who are not priests have the title *brother.*

Capitalize *pope* only when it is used as a title before a name: *Pope John Paul II, Pope John Paul.*

The forms for other titles: *Cardinal John O'Connor, Cardinal O'Connor, the cardinal. Archbishop Gregory Langan,* or *the Most Rev. Gregory Langan, archbishop of Cincinnati; Archbishop Langan, the archbishop. Bishop James Kearney,* or *the Most Rev. James Kearney, bishop of Rochester; Bishop Kearney, the bishop.*

MONSIGNORS: *Msgr. Gregory Langan, the monsignor. The Rt. Rev.* and *the Very Rev.* are no longer used to distinguish between types of monsignors.

PRIESTS: *the Rev. Eric Martin;* on second reference, *Father Martin.*

DEACONS: *Deacon James Goble, Deacon Goble, the deacon.*

BROTHERS: *Brother Jeffrey Beller, Brother Beller, the brother.*

NUNS: *See* the separate entry **sister.**

See **religious titles.**

Romania Not Rumania.

Romanian Orthodox Church The Romanian Orthodox Church in America is an autonomous archdiocese of the Romanian Orthodox Church. The Romanian Orthodox Episcopate of America is an autonomous archdiocese within the Orthodox Church in America.

See **Eastern Orthodox churches.**

Rome The capital of Italy stands alone in datelines.

Ronald Reagan National Airport It is in Washington; also: *Reagan National Airport.*

room numbers Use figures and capitalize *room* when used with a figure: *Room 2, Room 211.*

rooms Capitalize the names of specially designated rooms: *Blue Room, Lincoln Room, Oval Office, Persian Room.*

rosary It is *recited* or *said,* not *read.*

Rosh Hashana The Jewish New Year. Occurs in September or October.

ROTC The abbreviation is acceptable in all references for *Reserve Officers' Training Corps.*

Roto-Rooter It is a trademark for a sewer and drain-cleaning service.

round lot In securities trading, a *round lot* refers to 100 shares. In commodities trading, it is a quantity of a commodity equal to the corresponding futures contract.

See **odd lot.**

rounding off

See **dollars and cents.**

round trip (n.), **round-trip** (adj.)

round up (v.), **roundup** (n.) The noun is used to designate a Wall Street Journal news article drawn from a number of bureaus.

route numbers Don't abbreviate *route.*

See **highway designations.**

router In computer parlance, a *router* is a part-hardware, part-software device that directs traffic flow among segments of a network or between networks.

Royal Dutch/Shell Group Shell is acceptable on second reference, unless the intervening mention of Shell unit names may cause confusion with the parent.

royalty

See **nobility.**

rpm *See* **revolutions per minute.**

R.S.V.P. It is the abbreviation for the French *repondez s'il vous plait,* and means "please reply."

rubber stamp (n.), **rubber-stamp** (v. and adj.)

rubella It is also known as *German measles.*

Rule 144a This section of the U.S. Securities Act of 1933 allows the sale of securities to qualified institutional buyers without the SEC registration process for public offerings. The securities issues are considered private placements. Issuers often use *Rule 144a* to get securities to market quickly, including provision allowing the issuers to register the deals later.

runner-up, runners-up

running mate

rush hour (n.), **rush-hour** (adj.)

Russell 1000 and 2000 Published by Frank Russell Co., the indexes are measures of the stock-price performance of companies. *The Russell 1000* includes the 1,000 largest-capitalization companies, including those in the S&P 500. *The Russell 2000,* more widely followed, comprises the 2,000 companies smaller than those included in the Russell 1000.

Russia

See **Commonwealth of Independent States.**

See **Soviet Union** for the names of the 15 republics that formerly constituted the confederation.

Russian names When a first name in Russian has a close phonetic equivalent in English, use the equivalent in translating the name: *Alexander Solzhenitsyn* rather than *Aleksandr,* the spelling that would result from a transliteration of the Russian letters into the English alphabet.

Generally use the English spelling that most closely approximates the pronunciation in Russian, or follow the individual's preference.

Women's surnames have feminine endings, but use them only if the woman is not married or if she is known under that name.

Russian Orthodox Church

See **Eastern Orthodox churches.**

Russian Revolution Also: *the Bolshevik Revolution.*

ruthenium The platinum-group metal is used in alloys.

Ss

SA

The corporate designation, for *Societe Anonyme,* follows many French and Belgian company names, indicating that the company has shareholders.

See **foreign companies.**

Sabbath It is capitalized in religious references.

Sabena SA The Belgian airline may also be called simply *Sabena.*

saboteur

sacraments

Capitalize the proper names used for these Christian sacramental rites: *the Lord's Supper, Holy Communion, Communion, Holy Eucharist, Eucharist.*

Lowercase other sacraments: *baptism, confirmation, penance* (now often called *the sacrament of reconciliation*), *matrimony, holy orders* and *the sacrament of anointing the sick* (formerly called *last rites* or *extreme unction*).

sacrilegious

safe-deposit box Not *safety-deposit.*

Sahara Because the word means "desert," *Sahara desert* is considered redundant.

saint Abbreviate as *St.* in the names of saints, cities and other places: *St. Jude; St. Paul, Minn.; St. John's, Newfoundland; St. Lawrence Seaway.*

Exceptions: *Sault Ste. Marie, Mich.,* and *Saint John* in New Brunswick (to distinguish from *St. John's* in Newfoundland).

salable

sales In the corporate word, it is the amount of money a company received for the goods and services it sold. In some cases, this figure includes receipts from rents and royalties. In other cases, particularly when a company has a large volume of rents and royalties, these figures are listed separately from sales.

See **revenue** and **profit terminology.**

salesman, salesmen, salesperson, salespeople, saleswoman, saleswomen

salesroom

Sallie Mae The nickname is acceptable in second reference for *the Student Loan Marketing Association,* the government-chartered agency that makes low-cost loans to students through private lenders.

Salomon Smith Barney The New York brokerage firm is a subsidiary of Citigroup Inc.

Salt Lake City The capital of Utah stands alone in datelines.

Salvadorans They are the people of El Salvador.

salvo, salvos

SAM, SAMs The acronym is acceptable on second reference for *surface-to-air missile(s).*

same-store sales Also known as *comparable-store sales,* they are a more-reliable measure of a retailer's sales trends than total sales. While total sales account for sales in all of a company's stores, *same-store sales,* expressed as a percentage gain or decline, represent only the changes in sales at the stores currently in operation that were also operating a year earlier (sometimes longer, depending on a company's definition).

Major retailers report their monthly sales on the first Thursday of the following month.

Samurai bond It is a yen-denominated bond issued in Japan by a foreign country or company.

San Antonio The city in Texas stands alone in datelines.

sandbag (n.), **sandbagged, sandbagging** (v.), **sandbagger** (n.)

S

San Diego The city in California stands alone in datelines.

sanction Because the word can refer to approval or disapproval as a noun and verb, be sure the context makes the meaning clear.

S&L, S&Ls The short form is used with institution names and in second reference for *savings-and-loan associations.*

See **savings-and-loan associations.**

S&P, S&P 500

See **Standard & Poor's Corp.**

Sanforized A trademark for a preshrinking process for fabrics.

San Francisco The city in California stands alone in datelines.

sanitarium, sanitariums

San Marino Use alone in datelines on articles from the Republic of San Marino.

Sardinia Use instead of *Italy* in datelines on articles from communities on this island.

SAS The abbreviation for *Scandinavian Airlines System* is acceptable in all references if the airline context is clear.

Saskatchewan A province of Canada. Don't abbreviate. *See* **datelines.**

Satan But lowercase *devil* and *satanic.*

satellites

See **spacecraft designations.**

Sault Ste. Marie The cities in Ontario and Michigan are abbreviated this way, reflecting the full name *Sault Sainte Marie.*

saving(s) Don't use the plural in referring to a reduction. *A saving of 10%,* not *a savings of 10%.*

savings-and-loan associations They aren't *banks. The associations* or *the S&Ls* are acceptable on second reference. They also may be called *thrift institutions* or *thrifts.*

Use an ampersand in a proper name: *Continental Savings & Loan Association.*

SBC Communications Inc. Based in San Antonio, Texas, it is the parent of Pacific Bell,

Southwestern Bell, Southern New England Telecommunications Corp. and Ameritech.

SBIC The abbreviation is acceptable on second reference for *small-business investment company.*

Scandinavian Airlines System *SAS* is acceptable in all references clearly involving airlines.

scheme Because the word often has a negative connotation, use *transaction, plan, project* or other neutral words unless the plan involved is clearly devious.

See **Ponzi scheme.**

schizophrenia The mental illness is characterized by periodic delusion and disorientation. A so-called *split personality* is *not* part of the syndrome, and the word *schizophrenic* is better avoided in that context.

schoolchildren, schoolteacher

scientific names Italicize the taxonomic names of genera, species and varieties: The banyan tree (*Ficus bengalensis*) is prevalent in the area.

scissors The word takes plural verbs and pronouns.

scores

See **numbers.**

Scotch tape It is a trademark for a brand of transparent tape.

Scotch whisky It is distilled in Scotland from malted barley. Capitalize *Scotch* and use the spelling *whisky* only when the two words are used together. Lowercase *scotch* standing alone: *He ordered a scotch.*

Except for *Scotch whisky,* use the spelling *whiskey(s).*

scot-free

Scotland

See **datelines** and **United Kingdom.**

Scot, Scots, Scottish The people are *the Scots,* not *the Scotch.* Somebody or something is *Scottish.*

screen saver It is a program that automatically blanks out a computer screen, or provides a moving display covering the screen, when the computer remains unused for a few minutes. Originally, it was to keep the screen coating from deteriorating in places where bright images were constantly displayed, but with better screens today, the screen saver's function is to preserve the privacy of the user.

Scripture, Scriptures Capitalize the words when referring to the religious writings in the Bible. *See* **Bible.**

scuba The acronym for *self-contained underwater breathing apparatus* is acceptable in all references.

sculptor Use *sculptor* for both men and women.

scurrilous

Sea Islands The islands off the coast of South Carolina, Georgia and Florida.

search engine It is a software application that allows an Internet user to find a Web site by typing in the topic.

Sears, Roebuck & Co. In second reference to the retailer, use *Sears* or *Sears Roebuck,* dropping the comma, as is our style.

seasons Lowercase *spring, summer, fall, winter* and derivatives such as *springtime* unless part of a formal name: *Dartmouth Winter Carnival, Winter Olympics, Summer Olympics.*

Seattle The city in the state of Washington stands alone in datelines.

SEC

See **Securities and Exchange Commission.**

secondary boycott It occurs when workers refuse to handle or work on products made by a separate employer who has a labor dispute.

secondary offering It is the sale of stock by shareholders (typically venture-capital investors or management) rather than by the company. Additional offerings of stock by a company after an initial public offering, or IPO, should be referred to as *follow-on offerings.*

second hand (n.), **secondhand** (adj. and adv.) *The secondhand dealer had a watch with a second hand that he bought secondhand.*

second-rate

second reference In this book, the term applies to all subsequent references to an individual or organization within an article. Second- references, except as noted, are acceptable in headlines. Acceptable abbreviations and acronyms for many organizations are listed under the organizations' names. A generic term such as *the agency, the commission* or *the company* is often the better alternative for a second reference.

See **abbreviations and acronyms.**

secretary Capitalize it before a name only if it is an official corporate or organizational title. Don't abbreviate.

See **titles** and **cabinet titles.**

secretary-general Note the hyphen. Capitalize it as a formal title before a name: *Secretary-General Kofi Annan of the United Nations.*

See **titles.**

secretary of state Capitalize it as a formal title before a name.

See **titles** and **cabinet titles.**

secretary-treasurer With a hyphen. Capitalize as a formal title before a name.

See **titles.**

Secret Service The federal agency is administered by the Treasury Department.

sect Use the word advisedly, as it is considered pejorative when used in relation to established denominations.

Section 301 The section of the U.S. trade law that empowers the executive branch of government to unilaterally levy *trade sanctions* on countries it deems to be engaging in unfair trade practices.

sector fund It is a mutual fund that invests in a single industry sector, such as biotechnology, gold or the Internet.

secure (v.) Avoid *secure* as a synonym for *obtain,* because of ambiguity in such cases as *secure a loan.*

Securities and Exchange Commission Use *SEC* in headlines and *the SEC* or *the commission* in second reference. The government agency enforces securities laws and sets disclosure standards for publicly traded securities, including mutual funds.

See **Regulation FD.**

Securities Industry Association It is a trade group of brokers and dealers.

Securities Investor Protection Corp. It is a nonprofit organization supported by member securities traders and dealers. It provides reimbursements to individual customers of failed member firms.

Security Council In articles involving the United Nations, *Security Council* may be used in first reference. Use *U.N. Security Council* in other first references. Retain the capitalization in all references. But: *the council.*

Seder It is a Passover ceremony. The plural is *Seders.*

Seeing Eye dog It is a trademark for a guide dog.

seesaw

selenium The element, used in photocopiers and other electronic devices, is obtained mostly in the refining of lead, copper and nickel. It is also a dietary supplement.

self- Always hyphenate:

self-assured
self-government
self-defense

sell off (v.), **selloff** (n.) The unhyphenated noun is an exception to the dictionary. In securities or commodities trading, a *selloff* represents investors' fears of further price declines.

sell out (v.), **sellout** (n.)

sell side (n.), **sell-side** (adj.) In securities trading, the *sell side* comprises brokers and dealers. The *buy side* includes mutual-fund and other fund managers who purchase securities.

semi- Rules in **prefixes** apply, but in general, don't use a hyphen:

semifinal semi-invalid
semiofficial semitropical

semiannual It means twice a year and is preferred over *biannual.* Biannual is often confused with *biennial,* which means every two years.

semicolon (;)

IN A SERIES: Use semicolons to separate elements of a series when the individual segments contain material that must also be set off by commas: *The committee includes the president, Monica Goble; the vice president, David Maj; the secretary, Barbara Martin; and four outside directors.* Note that the semicolon is used before the final *and* in such a series.

TO LINK CLAUSES: Use a semicolon as an alternative to a coordinating conjunction such as *and, but* or *for* with independent clauses: *The annual meeting was delayed a week; it was held yesterday.*

semifinished steel The category includes steel shapes such as blooms, billets or slabs that later are rolled into finished products such as beams, bars or sheet.

See **steel.**

semiweekly It means twice a week. *Biweekly* means every two weeks.

senate Capitalize all references to specific governmental legislative bodies, regardless of whether the name of the nation or state is used: *the U.S. Senate, the Senate; the Virginia Senate, the state Senate; the Senate.*

Lowercase plural uses: *the Virginia and North Carolina senates.*

See **governmental bodies.**

The same principles apply to foreign bodies.

See **foreign legislative bodies.**

Lowercase references to nongovernmental bodies: *the student senate at Yale.*

senatorial

senator, Sen.

See **legislative titles** and **party affiliation.**

send off (v.), **send-off** (n.)

senior

See **junior, senior.**

senior and subordinate securities Many asset-backed securities are structured so that the interest in the underlying receivables is divided between *senior* and *subordinate* class certificates. Greater certainty of payment is provided to the senior holders.

See also **asset-backed securities.**

senior citizen Use the euphemism only in quotes or organization names. Instead, provide people's ages or age ranges, or use *older person* or *older people.*

See **elderly.**

September

See **months.**

sequence of tenses

See **tenses.**

Serbia It is a republic of Yugoslavia. The *Serbian Republic,* however, is part of *Bosnia and Herzegovina.*

sergeant

See **military titles.**

serial bonds They are municipal bonds that mature in successive years without interruption, for example, between 2010 and 2020.

server On the Internet, it is the computer that is host to a Web site.

serviceable

service clubs

See **fraternal organizations and service clubs.**

serviceman, servicewoman

set up (v.), **setup** (n. and adj.)

7-Eleven Stores Convenience stores operated by Southland Corp.

Seventh-day Adventist Church The head of the church's General Conference is *president* of the organization. Titles for ministers are *pastor* or *elder.* Capitalize them when used before a name. The term *the Rev.* is not used.

See **religious titles.**

Seven Up, 7 UP The trade name *7 UP* is owned by Dr Pepper/Seven Up Inc. in Plano, Texas, a subsidiary of London's Cadbury Schweppes PLC (although PepsiCo owns overseas rights to the brand).

Seven Wonders of the World The Egyptian pyramids, the hanging gardens of Babylon, the Mausoleum at Halicarnassus, the temple of Artemis at Ephesus, the Colossus of Rhodes, the statue of Zeus by Phidias at Olympia and the Pharos (or lighthouse) at Alexandria.

sewage, sewerage

Sewage is waste matter.

Sewerage is a waste-drainage system.

shah Capitalize as a royal title before a name; lowercase elsewhere: *Shah Mohammad Reza Pahlavi of Iran, the late shah of Iran.*

shake out (v.), **shakeout** (n. and adj.)

shake up (v.), **shake-up** (n. and adj.)

Shanghai China's largest city stands alone in datelines.

shape up (v.), **shape-up** (n. and adj.)

shareholder, share owner

shareholders' equity It represents a company's total assets minus total liabilities.

shareholder rights plan It typically involves rights to buy preferred shares distributed as a defensive maneuver against a hostile-takeover. The target company gives its stockholders the rights to purchase the new preferred shares, which the raider isn't eligible to buy. This dilutes the total number of voting shares enough to make the hostile acquisition difficult or impossible.

Shariah The legal code of Islam.

she Don't use in references to nations or hurricanes. Use the pronoun *it* instead.

Sheetrock A trademark for a brand of gypsum wallboard.

sheik, sheikdom

shelf registration It is the bulk registration of debt or equity securities with the Securities and Exchange Commission. Once the SEC approves a company's *shelf registration,* the company may offer the debt or equity at intervals it chooses, for up to two years, with a minimum of administrative preparation.

shell

See **weapons.**

Shell

See **Royal Dutch/Shell Group.**

shell company, shell corporation It is an incorporated entity with no significant assets or operations.

sheriff Capitalize it as s a formal title before a name.

See **titles.**

Shiite and Sunni The terms apply to members of the two so-called great sects of Muslims. *Sunni* is both singular and plural. *Sunni* adherents also may be called *Sunnites.*

shine, shined, shone Use *shined* for the past tense when it has an object: *The trooper shined a flashlight at the car.* Otherwise, use *shone: The sun shone on us.*

ships *See* **boats, ships.**

shirt sleeves (n.), **shirt-sleeve** (adj.)

shoeshine, shoestring

shopkeeper, shop owner

shop steward A *shop steward* is the representative of a union local elected to deal with the union members' employer.

shopworn

short In the investment world, the term describes the position held by an investor who sells securities or currencies that he doesn't yet own by borrowing them from a broker to deliver to the purchaser.

short covering The purchase of a security to replace shares previously borrowed for a short sale.

short sale The sale of borrowed securities by an investor who hopes to make a profit by buying an equal number of shares later at a lower price to replace the borrowed securities.

short interest The number of shares of a given stock that has been sold short and not yet repurchased.

short squeeze It occurs when the price of a security rises sharply, causing many short sellers to buy the security to cover their positions and limit losses. The buying leads to even higher prices, further aggravating the losses of short sellers who haven't covered their positions.

shorthand (n.), **short-handed** (adj.)

short-lived

short ton *See* **ton.**

shot *See* **weapons.**

shotgun *See* **weapons.**

showcase, showpiece, showplace, showroom

show off (v.), **showoff** (n.)

shrubs
See **plants.**

Sicily Use instead of *Italy* in datelines on articles from communities on this island.

side by side, side-by-side *They walked side by side. The articles received side-by-side display.*

Sierra Nevada, the Not *Sierra Nevada Mountains,* because *Sierra* means mountains.

sightseeing, sightseer

silicon Commonly found in clay, granite, quartz and sand, *silicon* is used in glassmaking and is the basic material of semiconductor elements used in computer circuits.

Silicon Valley The area of west-central California derived its name from its dense concentration of electronics and computer companies.

silver The precious metal is used in jewelry, photography and electronics.

Simoniz It is a trademark for a brand of auto wax.

Sinai Not *the Sinai.* But: *the Sinai Desert, the Sinai Peninsula.*

since To introduce a clause, use *since* if a time element is intended. Otherwise, use *because* or *as.*

Singapore It stands alone in datelines.

single file

single-handed

sinking fund It is set up under a bond-issuing contract. The bond issuer makes periodic deposits into the fund, to be used eventually to redeem the bonds.

Sir Graham Goble, Sir Graham
See **nobility.**

sister Capitalize it in references before the names of nuns. If no surname is given, the name is the same in all references: *Sister Monica.* If a surname is used in the first reference, drop the given name on second reference: *Sister Monica Goble* on first reference, *Sister Goble* in subsequent references.
See **religious titles.**

sister-in-law, sisters-in-law

sit in (v.), **sit-in** (n. and adj.)

sizable

skillful

ski, skis, skier, skied, skiing

skyline

slang
Try to avoid words the dictionary identifies as *slang.*

slaying
See **homicide, murder, manslaughter.**

sledgehammer

sleight of hand

slink (present tense), **slunk** (past tense and past participle)

Slovakia Its capital is Bratislava.

slowdown

slumlord

slush fund

small-arms fire

small-business investment company *SBIC* is acceptable in second reference.

small-business man, small-business owner

smash up (v.), **smashup** (n. and adj.)

smelter, smelting This operation extracts metal concentrates found in mined ore and separates the metal concentrates in the ore.

Smithsonian Institution The museum organization is in Washington, D.C.

smoke bomb, smoke screen

Smokies A second-reference form for *the Great Smoky Mountains.*

smoky, Smokey *A smoky room. Smokey Bear.* Not *Smokey the Bear.*

sneaked, snuck Sneaked is preferred as the past tense and past participle of sneak. Use *snuck* only in quotations.

snowdrift, snowfall, snowflake, snowman, snowplow, snowshoe, snowstorm, snowsuit

so called (adv.), **so-called** (adj.) Don't use quotation marks following this term.

socialist, socialism
See **political parties and philosophies.**

Social Security
Capitalize all references to the U.S. system.
Lowercase generic uses: *that nation's social-security program.*

Society for the Prevention of Cruelty to Animals *SPCA* is acceptable on second reference. *The American Society for the Prevention of Cruelty to Animals,* or *ASPCA,* is the name of the New York City organization.

Society of Friends
See **Quakers.**

soft-spoken

software It includes anything a computer can store electronically, including computer instructions and data. *See* **hardware.**

Soho, SoHo
Soho is a district in London.
SoHo is the area south of Houston St. in New York.

solicitor
See **lawyer.**

soliloquy, soliloquies

Solidarity
See **Poland.**

song titles
See **composition titles.**

son-in-law, sons-in-law

SOS Don't use points in the distress signal.

sources Newspapers in past years would routinely cite *reliable sources, highly placed sources, informed sources* and such. The modifiers

S

never conveyed much meaning. If sources aren't informed, they shouldn't be used.

The word *source* itself is usually best avoided. It often conveys the idea of either more or less authority than the person deserves. *Sources say* may suggest to the reader that we are uncertain that we have the facts straight, so we are putting the onus on an unnamed *source.* In other cases, *sources say* carries the connotation of *inside knowledge,* suggesting more credibility than the person may warrant.

The mundane words *people* and *individuals,* therefore, are preferable to *sources* if we can't be more specific. That goes for headlines and summary columns as well as articles. In headlines, any use of *sources say* and its variations should be avoided.

Spokesman or *representative* is sometimes a suitable alternative: *a police spokesman, a White House representative.*

ANONYMOUS SOURCES: Accepting a source's request for anonymity sometimes is the only practical way to obtain important information, but we must be circumspect. On-the-record sources are always preferable because they may be held personally accountable for what they say and are therefore generally more certain to be scrupulously accurate. Also, readers are able to make judgments about the reliability of those whose identities are provided.

In cases where the person's identity is to be protected, take pains to indicate where his or her biases might lie: *an executive working for a competitor* . . . *an executive who left the company in a management shakeup* . . . *a laid-off employee* . . . or *a close relative of the plaintiff.*

South The 16 states, by Census Bureau definition: Alabama, Arkansas, Delaware, Florida, Georgia, Kentucky, Louisiana, Maryland, Mississippi, North Carolina, Oklahoma, South Carolina, Tennessee, Texas, Virginia and West Virginia.

South America

South Asia It comprises India, Pakistan, Sri Lanka, Bangladesh, Afghanistan and the Maldives.

See **Asian geographic terms.**

South Carolina Abbreviate as *S.C.* after city names. Residents are *South Carolinians.*

See **state names.**

South Dakota Abbreviate as *S.D.* after city names. Residents are *South Dakotans.*

See **state names.**

Southeast Asia It comprises Cambodia, Laos and Vietnam and the islands of Indonesia, Malaysia, Brunei, Myanmar, the Philippines, Singapore and Thailand.

See **Asian geographic terms.**

southern, southeast, southwest Capitalize them when they refer to U.S. areas.

See **directions and regions.**

South-West Africa It now is *Namibia.*

Soviet Union The republics that once constituted the Soviet Union now are known as Armenia, Azerbaijan, Belarus, Estonia, Georgia, Kazakstan, Kyrgyzstan, Latvia, Lithuania, Moldova, Russia, Tajikistan, Turkmenistan, Ukraine and Uzbekistan.

See **Commonwealth of Independent States.**

soybean oil, soybean meal

Soybean oil is used mainly in cooking and in food products such as margarine.

Soybean meal is used mainly to feed livestock.

Futures and options related to the two products are traded on the Chicago Board of Trade.

SpA Follows many Italian company names.

Space Age It began with the launching of the first sputnik Oct. 4, 1957.

space agency

See **National Aeronautics and Space Administration.**

space centers

See **John F. Kennedy Space Center** and **Lyndon B. Johnson Space Center.**

spacecraft For designations, use Arabic figures and capitalize the name: *Gemini 7, Apollo 11.*

spaceship

space shuttle

Spanish-American War

Spanish surnames The family names of both the mother and father are usually used. The normal sequence is the given name, father's family name and mother's family name: *President Vicente Fox Quesada.* In second reference, use only the father's family name, *Mr. Fox,* or *President Fox.*

But some people use a multiple surname: *Porfirio Diaz Pizzaro, Mr. Diaz Pizzaro.*

Other people use a *y* (for *and*) between the two surnames: *Porfirio Diaz y Pizzaro.* In second reference, include the *y* if the person uses both names: *Mr. Diaz y Pizzaro.* A married woman frequently uses her father's family name followed by *de* and her husband's name. If *Maria Diaz* married *Ernesto Pizzaro,* she thus would be known as *Maria Diaz de Pizzaro.* Use *Mrs. Pizzaro* in second reference.

spartan Lowercase the adjective meaning stoical and frugal—an exception to Webster's New World.

speaker Capitalize it only as a formal title before a name: *Speaker Dennis Hastert; the speaker.*

specialist On the stock exchanges, it refers to an exchange member designated to maintain a fair and orderly market in a specified stock.

species Use singular or plural verbs depending on the sense: *The species is extinct. Both species are extinct.*

speechmaker, speechmaking, speechwriter, speechwriting

speed up (v.), **speedup** (n. and adj.)

spin off (v.), **spinoff** (n. and adj.) A *spinoff* involves the distribution to a company's shareholders of the stock in a division or subsidiary. The term should not be applied to the *sale* of company assets.

spokesman, spokeswoman But don't use *spokesperson.* Use *representative* if you don't know the sex of the individual.

In most instances, news and comment may be attributed to *the company* rather than to *a spokesman* or *a spokeswoman.* Use the representative's name whenever possible in attributing news or comments that aren't strictly routine or deal with potentially controversial matters.

spot market This refers to the market for buying or selling of commodities or foreign exchange for immediate delivery and for cash payment.

spot price This is the price of a commodity available for immediate sale and delivery. The term is also used in foreign-exchange transactions.

spread In securities trading, it is the difference between prices linked closely by market patterns or market trading strategy. In *fixed-income securities,* it is the yield differential between two comparable securities or investment instruments.

spreadsheet A *spreadsheet* is a ledger sheet, now usually in a computer program, laying out a company's financial data in rows and columns.

spring
See **seasons.**

springtime

spring wheat It is planted in the spring and harvested in the fall.

squall
See **weather terms.**

Sri Lanka The people may be called either *Sri Lankans* or *Ceylonese.*

SST It is acceptable in second reference for a *supersonic transport.*

stadium, stadiums

stanch, staunch
Use *stanch* as a verb: *Stanch the flow of blood.*
Use *staunch* as an adjective: *a staunch supporter.*

Standard & Poor's Corp. *S&P* is acceptable in second reference for the division of McGraw-Hill Cos. Along with Moody's Corp.'s Moody's Investors Service, it is a leading ratings agency. S&P rates commercial paper, common and preferred stock and short-term municipal issues. It also publishes investment advisory periodicals and compiles stock indexes, including the *Standard & Poor's Composite Index* of 500 stocks, commonly known as *the S&P 500.*

Another S&P division, *Standard & Poor's Ratings Service,* rates bond-market instruments.

See **Moody's Investors Service Inc.**

standard-bearer

standard time Capitalize *Eastern Standard Time, Pacific Standard Time,* etc., but lowercase *standard time* when standing alone. Abbreviations are normally used with clock readings: *noon EST, 9 p.m. PST.*

See **time zones.**

standby loan The International Monetary Fund commonly makes *standby loans* to members in support of economic stabilization programs. They are usually for 12 to 18 months.

stand in (v.), **stand-in** (n. and adj.)

stand off (v.), **standoff** (n. and adj.)

stand out (v.), **standout** (n. and adj.)

"The Star-Spangled Banner"

start up (v.), **start-up** (n. and adj.)

state Lowercase *state* in such constructions as *the state of Maine, the states of Maine and Vermont, New York state, Washington state.*

statehouse
Capitalize all references to a specific statehouse, with or without the name of the state: *The Massachusetts Statehouse is in Boston. The governor will visit the Statehouse today.*

Lowercase plural uses: *the Massachusetts and Rhode Island statehouses.*

state names
STANDING ALONE: Spell out the names of the 50 U.S. states when they stand alone (without a city or county name), even in headlines.

EIGHT NEVER ABBREVIATED: The names of eight states are never abbreviated in datelines or text: *Alaska, Hawaii, Idaho, Iowa, Maine, Ohio, Texas* and *Utah.*

ABBREVIATIONS REQUIRED: Use abbreviations for other states as follows:

—In conjunction with the name of a city, town, village or military base in most datelines.

See **datelines** for examples and exceptions for certain large cities.

In conjunction with the name of a city, county, town, village or military base in text. *See* examples in PUNCTUATION below.

See **datelines** for guidelines on when a city name may stand alone in the text of an article.

—In short-form listings of party affiliation: *(D., Mont.)*.

See **party affiliation** for details.

The abbreviations, which also appear in the entries for each state, follow:

Ala.	Md.	N.D.
Ariz.	Mass.	Okla.
Ark.	Mich.	Ore.
Calif.	Minn.	Pa.
Colo.	Miss.	R.I.
Conn.	Mo.	S.C.
Del.	Mont.	S.D.
Fla.	Neb.	Tenn.
Ga.	Nev.	Vt.
Ill.	N.H.	Va.
Ind.	N.J.	Wash.
Kan.	N.M.	W.Va.
Ky.	N.Y.	Wis.
La.	N.C.	Wyo.

PUNCTUATION: Place commas before and after the state name or abbreviation following a city name.

MISCELLANEOUS: Use *New York state* when necessary to distinguish the state from New York City. and use *Washington state* when necessary to distinguish the state from the District of Columbia.

State of the Union address Capitalize references to the president's annual address. Lowercase otherwise.

state police Capitalize only if it includes the name of the state: *the New York State Police, the state police.*

states' rights

statewide

stationary, stationery
To stand still is to be *stationary.*
Writing paper is *stationery.*

station wagon

staunch
See **stanch, staunch.**

stearin *See* **palm oil.**

steel Iron is alloyed with small amounts of carbon and often other metals, including nickel and chromium or manganese, to produce steel's hardness and resistance to rusting.

Cold-rolling of steel, without a reheating, reduces thickness, producing a smoother surface.

Hot-rolling of steel into flat-rolled steel follows reheating.

Flat-rolled steel is processed on rolls with flat faces as opposed to grooved or cut faces. Flat-rolled products include sheet, strip and tin plate, among others.

Steel sheet is flat-rolled steel less than 1/8-inch thick; *steel plate* is more than 1/8-inch thick.

Steel slab is semifinished, flat-rolled steel prepared for rolling down to plate or sheet.

Specialty steel includes electrical, alloy or stainless steel, usually produced to meet the specific needs of customers.

Tempering, also known as *drawing,* is the softening of steel or iron by reheating it at a considerably lower temperature than was used for its original hardening.

Slag is the nonmetallic material forming a molten layer atop molten steel in a steel furnace. It is made by charging suitable materials and plays an important role in the refining of the steel. *Slag* also applies generally to any waste material drawn off in molten form.

steelmaker, steelworker

stepbrother, stepfather, stepsister, stepmother

steppingstone

stifling

St. John's The city is in the Canadian province of Newfoundland.

St. Louis The city in Missouri stands alone in datelines.

stockbroker, stockholder, stockholdings
See **brokers.**

Stockholm The capital of Sweden stands alone in datelines.

stock indexes Don't use a comma in stock indexes up to 99999. For any indexes of 100,000 and up, insert a comma. *The Dow Jones Industrial Average rose 78 points to 10470.23. The Nikkei Stock Average of 225 selected issues closed at 15019.88, up 15.59 points.*

stock prices Whenever the day's news has affected (or may affect) stock prices, provide the market price in articles, generally using a 4 p.m. price: *At 4 p.m. in New York Stock Exchange composite trading, DaimlerChrysler shares rose 56.25 cents to $52.81.* The word *composite* takes into account trading off the exchange. With Nasdaq quotes, drop the word *composite,* because there isn't any material trading of Nasdaq stocks outside of Nasdaq. (*See* below for guidance on when to use after-hours quotes.)

S

—With the move to decimal pricing from fractions by the U.S. stock markets, use dollar and cents for stock-price descriptions in news articles and daily stock-market columns. (The exception is when the routine Abreast of the Market column or the Small Stock Focus column runs entirely inside the section, or in the case of a Friday's Market Activity add-on item about stock action. In those cases, to avoid having an article with scores of dollar signs, use the dollar sign in only the first reference to a stock price, and drop it for the rest of the item: *Intel rose 13 cents to 132.68.*)

—Decimals are rounded off to two decimal places: *$107.88, up 13 cents,* rather than the past practice of using *$107.875* in articles.

—When a stock price or change is less than $1, use the number of cents: *The stock rose 13 cents* (instead of 12.5,); *later it fell nine cents* (rather than 8.75). Consider the rounded numeral in decimal form (0.13 in the first example and 0.09 in the second) and then change it to cents.

—The offer price for an initial public offering always takes a dollar sign and decimals, rounded to two places.

AFTER-HOURS TRADING: Provide stock prices in after-hours trading when a company announces news after the markets' 4 p.m. close. The statistics department puts out an "after-hours" snapshot on our intranet after 6:30 p.m. Until that hour, when an after-hours stock quote is needed, get it from Instinet, and cite Instinet as the source. But update this for later editions with our intranet quote, without the need to mention the source: *Intel rose to $132.68 in after-hours trading.*

STOCK-QUOTE STYLE: Here is the preferred wording when citing stock quotes: *At 4 p.m. in New York Stock Exchange composite trading, DaimlerChrysler shares rose 56 cents to $52.81.* The one difference with describing a Nasdaq price is to drop the the word *composite,* because there's no material trading of Nasdaq stocks outside of Nasdaq, as there is for trading on the NYSE and Amex.

See **bid and asked; dollars and cents; composite trading;** and **third market.**

stock splits and stock dividends A *split* doesn't change the total value at which the company carries its capital stock in the balance sheet; all that changes is the number of shares. A *stock dividend* "capitalizes" part of the surplus; that is, the company increases its balance-sheet stock account by taking an amount out of surplus proportionate to the additional stock issued to shareholders.

Stone Age

stopgap

stop order In securities markets, it is an order to a broker to buy or sell a security when the market price reaches a given level.

story To most people, it refers to a work of fiction. *Article* is preferred to refer to pieces in the paper.

straddle In options trading, it is an option composed of both a put and a call on the same stock or other instrument. In futures trading, a *straddle,* or *spread,* is a two-part transaction that consists of buying a commodity for delivery in one month and selling it for delivery in another month, hoping to profit from a change in the difference between the two months' prices.

straight-laced, strait-laced
Use *straight-laced* for strict behavior.
Use *strait-laced* for confinement.

strait Capitalize as part of a proper name: *Bering Strait, Strait of Gibraltar.* But: *the Bosporus* and *the Dardanelles*, not followed by *strait.*

straitjacket Not *straightjacket.*

street
See **addresses.**

strikebreaker

strike price It is the price at which an option contract allows the underlying instrument to be bought or sold. It is also known as *the exercise price.*

See **call; options; put.**

strips In the securities business, they are derivative securities separated into interest-only and principal-only *strips,* traded separately.

See **derivatives.**

strong-arm (v. and adj.)

strongman A dictator.

strong-willed

stubs, stub stocks They are the publicly traded shares of companies that have drastically reduced their stock-market values, typically by taking on debt for leveraged buyouts or by paying a big one-time dividend. Stubs' market prices tend to fluctuate more than those of other shares because of the companies' greater debt leverage.

Stub may also refer to the remaining company itself after a sell-off of certain assets. As in this instance: *They began looking at ways that a stub of RJR, or parts of it, could remain in public shareholders' hands.*

See **shell company.**

student
See **pupil, student.**

Student Loan Marketing Association The government-chartered company makes low-cost student loans available through private lenders. The nickname *Sallie Mae* is acceptable on second reference.

Styrofoam A trademark for a brand of plastic foam used in industrial applications. Use the generic term to refer to consumer products: *a plastic-foam coffee cup.*

sub- The rules in **prefixes** apply, but in general, no hyphen. Some examples:

subbasement	subculture
submachine gun	subtotal
subcommittee	subdivision
suborbital	subzero

subcommittee
See **congressional committees and subcommittees.**

Capitalize only when a subcommittee has a proper name of its own: *the Senate Permanent Subcommittee on Investigations.*

subheads They are inserted into longer articles by editors, at least two to an article (or to the jump of an article) unless artwork takes the place of one subhead. They shouldn't begin with numerals. Single quotation marks (') are used, not double quotes (").

subject *See* **citizen, resident, subject, national, native.**

subjunctive mood Use the subjunctive mood of a verb for contrary-to-fact conditions and for wishes or regrets: *If I were king, I would change the laws. I only wish she were younger.* In expressing a hypothesis, use the subjunctive if there is little likelihood it might come true.

submachine gun
See **weapons.**

subpoena, subpoenaed, subpoenaing

subsidiary It normally is a company whose voting stock is more than 50% owned by a parent company.

Sucaryl A trademark for a brand of noncaloric sweetener.

successor

suit, suite
A *suit* of clothes, a *suit* of cards, a *suit* in court.

Suites apply to music, rooms and furniture.

Sukkot

Sun Microsystems Inc. It is based in Palo Alto, Calif.

support level In securities trading, it is the price level at which a falling market turns back upward. Support levels usually are seen as buying opportunities.

See also **breakout; resistance level; technical analysis.**

surplus
See **deficit.**

swap *See* **derivatives.**

S

Tt

Tabasco It is a trademark for a brand of hot-pepper sauce.

tablecloth

tablespoon, tablespoonfuls

taglines They are the lines at the end of articles, crediting those who contributed. They appear in italics, preceded by a dash. They should include the reporter's city only if it is different from the dateline or if the article has a byline box that situates the other reporters:

—Jerry Seib in Washington contributed to this article.

tailings In mining, *tailings* are the end-product or waste piled up near the mine. Some contain metal residues that can be extracted from them.

tailspin

tail wind

Taiwan Use *Taiwan* in datelines after city names. Its capital is Taipei.

See **China.**

Tajikistan

See **Commonwealth of Independent States.**

take, bring

Take denotes movement that is not toward the speaker.

Bring denotes movement toward the speaker or toward the dateline city or toward the U.S. In headlines, *bring* normally refers to movement toward the U.S. from abroad.

take-home pay

take off (v.), **takeoff** (n. and adj.)

take out (v.), **takeout** (n. and adj.)

take over (v.), **takeover** (n. and adj.)

Talmud The collection of writings constitutes the Jewish civil and religious law.

Tammany, Tammany Hall

tankan Lowercase this reference to the Bank of Japan's quarterly survey of business sentiment. Use italics in first reference: *He referred to the first-quarter* tankan *survey of sentiment in Japan.* The surveys are widely watched for clues about future capital investment and monetary policy. The reports include detailed surveys of smaller companies.

tanks Use Arabic figures, separated from letters by a hyphen: *M-60, M-60s.*

tap, bug
A *tap* is a device attached to a telephone circuit to pick up conversations on the line, or the act of using such a device.
A *bug* is a concealed listening device designed to pick up sounds, or the act of using such a device.

tape recording (n.), **tape-record** (v.)

tattletale

taxable-equivalent yield It is the interest rate that must be received on a taxable security to provide the holder the same after-tax return as that earned on a comparable tax-exempt security. It's calculated by dividing the tax-exempt yield by the investor's marginal tax rate.

taxable income
See **adjusted gross income.**

tax-anticipation notes They are issued by states or municipalities to finance current operations in anticipation of tax receipts.

Tax Court
See **U.S. Tax Court.**

taxonomic names Names of organisms are italicized, with the genus name capitalized and the specific epithet lowercased: *Canis familiaris, Borrelia burgdorferi.*

Tbilisi It is the capital of Georgia, the former Soviet republic.

teachers college No apostrophe.

teammate

Teamsters union, the Teamsters, a Teamster The terms are acceptable in all references to *the International Brotherhood of Teamsters, Chauffeurs, Warehousemen and Helpers* and its members.

tear gas Two words.

teaspoon, teaspoonfuls

techie It is slang for a computer technician. Not *tekkie.*

technical analysis In securities investing, it is the study of price patterns as a way of forecasting price movements.

Technicolor A trademark for a process of making color motion pictures.

teen, teenager (n.), **teenage** (adj.) Don't use *teenaged.*

Teflon A trademark for a type of non-stick coating.

Tehran, Iran

Tel Aviv The city in Israel stands alone in datelines.

telecast (n.), **televise** (v.)

telecommuter, telecommuting

telemarketer, telemarketing

telephone numbers Use figures. The form: *212-416-2591.* (No parentheses around the area code.)

teleprompter It has become a generic term for prompting devices used in television studios.

teletext A type of videotex, for delivery of information to home TV sets.

Teletype A trademark for a brand of teleprinters and teletypewriters.

television-program titles Use quotation marks and follow the guidelines listed under composition titles.

television set, TV set Including the word *set* is preferred when referring to the receivers.

television station The call letters alone are frequently adequate, but when this phrase is needed, use lowercase: *television station WGAL,* or *station WGAL-TV.*

telltale

temblor *See* **earthquakes.**

temperatures Write out *zero* through *nine: five-degree temperatures, temperatures fell five degrees, temperatures in the 30s.*

Temperatures get *higher* or *lower,* but they don't get *warmer* or *cooler.*

See **Fahrenheit; Celsius;** and **weather terms.**

Temple Mount In Jerusalem, it is Judaism's holiest site. It is known by Muslims as *al-Haram al-Sharif,* meaning Noble Sanctuary.

Ten Commandments Don't abbreviate or use figures.

tenderhearted

tender offer It is an offer to buy shares in a company, usually at a premium, often with the purpose of taking control of the target company. The *tender offer* seeks to have stockholders of the target company *tender* their shares to the potential purchaser.

tendinitis Not *tendonitis,* for inflammation of the tendons.

tenfold

Tennessee Abbreviate as *Tenn.* after city names. Residents are *Tennesseeans.*

See **state names.**

Tennessee Valley Authority *TVA* is acceptable on second reference.

tenses Main verbs in newspaper writing are usually in the past tense, but in Journal features and some columns, the present tense is usually used. Rules governing *the sequence of tenses* call for a verb in a subordinate clause to be in the past or past-perfect tense if the main verb is in the past tense. However, when the subordinate clause refers to a continuing condition, the subordinate verb should be in the present tense to make this clear. *I said I am married* conveys the meaning of a continuing married state, whereas *I said I was married* indicates that the married condition was in the past.

tenterhooks, on References to the condition of uneasiness or strain often misspell it "tenderhooks."

terrorist The term applies to participants and organizations planning and executing acts of violence against civilian or noncombatant targets. Groups that admit to terrorist acts are said to take *responsibility,* not *credit,* for them.

Texas Don't abbreviate. It is second to Alaska in land area. Residents are *Texans.*

See **state names.**

Thai It is a native or the language of Thailand. *Siam* and *Siamese* are the former terms. *Siamese* still applies to such things as *Siamese cats* and *Siamese* twins.

Thanksgiving, Thanksgiving Day

that (conjunction) The conjunction *that* usually is helpful to the reader in introducing a dependent clause, but it may be omitted following forms of the verb *to say: The company said it will raise the dividend.*

Use *that* in both or all dependent clauses if it is used in one of the clauses: *The company said* that *it will raise the dividend and* that *it expects higher earnings this year.*

Include *that* if a time element is used between the verb and the dependent clause:

The company said last week that it will raise the dividend in the next quarter.

that, which

That is preferred in introducing essential clauses: *The company that publishes The Wall Street Journal is Dow Jones & Co.*

Which is preferred in introducing nonessential clauses: *Dow Jones & Co., which publishes The Wall Street Journal, is based in New York.* Such a nonessential clause, between the commas, can be discarded without changing the meaning of the sentence.

See **essential clauses.**

that, who For people, use *who* or *whom.* For objects, plants and animals, use *that* or *which.* But for animals that are given names or otherwise personalized, use *who* or *whom.*

the Don't use the article with company names except railroads, and then only if Co. or Corp. isn't used.

In newspaper names, capitalize *the* only for *The Wall Street Journal.*

theater Use this spelling except where the formal name of a theater or company is spelled *theatre.*

theatergoer

theft

See **burglary, larceny, robbery, theft.**

T

thermos It has become a generic term for a vacuum bottle.

third market It consists of all off-exchange trading in listed stocks by large brokerage houses. Articles involving significant corporate announcements made after the 5 p.m. close of composite trading should contain third-market quotes from a firm that engages in third-market trading, such as Jefferies Group of Los Angeles.

On Nasdaq's National Market System, a computerized network over which shares are traded between 9:30 a.m. and 4 p.m. Eastern time, any trading after 4 p.m. is considered to be third-market trading.

See **composite trading.**

Third World The reference to the economically developing nations of Africa, Asia and Latin America is often considered inappropriate or even pejorative. Generally avoid it.

3Com Corp. Based in Santa Clara, Calif., *3Com Corp.* is a provider of systems and services that connect people to information across networks, including the Internet. Try to avoid starting sentences and headlines with the company name, because of the numeral.

3M Co. Based in St. Paul, Minn., the diversified industrial company was formerly known as *Minnesota Mining & Manufacturing Co.* Try to avoid starting sentences and headlines with the company name, because of the numeral.

threesome

thrift institutions The term applies to savings banks and savings-and-loan associations. In the industry jargon, they are *thrifts.*

throwaway

Thursday

See **days of the week.**

Tiananmen Square The large public square is in Beijing.

tidal wave It is induced primarily by lunar gravity pull. *Tsunami* is the preferred term for a giant wave caused by earthquakes or undersea landslides.

tidbit

tie-dye, tie-dyed, tie-dyeing

tie in (v.), **tie-in** (n. and adj.)

tie, tied, tying

tie up (v.), **tie-up** (n. and adj.)

time element Generally avoid specifying the day on which routine announcements are made or on which routine actions occur. When the time element is needed, use *today, yesterday* and *tomorrow* as appropriate, or the days of the week within seven days before or after the current date. Use the date beyond that range.

See **dates.**

To prevent ambiguity, generally avoid terms such as *last Tuesday* or *next Tuesday* and *last March* or *next March* when the references are to the current week or year. The past, present or future tense of the verb usually provides adequate indication of which Tuesday is meant.

See **last** and **next.**

time of day The specific time of day that an event happens or will happen shouldn't be given unless required in context. When a clock reading is given, it should be the time that applies in the datelined community, and specify the time zone. If the article is undated, use the time where the event happened, and specify the time zone.

times Use figures except for *noon* and *midnight.* Use a colon to separate hours from minutes: *11 a.m., 1 p.m., 3:30 p.m. EST.* The construction *4 o'clock* should generally be used only in quotations.

Avoid redundancies such as *10 p.m. tonight.*

time zones Capitalize the full name: *Eastern Standard Time, Eastern Daylight Time; Central Standard Time, Central Daylight Time; Mountain Standard Time; Mountain Daylight Time; Pacific Standard Time; Pacific Daylight Time.* But short forms: *Eastern time, Mountain time, Alaska time, Hawaii Standard Time* (Hawaii doesn't switch to daylight time).

With clock readings, the abbreviations for zones within the continental U.S., Canada and Mexico are acceptable in first and other references *noon EST, 9 a.m. PDT, 4 p.m. MST.* Don't use a comma between the clock reading and the time zone, and don't use periods in the zone abbreviations.

Spell out references to time zones outside the contiguous states of the U.S.: *The program is broadcast at 9 p.m. Alaska Standard Time.* (*Greenwich Mean Time* has been replaced as the world standard by *Coordinated Universal Time.*)

tin The base metal, traded on the London Metal Exchange and the Kuala Lumpur Tin Market, is used mostly as a coating for cans. *Tinplate* is thin steel sheet with a very thin coating of tin, used primarily in can-making.

titanium The minor metal, used in specialty steels, notably in the aerospace industry and in high-performance engines, is very strong and lightweight.

tiptop

title (v.)

See **entitle, title.**

titleholder

titles

WITHOUT NAMES: Lowercase titles and spell them out when they aren't used with an individual's name: *The president announced his nomination for secretary of state. They had an audience with the pope.*

Also: *The chairman, Peter Kann, made the announcement. The vice president, Dick Cheney, presided over the Senate session.*

EXCEPTION: The editorial page capitalizes *President, Vice President, First Lady, Governor, Senator* and *Representative*, even when they are not followed by a name.

BEFORE NAMES: Capitalize formal titles directly before an individual's name. *Pope John Paul, President Washington, Vice Presidents Drew Martin and Elaine Brodie.* Formal titles indicate a scope of authority or professional activity that is integral to identity: *President Bush, Pvt. James Goble.* Many other titles are essentially occupational descriptions and are lowercased: *astronaut John Glenn, copy editor Barry Kramer.*

When in doubt about whether a title is formal, use a construction that sets off the name or the title with commas.

LONG TITLES: Separate a long title from a name by a construction that requires a comma: *George High, the undersecretary of the Treasury for economic affairs, spoke.* Or: *The undersecretary of the Treasury for economic affairs, George High, spoke.*

See **cabinet titles; composition titles; legislative titles; military titles; nobility; religious titles;** and **Mr., Mrs., Miss, Ms.**

TNT It stands for the explosive *trinitrotoluene,* as well as for *Turner Network Television.*

tobacco, tobaccos

Tobago
See **Trinidad and Tobago.**

toe the line *Toe,* not tow.

Tokyo Japan's capital city stands alone in datelines.

tollhouse, tollhouse cookies

tom-tom

ton

A *short ton,* the U.S. standard, is equal to 2,000 pounds.

A *long ton,* or *British ton,* is equal to 2,240 pounds.

A *metric ton* is equal to 1,000 kilograms, or 2,204.62 pounds.

Conversions:

Short ton to long, multiply by 0.89.

Short ton to metric multiply by 0.9.

Long ton to short, multiply by 1.12.

Long ton to metric, multiply by 1.02.

Metric ton to short, multiply by 1.1.

Metric ton to long, multiply by 0.98.

See **metric system.**

topsy-turvy

tornado
See **weather terms.**

Toronto The city in Canada stands alone in datelines.

tortuous, torturous
Tortuous means twisting or winding.
Torturous means anguishing.

Tory, Tories

total, totaling, totaled

tot, totted, totting To add.
Tote means to carry.

tout Use the word with care. An advertisement may *tout* a product, but an analyst's recommendation doesn't normally *tout* a stock.

toward Not *towards.*

town Apply the capitalization principles listed under **city.**
See also **cities and towns.**

town council Apply the principles listed under **city council.**

Toys "R" Us Inc. In headlines, use single quotes around the R.

tradable

trade in (v.) **trade-in** (n. and adj.)

trademark A trademark is a brand or symbol or the like, registered by a manufacturer or dealer and protected by law to prevent a competitor from using it: *Mountain Dew* for a beverage, for example. A generic equivalent is usually better. *See* **brand names.**

trade off (v.), **trade-off** (n. and adj.)

traditional, traditionally Generally avoid as synonyms for *usual* or *usually.*

traffic, trafficked, trafficking

trailing 12 months In corporate financial reporting, it refers to the most-recent 12 months of results. *Utilities* report earnings on the basis of the *trailing 12 months,* instead of the fiscal year, because of the seasonal nature of gas and electricity usage.

trampoline Formerly a trademark, now a generic term.

trans- The rules in **prefixes** apply, but in general, no hyphen.

Some examples:

transcontinental	transoceanic
transsexual	trans-Siberian
transmigrate	trans-Atlantic
transship	trans-Pacific

(The last two are exeptions to Webster's New World listings.)

transfer, transferred, transferring

Trans World Airlines *TWA* is acceptable on second reference.

traveler's check(s)

travelogue

travel, traveled, traveling, traveler

treasurer Capitalize it when it is used as a formal title before a name. *See* **titles.**

Treasury borrowings The U.S. Treasury raises funds by selling *Treasury bills* (usually maturing in three, six or 12 months), *Treasury notes* (usually maturing in one to 10 years) and *Treasury bonds* (maturing in 10 years or more).

Some terms involved in Treasury auctions of its debt issues:

bid-to-cover ratio The total of all bids received, divided by the amount accepted. It can help define demand for a particular issue. Example: *The auction carried a 2.1-to-1 bid to cover.*

competitive bid A bid that details a specific price/yield a participant is willing to pay for a security.

coupon The annual rate of interest the U.S. will pay a holder.

foreign add-on The additional amount of a security sold to foreign entities, above and beyond the amount accepted at the auction.

noncompetitive bid A participant's bid that says he/she will take the average of all awarded bids.

stopout The highest rate at which a security is sold. Use quotation marks and explain.

tail The difference between an average yield and *stopout rate,* expressed in basis points. A *wide tail* suggests a thinly bid auction.

when-issued The basis for trading activity that takes place before a security's sale. When-issued activity begins immediately after a security is announced by the Treasury and is expressed in yield. After the auction is completed and the coupon is announced, the debt is traded by price, on a *when-issued* basis until the settlement date.

Treasurys This plural for Treasury-issued debt instruments follows the normal plural form for proper nouns ending in *y*.

trees
See **plants.**

tribes
See **nationalities and races.**

trickle-down (adj.) In referring to the economic theory, use quotation marks in the first reference.

trigger-happy

Trinidad and Tobago In datelines on stories from this island nation, use a city name followed by either *Trinidad* or *Tobago,* depending on the city's location.

triple witching The term is applied to the times each quarter when index options, index futures and stock options all expire in the same Thursday–Friday period. *Triple witchings* can cause stock-market volatility on the Fridays involved, as stocks are bought or sold to offset expiring options positions. *Double witchings* occur when index and stock options expire together.

triweekly It means both *every three weeks* and *three times a week.* To avoid confusion, use one of these more precise terms instead.

Trojan horse, Trojan War

troop, troops, troupe
A *troop* is a group of people or animals.
Troops are combined groups, particularly of soldiers.
Use *troupe* for ensembles of actors, dancers, or singers.

tropical depression
See **weather terms.**

trustee Don't capitalize it, even before a name.

try out (v.), **tryout** (n.)

tsar Use *czar.*

T-shirt

tsunami It is the scientific term for a sea wave induced by an earthquake or undersea landslide. Explain the term in articles. A *tidal wave* is related to the ocean tides.

tuberculosis *TB* is acceptable on second reference.

Tuesday
See **days of the week.**

tune up (v.), **tuneup** (n. and adj.)

turboprop
See **aircraft terms.**

turnpike Capitalize as part of a proper name: *the Pennsylvania Turnpike.* Lowercase *turnpike* when it stands alone.
See **highway designations.**

TV Acceptable as an adjective or in constructions such as *cable TV.* But don't normally use as a noun except in a quotation or a headline. The receiver is a *TV set.*

TVA
See **Tennessee Valley Authority.**

twisted pair It is telecommunications jargon for the two copper wires used in old-style analog household telephone wiring. Because telephone companies deliver high-speed services over a speedy digital connection such as an ISDN, or integrated services digital network, the twisted pair can cause a bottleneck. Explain the term if you use it.
See **last mile.**

U u

UFO, UFOs The abbreviations are acceptable in second reference for *unidentified flying object(s).*

UHF It is acceptable in all references for *ultrahigh frequency.*

Ukraine Don't use the article *the*. Its capital is Kiev. *See* **Commonwealth of Independent States.**

ukulele

Ulster It is used colloquially used as a synonym for *Northern Ireland.*

See **United Kingdom.**

ultra- The rules in **prefixes** apply, but in general, no hyphen is used:

ultramodern
ultranationalism
ultraviolet

ultrahigh frequency *UHF* is acceptable in all references.

UMTS It stands for *universal mobile telecommunications services.* The full name should be included in articles

un- The rules in **prefixes** apply, but in general, a hyphen is used only before a proper noun.

un-American	unarmed
unnecessary	unshaven

U.N.

See **United Nations.**

UNAids It administers an interagency United Nations program dealing with AIDS. The capitalization is an exception to the rule that only the first letter is capitalized in acronyms of more than four letters.

under- The rules in **prefixes** apply, but in general, no hyphen is used.

underdog	underrepresented
underground	undersold
underrated	

undersecretary One word. *See* **titles.**

under way In most cases, use the two words: *The project is under way. The naval maneuvers are under way.*

It is one word only when used as an adjective before a noun in a nautical sense: *an underway flotilla.*

underwriter In the insurance business, an *underwriter* assumes risk for a fee. In securities markets, an *underwriting firm* or *syndicate* is one that agrees to purchase a new bond or stock offering from the issuer, for resale.

unemployment rate As compiled by the Labor Department, it is the percentage of people in the work force who are looking for jobs, adjusted for seasonal variations. Although the government now emphasizes the overall figure, including the military, the Journal continues to use primarily the civilian work-force figure, on the theory that there aren't many unemployed soldiers.

Unesco It is acceptable on first reference for *the United Nations Educational, Scientific and Cultural Organization,* but in most instances, a subsequent reference should give the full name.

Unicef It is acceptable in all references for *the United Nations Children's Fund.* The words *International* and *Emergency,* originally part of the name, have been dropped.

Unification Church The short form is acceptable in all references to *the Holy Spirit Association for the Unification of World Christianity.* It was founded by the Rev. Sun Myung Moon.

Uniform Code of Military Justice The code of laws covers members of the U.S. armed forces.

uninterested
See **disinterested, uninterested.**

union Capitalize *union* when used as a proper name for the Northern states during the Civil War.

U

union names Long formal names of unions may be condensed to conventionally accepted short forms that retain capitalization of the key word but lowercase *union: Teamsters union.*

Generically, however, use the possessive form: *drivers' union.*

Abbreviations used on subsequent references and in headlines do not take periods: *UAW, UMW.*

See **United Auto Workers.**

Union of Needletrades, Industrial and Textile Employees In second reference, *Unite* is acceptable. *See* **closed shop.**

union shop

unique It means *one of a kind.* Don't describe something as *rather unique* or *most unique.*

unit In headlines and in second references in articles, *unit* is acceptable to refer to a *subsidiary* or *division,* but try to be specific on first reference in articles. *Unit* shouldn't be used in reference to an *affiliate.*

United Arab Emirates The abbreviation *U.A.E.* is acceptable on second reference.

United Auto Workers This short form is acceptable in all references to *the United Automobile, Aerospace and Agricultural Implement Workers of America. UAW, Auto Workers* and *Auto Workers union* are acceptable in second reference. Use *auto workers* in generic reference to workers in the industry.

United Food and Commercial Workers International Union

United Kingdom It may be abbreviated *U.K.* after the initial reference in an article and in headlines if *United Kingdom* is used in the article. It comprises Britain and Northern Ireland. *Britain* comprises England, Scotland and Wales. *Ireland,* formally the Irish Republic, is independent of the United Kingdom.

See **datelines** and **Ireland.**

United Mine Workers of America The shortened forms *United Mine Workers* and

United Mine Workers union are acceptable in all references. *UMW* and *Mine Workers* are acceptable in headlines and in second reference.

United Nations It is used alone for datelines. Use *U.N.* in second reference in articles. Capitalize *Secretariat, Security Council* and *General Assembly* even when they aren't preceded by *U.N.*

Union Pacific Corp. Based in Dallas, it is the parent of *the Union Pacific Railroad.*

Uniroyal Technology Corp. It is based in Sarasota, Fla.

United Service Organizations *USO* is acceptable in second reference.

United States Spell out only in quotes or for special effect. Otherwise, including in corporate names, always abbreviate *U.S.*

United Steelworkers of America *United Steelworkers* and *United Steelworkers union* are acceptable in all references. Capitalize *Steelworkers* in all references to the union or its members. Use *steelworker* in generic references to workers in the industry.

unit trusts They are mutual funds.

universal mobile telecommunications services *UMTS* is acceptable on second reference.

UNIX This *multitasking operating system* is the main operating system for workstations.

See **workstation.**

unlisted stocks These formerly were considered to be those not listed on a formal exchange. Now, if the stocks are carried on the Nasdaq Stock Market, they are termed *Nasdaq stocks.* Only shares listed on the so-called Pink Sheets and not on the Nasdaq tables are considered to be *unlisted.*

up- In general, no hyphen: *upend, uptown, upgrade.*

-up Follow Webster's New World Dictionary.

In these examples, use *two words* for the *verb* forms:

breakup	setup
makeup	crackup
buildup	shake-up
mix-up	follow-up
call-up	shape-up
mock-up	frame-up
change-up	smashup
pileup	grown-up
checkup	speedup
push-up	holdup
cleanup	start-up
roundup	letup
close-up	walk-up
runners-up	lineup
cover-up	windup

upcoming Use *coming* instead, except in a quotation.

uppercase It is one word (n., v., adj.) when referring to the use of capital letters.

upside down (adv.), **upside-down** (adj.) *The car turned upside down. It's an upside-down world.*

upstate Always lowercase: *upstate New York.*

uptick

See **program trading.**

up-to-date All uses.

U

up, ups, upping, upped Don't use *up* and its variants as verbs for *increase or raise.*

upward, upward of Use *upward,* not upwards. And avoid *upward of* to mean *more than* unless the intended meaning is unquestionably clear in context.

uranium It is used as a fuel for nuclear reactors.

URL Referring to an Internet address, it stands for *Uniform Resource Locator.* In a URL, *http* is the protocol, or method of transfer; // indicates a computer name follows, and subsequent words refer to the server, the domain, the folder and the file (*html* is a type of file).

U.S. Use the abbreviation in all cases, generally, including corporate names. Spell it out only in quotes or for special effect.

U.S. Air Force *See* **air force; military academies; military titles.**

US Airways

U.S. Army *See* **army; military academies; military titles.**

U.S. Claims Court Based in Washington, this court handles claims against the federal government.

U.S. Coast Guard

See **coast guard; military academies; military titles.**

U

U.S. Conference of Mayors The members are the mayors of cities with 30,000 or more residents. *See* **National League of Cities.**

U.S. Court of Appeals The court is divided into 13 circuits: the District of Columbia Circuit and the Federal Circuit, based in Washington, D.C., and the First Circuit through the 11th Circuit. The First Circuit is based in Boston; Second Circuit, New York; Third Circuit, Philadelphia; Fourth Circuit, Richmond, Va.; Fifth Circuit, New Orleans; Sixth Circuit, Cincinnati; Seventh Circuit, Chicago; Eighth Circuit, St. Louis; Ninth Circuit, San Francisco; 10th Circuit, Denver; 11th Circuit, Atlanta.

The courts sometimes hold sessions in other major cities within their regions. Always mention the base location or the hearing site.

First and other references may use a phrase such as *a federal appeals court in St. Louis.* The formal name should use *U.S.* or *Federal Court of Appeals* or a full name such as *Eighth U.S. Circuit Court of Appeals* or *the U.S. Court of Appeals for the Eighth Circuit.* Be sure to provide the location.

In subsequent references: *the appeals court, the appellate court(s).*

The jurists themselves use the title *judge: U.S. Circuit Judge John Denton* or *U.S. Appeals Judge John Denton.*

See **judge.**

U.S. Court of Appeals for the Federal Circuit It handles appeals on many trade, patent, trademark and copyright cases, as well as appeals from the claims court.

U.S. Court of International Trade Based in New York City, this court handles disputes over customs, tariffs and trade that arise at any U.S. port of entry.

U.S. Court of Military Appeals This court is a civilian body established by Congress to hear appeals of courts-martial and other actions of the armed forces. It is based in Washington.

U.S. District Court In shortened references to any of the 94 federal district courts: *the district court, the court, the federal court.* District-court jurists use the title *judge: U.S. District Judge Greg Langan.*

See **judge.**

Usenet It is a world-wide system of Internet discussion areas called *newsgroups.*

usher Use *usher* for both men and women.

U.S. Information Agency Use *U.S. Information Agency* on first reference. Lowercase *the information agency* or *the agency* in second reference.

U.S. Military Academy
See **military academies.**

U.S. Navy
See **navy; military academies; military titles.**

U.S. Patent and Trademark Office Not *U.S. Patent Office.*

U.S. Postal Service Use *U.S. Postal Service* or *the Postal Service* on first reference. Retain capitalization of *Postal Service* in subsequent references to the agency. Lowercase *the service* when it stands alone. Lowercase *post office* in generic references to the agency and to an individual office.

U.S. Postal Service Directory of Post Offices It is the reference for U.S. place names not covered in this book.

USS It stands for *United States Ship,* preceding the name of a vessel: *the USS Iowa.*

U.S. Supreme Court Capitalize *Supreme* Court with or without the U.S.

Chief Justice William Rehnquist is the *chief justice of the U.S.* (rather than of the Supreme Court). The other members are *associate justices* of the Supreme Court and may be referred to as *justices: Justice Clarence Thomas.*

U.S. Tax Court, the Tax Court This is a special federal court for tax cases.

Utah Don't abbreviate. Residents are *Utahns* or *Utahans.*
See **state names.**

utilize Use *use* instead whenever possible.

Uzbekistan
See **Commonwealth of Independent States.**

U

V v

VA *See* **Veterans Affairs.**

v. and vs. In abbreviating *versus,* limit *v.* to names of court cases: *the State of New Jersey v. the Commonwealth of Pennsylvania.*

In headlines, lowercase the abbreviations, and use *vs.* only for occasional special effect: *A Case of Good vs. Evil.*

See **versus.**

valley Capitalize it as part of a full name: *the Mississippi Valley.* In plural uses: *the Columbia and Mississippi valleys.*

vanadium The minor metal is used mainly to strengthen steel.

Vandyke beard, Vandyke collar

Varig *Varig Brazilian Airlines* may also be referred to as: *Varig, a Brazilian airline.*

Vaseline It is a trademark for a brand of petroleum jelly.

Vatican City It stands alone in datelines.

VCR It stands for *videocassette recorder. VCRs* is the plural.

V-E Day May 8, 1945, was designated by the Allies as the day victory was won in the European phase of World War II.

Velcro It is a trademark for a brand of fastener.

vendor

Venice The city in Italy stands alone in datelines.

venture capitalists They invest pools of money in businesses in exchange for roles in running the businesses and obtaining shares of the profits.

See **initial public offering.**

verbal

See **oral, verbal, written.**

veritable The nonce word is better avoided, except in quotes.

Vermont Abbreviate as *Vt.* after city names. Residents are *Vermonters. See* **state names.**

versus Spell it out in most contexts: *The contest involved Dartmouth versus Harvard.* Abbreviate as *vs.*, lowercase, for special effect in headlines and text: *It was a case of bull vs. bear.* But in referring to names of legal cases, use *v.*: *the State of New Jersey v. the Commonwealth of Pennsylvania.*

vertical portal

See **vortal.**

vertical-takeoff aircraft
See **V-STOL** and **VTOL.**

very high frequency *VHF* is acceptable in all references.

vet Don't use for an armed-services veteran. The verb form, derived from *veterinarian,* means *to examine* or *investigate.*

Veterans Affairs Formerly the Veterans Administration, it now is the cabinet-level *Department of Veterans Affairs. VA* may still be used on second reference.

Veterans Day Formerly Armistice Day, it is observed Nov. 11.

Veterans of Foreign Wars *VFW* is acceptable in second reference.

veto, vetoes, vetoing

VHF Acceptable in all references for *very high frequency.*

Viacom Inc. The entertainment company is based in New York. Its holdings include CBS broadcast and cable networks and the UPN Television Network, as well as Paramount Pictures and Simon & Schuster.

vice Use two words: *vice admiral, vice chairman, vice chancellor, vice consul, vice president, vice principal, vice regent, vice secretary.* (Several are exceptions to Webster's New World.)

vice president (of the U.S.) In the news pages, capitalize it only if it precedes a name: *Vice President Dick Cheney, the vice president.* The editorial pages capitalize *Vice President* in all references to the U.S. officeholder.

Don't drop the first name in first reference, as you do with *the president.*

See **president** and **titles.**

vice versa

videocassette recorder *VCR* is acceptable in second reference.

videocassette, videodisc, videotape

videotex It refers to the electronic delivery of textual information to home TV sets.
See **teletext.**

Vienna The capital of Austria stands alone in datelines.

Viet Cong During the Vietnam War, they were pro-Hanoi guerrillas in South Vietnam.

Vietnam

Vietnam War It spanned 1954–75.

vie, vied, vying

village Apply the capitalization principles listed under **city.**

Virginia Abbreviate as *Va.* after city names. Residents are *Virginians.*
See **state names.**

Virgin Islands Use in datelines after a city name in articles from the U.S. Virgin Islands. Don't abbreviate.
See **datelines** and **British Virgin Islands.**

vitamins Lowercase *vitamin,* use a capital letter and a hyphen and number if required: *vitamin A, vitamin B-12.*

V-J Day Aug. 15, 1945, was designated by the Allies as the day of victory over the Japanese, ending World War II.

V-neck (n. and adj.)

voice mail Electronic systems store and replay *voice-mail messages.*

Voice of America

Volkswagen of America Inc. The name of the U.S. subsidiary of the German company *Volkswagen AG. VW* may be used to refer to the company or its cars if the context is clear.

volley, volleys

volt The unit of electrical force indicates the rate at which power is moving. Appliances and equipment are rated according to how many volts they require to operate.

Volunteers in Service to America *Vista* is acceptable on second reference.

voodoo

vortal It is the techie term for *vertical portal,* or an Internet site with a tight focus geared toward users with specific interests. Broad-interest portals such as Yahoo are *horizontal portals.* Don't use the terms without explaining them.

votes In articles and headlines, use figures and a hyphen for pairs of numbers up to 1,000: *The vote in the Senate was 79–8, with 2 abstentions.*

Spell out numbers below 10 in other phrases related to voting: *by a five-vote majority, with three abstentions, four votes short of the necessary two-thirds majority.*

For totals above 1,000 votes, separate the figures with the word *to* and avoid hyphenated adjectival constructions: *a vote of 12,300 to 10,500.*

See **numbers.**

V-STOL It is acceptable in second reference for an aircraft capable of *vertical or short takeoff or landing.*

VTOL It is acceptable in second reference for an aircraft capable of *vertical takeoff or landing.*

vulgarities

See **obscenities, profanities, vulgarities.**

V

Ww Xx

waiter, waitress

Wales
See **United Kingdom** and **datelines.**

walk up (v.), **walk-up** (n. and adj.)

Wall Street When the reference is to the New York financial community, *the Street* is an acceptable short form in second reference.

Wall Street Journal, The The *The* is capitalized. But make it *the Journal* on second reference. Online, it is *The Wall Street Journal Online*. The overseas editions are *The Asian Wall Street Journal* and *The Wall Street Journal Europe.*

Wal-Mart Stores Inc. The retailer is based in Bentonville, Ark.

WAN *See* **wide-area network.**

war Capitalize it when it is part of the name for a specific conflict, such as *the Civil War, the Persian Gulf War, the Gulf War, the Korean War, the Vietnam War, the War of 1812, World War II.*

warden Capitalize it as a formal title before a name. *See* **titles.**

wards *See* **political divisions.**

warhead

war horse, warhorse Use two words for a horse used in battle, but one word for a veteran of many battles: *He is a political warhorse.*

warlike, warlord, wartime

warrant In the investment world, it is a certificate giving the holder the right to buy securities at stipulated prices, usually within a specified time limit.

warranty It is the same as a *guaranty.*

Warsaw The capital of Poland stands alone in datelines.

Washington Abbreviate the state as *Wash.* after city names.

Never abbreviate references to the U.S. capital. The city stands alone in datelines. Use *state of Washington, Washington state; Washington, D.C.,* or *District of Columbia* when the context requires a distinction between the state and the federal district. Residents of each are *Washingtonians.*

See **state names.**

Washington's Birthday *Presidents Day* (no hyphen or apostrophe) is the commonly used name for the holiday celebrated on the third Monday in February, in some states honoring President Lincoln as well as President Washington.

WASP The acronym for *white Anglo-Saxon Protestant* is considered objectionable by some, so use it advisedly.

wastebasket, waste water

watt It is the basic unit for measuring the volume of electricity. The generating capacity of power plants is usually given in megawatts, equal to a million watts, or 1,000 kilowatts. One megawatt can power about 500 households.

See **kilowatt-hour.**

weak-kneed

weapons

antiaircraft A cannon that fires explosive shells: *a 105mm antiaircraft gun.* Smaller antiaircraft guns such as the 20mm Vulcan Phalanx rotary cannon are used on Navy ships.

artillery Carriage-mounted cannons.

automatic A pistol with cartridges held in a magazine: *a .22-caliber automatic.*

bullet A projectile fired by a rifle, pistol or machine gun.

caliber A measurement of the diameter of the inside of a gun barrel (except for most shotguns) and the ammunition. Measurement is in millimeters or decimal fractions of an inch. The word *caliber* is not used when giving the metric measurement. The forms: *a 9mm pistol, a .22-caliber rifle.* A 38-caliber bullet is actually 0.357 inch.

cannon A weapon mounted on a carriage or ship that fires explosive projectiles: *a 105mm cannon.*

carbine A short-barreled rifle: *an M-3 carbine.*

cartridge It comprises a *bullet, metal casing, primer* and *propellant.*

Colt Named for Samuel Colt, it designates a make of handgun: *a Colt .45-caliber revolver.*

gauge This describes the size of a shotgun's bore. The bigger the number, the smaller the shotgun: *a 12-gauge shotgun, a .410-gauge shotgun.* The .410 is actually a caliber but is commonly called a gauge.

The forms: *a 12-gauge shotgun, a .410-gauge shotgun.*

Gauge	*Interior Diameter*
10	0.775 inch
12	0.729 inch
16	0.662 inch
20	0.615 inch
28	0.550 inch
.410	0.410 inch

gun Any firearm may be called a gun.

howitzer A cannon shorter than a gun of the same caliber employed to fire projectiles at relatively high trajectories at a target: *a 105mm howitzer.*

M-1, M-16 Rifles used by the military: *an M-1 rifle, an M-1, an M-16 carbine, an M-16.*

machine gun An automatic gun that fires continuously while the trigger is depressed.

Magnum A trademark for a cartridge with a larger powder charge than other cartridges of similar caliber: *a .357-caliber Magnum, a .44-caliber Magnum.*

musket A large-caliber shoulder firearm that fires musket balls by using a matchlock, a wheel lock, a flintlock or a percussion lock.

pistol A hand-held revolver or an automatic: *a.38-caliber pistol.*

revolver A pistol using cartridges held in revolving chambers: *a .45-caliber revolver.*

rifle A firearm using bullets or cartridges: *a .22-caliber rifle.*

Saturday Night Special A cheap pistol so-called because impulsive crimes often occur on Saturday nights.

shells Ammunition used in military weapons and shotguns.

shot Small lead or steel balls used as ammunition in shotguns. Buckshot applies to the largest shot sizes. Ballistics tests aren't possible with shot.

shotgun A gun with one or two smoothbore barrels, usually using shot: *a 12-gauge shotgun.* Shotguns may also use projectiles called *slugs,* often used for deer hunting.

submachine gun A lightweight automatic gun.

weather-beaten

weather bureau
See **National Weather Service.**

weatherman The preferred term is *weather forecaster.*

weather terms The terms are based on definitions used by the National Weather Service.

blizzard It involves wind speeds of 35 mph or more and considerable falling or blowing of snow with little if any visibility.

coastal waters They are waters within about 20 miles of the coast.

cyclone It involves strong winds rotating about a moving center of low atmospheric pressure. The term is sometimes used loosely to refer to a *tornado* or *hurricane.*

degree-day It measures the temperature against a standard average and is used to estimate the amount of heating or cooling needed for a building.

flash flood It follows heavy rains or melting snow within a few hours.

freeze It describes conditions when the temperature at or near the surface is expected to be below 32 degrees Fahrenheit during the growing season.

frost It involves the formation of thin ice crystals from moisture in the atmosphere.

funnel cloud This violent, rotating column of air does not touch the ground.

gale It involves sustained winds of 39 to 54 mph.

heavy snow It involves snowfall accumulating to at least 4 inches or more in depth in 12 hours, or accumulating to at least 6 inches in 24 hours.

high wind It usually indicates sustained winds of at least 39 mph that are expected to persist for at least an hour.

hurricane or **typhoon** Either one is a warm-core tropical cyclone in which the minimum sustained surface wind is at least 74 mph. *Hurricanes* develop east of the international dateline, *typhoons* west of the line.

When a hurricane or typhoon loses strength after landfall, it is reduced to *tropical storm* status.

hurricane eye It is the relatively calm area in the center of the storm, where winds are light and the sky only partly cloudy.

ice storm It involves rain or drizzle that freezes as it strikes objects.

National Hurricane Center The National Weather Service's center in Miami tracks hurricanes and lesser storms. The service's center in Honolulu tracks Pacific storms.

nor'easter It is a storm or strong wind from the northeast, in the eastern U.S.

offshore waters They extend about 250 miles from the coast.

sandstorm It involves visibility of a half mile or less caused by sand and wind speeds of 30 mph or more.

sleet It involves generally solid grains of ice from freezing of raindrops or the refreezing of melted snowflakes.

squall It is a sudden increase of wind speed by at least 16 knots and rising to 25 knots or more and lasting for at least one minute.

temperature-humidity index It indicates the effect of heat and moisture on human comfort. Readings above 70 indicate increasing levels of discomfort.

tornado It is a violent rotating column of air, usually from a cumulonimbus cloud, and touching the ground. It often starts as a funnel cloud and is accompanied by a roaring noise.

tropical depression It is a tropical cyclone in which the sustained surface wind is 38 mph or less.

tropical storm It is a warm-core tropical cyclone with surface wind of 39 to 73 mph.

typhoon *See* **hurricane** or **typhoon.**

tsunami It is a seismic sea wave caused by underwater earthquakes or volcanic eruptions. It is often erroneously called a *tidal wave,* but it is unrelated to the tides.

waterspout It is a tornado over water.

wind-chill factor The index is calculated to gauge the combined effect of the wind and cold temperatures on exposed skin. The index would be minus 22 degrees, for example, if the temperature was 15 degrees Fahrenheit and the wind speed was 25 mph.

wind shear It is a sudden shift in wind direction caused when a mass of cooled air from a thunderstorm hits the ground and rushes outward in all directions.

weather vane

Web, the *The Web* is acceptable in all references to the World Wide Web. Also: *Web site, Web pages, Web server.* But *Webcast* for publishing on the Web.

See **World Wide Web.**

Wednesday *See* **days of the week.**

weekend

weeklong

weird

well Hyphenate as part of a compound modifier before the noun: *She is a well-known actress.*

See **hyphen** (-) for guidelines on compound modifiers.

well-being

well-to-do

well-wishers

welsh In the slang sense of *evade an obligation,* avoid forms of the word except in quotes.

Western Hemisphere It comprises the continents of North and South America and the islands near them.

Western Wall The wall in Jerusalem formerly was called *the Wailing Wall.*

West Indian The term applies to people from the former British colonies in the Caribbean. It doesn't apply to those from Cuba or Puerto Rico.

West Point It is an acceptable alternative reference for the *U.S. Military Academy* at West Point, N.Y. *See* **military academies.**

West Texas Intermediate crude It is the most commonly traded domestic crude-oil grade.

West Virginia Abbreviate as *W.Va.* (no space between *W.* and *Va.*) before city names. Residents are *West Virginians.*

See **state names.**

west, western Capitalize *West* and *Western* when referring to Western U.S. or to the Western part of the world. But: *western Pennsylvania, a TV western.*

States in the West, by Census Bureau definition: Alaska, Arizona, California, Colorado, Hawaii, Idaho, Montana, Nevada, New Mexico, Oregon, Utah, Washington and Wyoming.

Wharton School It is the business school of the University of Pennsylvania.

wheelchair

wheeler-dealer

whence It means *from where.* Avoid the redundancy *from whence.*

whereabouts It takes a singular verb: *His whereabouts is a mystery.*

wherever

which

See **essential clauses, nonessential clauses; that, which.**

whip Capitalize it only when it is used as a formal title before a name.

See **legislative titles** and **titles.**

whiskey, whiskeys Use the spelling *whisky* only when it is used with *Scotch whisky.*

See **Scotch whisky.**

white The racial designation is lowercase, as are *black* and *yellow*.

white-collar (adj.)

white knight In corporate-takeover lingo, a *white knight* is a friendly suitor who helps a company fend off a hostile takeover.

white paper It is a special report.

whitewash It is always one word.

whoever, whomever *Give this to whoever answers the door. Give this to whomever they designate.* The object of the preposition is the entire clause, and whether you use *whoever* or *whomever* depends on whether that word is the subject or object of the clause.

wholehearted

wholesale price index

See **producer price index**, which has replaced this indicator.

whole-wheat

who, whom

Use *who* and *whom* as pronouns to refer to humans and to animals with names. Otherwise, use *that* and *which.*

Who is used as subject of a sentence, clause or phrase: *The woman who headed the division was responsible. She is the woman who heads the division.*

Whom is used as the object of a verb or preposition: *She was the one to whom the vice president reported. Whom do you talk to?*

See **essential clauses, nonessential clauses** for guidelines on how to punctuate clauses introduced by *who, whom, that* and *which.*

-wide No hyphen. Some examples:

citywide	nationwide
industrywide	countrywide
continentwide	statewide

Exceptions: *world-wide* and proper-noun combinations: *Asia-wide.*

wide-area network It is a system linking an organization's individual computer workstations world-wide, using telecommunications to share files.

widths

See **dimensions.**

wigwag

wildcat (adj.) When applied to strikes, it means unauthorized. Be sure it is unauthorized before you call a strike a *wildcat strike.*

wildlife

Wilkes-Barre, Pa.

Wilshire 5000 It is the broadest U.S. stock index, covering all Nasdaq Stock Market stocks and all stocks traded on the New York and American stock exchanges.

Windbreaker A trademark for a wind-resistant sports jacket.

window dressing (n.), **window-dress** (v.)

wind-swept

wind up (v.), **windup** (n. and adj.)

wine Capitalize wine names when referring to a specific wine, grape variety or proprietary name. *Cabernet Sauvignon, Chardonnay, Chenin Blanc* and the like are uppercase. *Burgundy* and *Chablis* are uppercase when referring to a specific wine or wine from the specific regions of France, but lowercase when referring to a generic type or a knock-off type: *J. Moreau Chablis, a house chablis; a French Burgundy, a domestic burgundy.*

wingspan

winter *See* **seasons.**

wintertime

winter wheat Wheat planted in the fall and harvested in late spring.

wiretap, wiretapped, wiretapping, wiretapper

Wisconsin Abbreviate as *Wis.* after city names. Residents are *Wisconsinites.*

See **state names.**

-wise Use no hyphen when it means *in the direction of* or *with regard to:*

clockwise	lengthwise
contrariwise	slantwise
otherwise	

Avoid contrived combinations such as *moneywise, religionwise.*

The term *penny-wise* is hyphenated because it is a compound modifier in which *wise* means *smart,* rather than a use of the suffix *-wise.* The same for *street-wise.*

wishy-washy

witch doctor

Woman's Christian Temperance Union *WCTU* is acceptable in second reference.

women Don't use physical descriptions, sexual references, family status and stereotypical wording, especially if parallel wording wouldn't be used in references to men.

—Try to use plural nouns and pronouns when both sexes are involved. *Taxpayers are expected to verify their deductions.* Rather than: *The taxpayer is expected to verify his deductions.*

—Don't gratuitously mention irrelevant family relationships, as in: *Roberta Gardner, a grandmother of three, was named president of the co-op.*

See **Mr., Mrs., Miss, Ms.; divorcee;** and **people.**

word-of-mouth (n. and adj.)

workbook, workday, workhorse, workload, workplace, workstation, workweek But: *work force, work sheet.*

workers' compensation

working class (n.), **working-class** (adj.)

work out (v.), **workout** (n.)

workstation This type of computer system is used for engineering applications, desktop publishing, software development and other applications that require high-quality-graphics capabilities. In computer networking, the term applies to any computer that is connected to a local-area network.

See **local-area network, operating system** and **UNIX** entries.

World Bank *The World Bank* is acceptable in all references for *the International Bank for Reconstruction and Development.* Based in Washington and affiliated with the United Nations, it assists economic development of member

W X

nations by making loans when private capital isn't available. *The International Finance Corp.,* a World Bank affiliate, encourages private enterprise in less-developed countries, using funds from the World Bank and private capital markets. World Bank members are also members of the International Monetary Fund.

World Council of Churches It is an organization of Protestant and Orthodox churches.

world court This is an informal name for *the International Court of Justice.*

World Health Organization *WHO* is acceptable in second reference. Headquarters is in Geneva.

World Series Or *the Series* in second reference.

World Trade Organization Based in Geneva, it succeeded *the General Agreement on Tariffs and Trade* in 1995. *WTO* is acceptable in second reference.

World War I, World War II

world-wide

World Wide Web It is the information-retrieval system for the Internet; *the Web* is acceptable in all references. A *Web site* is an information page on the Web. A *Web browser* is a software application that locates and displays *Web pages.*

See **Internet.**

worse, worst The idiom is *if worst comes to worst,* not *if worse comes to worst.*

worship, worshiped, worshiping, worshiper

worth In giving evaluations, generally use *valued at* instead of *worth.* Avoid such constructions as *$22 million worth of jewelry,* because the item in question could be valued at more or less than the stated figure. Usually *worth* can be dropped without harm: *$22 million of jewelry.*

worthwhile

wrack *See* **rack, wrack.**

wrap up (v.), **wrap-up** (n. and adj.)

write down (v), **write-down** (n. and adj.)

write in (v.), **write-in** (n. and adj.)

write off (v.), **write-off** (n. and adj.)

wrongdoing

Wyoming Abbreviate as *Wyo.* after city names. Residents are *Wyomingites.*

See **state names.**

Xerox It is a trademark of Xerox Corp., Stamford, Conn., for a brand of photocopying machine. For a verb, use *photocopy* instead.

X-rated It is an informal reference to pornographic films.

See **movie ratings.**

X-ray (n., v., adj.) The term applies to the photographic process, the radiation particles themselves and a picture they produce.

Yy Zz

Yahoo Inc. Based in Santa Clara, Calif., it is an Internet communications company.

Yankee bond A dollar-denominated issue, it is registered with the Securities and Exchange Commission and sold in the U.S. by foreign companies or governments.

yard It is equal to three feet. The metric equivalent is approximately 0.91 meter.

To convert to meters, multiply by 0.91.

See **foot** and **meter.**

year end, year's end (n.), **year-end** (adj.)

yearling It refers to an animal one year old or in its second year. The birthdays of all thoroughbred horses are arbitrarily set at Jan. 1. On that date, any foal born in the preceding year is reckoned to be a year old.

yearlong

years Use figures, without commas: *1975.* Use an *s* without an apostrophe to indicate spans of decades or centuries: *the 1800s, the 1890s, the '90s.* For spans, use *1985–92.*

See **A.D.; B.C.; century;** and **months.**

yesteryear

yield It is the annual rate of return on an investment as paid in dividends or interest. For stocks and bonds, it is expressed as a percentage, generally obtained by dividing the current market price for the security into the annual dividend or interest payment.

Current yield is the rate of interest, or coupon, on a bond, divided by the purchase price. When the bond's coupon rate remains constant, the yield rises as the purchase price falls and falls as the purchase price rises.

Yield to maturity determines the amount to be earned if the bond purchaser keeps the bond to its maturity date. The complex equation takes into account the purchase price, redemption value, time to maturity, coupon rate and time between interest payments.

Yield to call calculates the yield based on the assumption that the bond issuer will redeem the bond at the first redemption date.

Yield to average life calculates the yield on bonds that the issuer retires systematically through the life of the issue.

Yield spread is the difference between one yield and another, used for comparisons between a corporate bond and a similar government bond.

yield curve A *yield curve* is a graph showing the relationship at a given time between the yields and maturities of securities that all carry the same credit rating. The *U.S. Treasury yield curve* shows yields on maturities from two years to 30 years.

yogurt

Yom Kippur The Jewish Day of Atonement *Yom Kippur* occurs in September or October.

Young Men's Christian Association *YMCA* is acceptable in second reference.

Young Women's Christian Association *YWCA* is acceptable in second reference.

yo-yo

yuan Use *yuan* to refer to the currency of China, though *renminbi* is also used by some.

Yugoslavia It comprises the republics of Serbia and Montenegro. Its capital is Belgrade.

Yukon It is a territorial section of Canada. Don't abbreviate. Use in datelines after the names of all cities and towns in the territory. *Yukon* is also the name of a river in this territory and Alaska. *See* **Canada.**

yule, yuletide

zero-coupon bonds They pay no interest but are issued at a deep discount. Investors' gains come from the difference between the discounted purchase price and the face value received at maturity.

zero, zeros (n.), **zero, zeroes** (v.)

zigzag

zinc The base metal, traded on the London Metal Exchange, is used mainly as a plating for rust protection, particularly in the auto industry.

ZIP Codes

Zurich The city in Switzerland stands alone in datelines.

APPENDIX

WORLD CURRENCIES

NATION	CURRENCY	SWIFT CODE/ ABBREVIATION
Afghanistan	Afghani	AFA
Albania	lek	ALL
Algeria	Algerian dinar	DZD
American Samoa	U.S. dollar	US$
Andorra	peseta/Spanish peseta/French franc	ADP/ESP/FRF
Angola	kwanza	AON
Antigua & Barbuda	East Caribbean dollar	XCD
Argentina	Argentinian peso	ARS
Armenia	Armenian dram	AMD
Aruba	Aruban florin	AWG
Australia	Australian dollar	A$
Austria	schilling and euro	ATS
Azerbaijan	Azerbaijani manat (plural *manat*)	AZM
Bahamas	Bahamian dollar	BSD
Bahrain	Bahraini dinar	BHD
Bangladesh	taka	BDT
Barbados	Barbados dollar	BBD
Belarus	Belarussian rubel	BYB
Belgium	Belgian franc and euro	BEF/EVR
Belize	Belizean dollar	BZD
Benin	CFA franc	XOF
Bermuda	Bermudian dollar	BMD
Bolivia	boliviano	BOB
Bosnia-Herzegovina	convertible marka	BAD
Botswana	pula (plural *pula*)	BWP
Brazil	Brazilian real	BRR
Brunei	Brunei dollar	BND
Bulgaria	lev (plural *leva*)	BGL
Burkina Faso	CFA franc	XOF

NATION	CURRENCY	SWIFT CODE/ ABBREVIATION
Burundi	Burundi franc	BIF
Cambodia	riel	KHR
Cameroon	CFA franc	XAF
Canada	Canadian dollar	C$
Cayman Islands	Cayman Islands dollar	KYD
Central African Republic	CFA franc	XAF
Chad	CFA franc	XAF
Chile	Chilean peso	CLP
China	yuan (plural *yuan*)	CNY
Christmas Island	Australian dollar	A$
Cocos Islands	Australian dollar	A$
Colombia	Colombian peso	COP
Comoros	Comorian franc	KMF
Congo, Republic of	CFA franc	XAF
Congo, Democratic Republic of (formerly Zaire)	Congo franc	CDF
Cook Islands	New Zealand dollar	NZ$
Costa Rica	Costa Rica colon	CRC
Croatia	Croatian kuna	HRK
Cuba	Cuban peso	CUP
Cyprus	Cyprus pound	CYP
Czech Republic	Czech koruna (plural *koruna*)	CZK
Denmark	Danish krone (plural *kroner*)	DKK
Djibouti	Djibouti franc	DJF
Dominica	Eastern Caribbean dollar	XCD
Dominican Republic	Dominican peso	DOP
East Timor	Indonesian rupiah	IDR
Ecuador	Eurodorican sucre and U.S. dollar	ECS
Egypt	Egyptian pound	EGP
El Salvador	El Salvador colon and U.S dollar	SVC
Equatorial Guinea	CFA franc	GQE
Eritrea	nakfa	ERN
Estonia	kroon (plural *kroon*)	EEK
Ethiopia	birr	ETB
European Union	euro and others	EUR
Faeroe Islands	Danish krone	DKK

NATION	CURRENCY	SWIFT CODE/ ABBREVIATION
Falkland Islands	pound	FKP
Fiji	Fiji dollar	FJD
Finland	markka (plural *markkaa*)	FIM
France	French franc and euro	FRF/EUR
French Polynesia	franc	XPF
Gabon	CFA franc	XAF
Gambia	dalasi (plural *dalasi*)	GMD
Georgia	lari	GEL
Germany	mark and euro	DEM/EUR
Ghana	cedi (plural *cedi*)	GHC
Greece	drachma and euro	GRD/EUR
Greenland	Danish krone	DKK
Grenada	East Caribbean dollar	XCD
Guadeloupe	French franc	FRF
Guam	U.S. dollar	US$
Guatemala	quetzal and U.S. dollar	GTQ/US$
Guernsey	British pound	GBP
Guinea	Guinean franc/syli	GNF/GNS
Guinea-Bissau	CFA franc	XAF
Guyana	Guyana dollar	GYD
Haiti	gourde and U.S. dollar	HTG, US$
Heard and McDonald Islands	Australian dollar	A$
Honduras	lempira	HNL
Hong Kong	Hong Kong dollar	HK$
Hungary	forint	HUF
Iceland	Icelandic krona (plural *kronur*)	ISK
India	rupee	INR
Indonesia	rupiah (plural *rupiah*)	IDR
Iran	Iranian rial	IRR
Iraq	Iraqi dinar	IQD
Ireland	punt and euro	IEP
Isle of Man	British pound	GBP
Israel	shekel	ILS
Italy	lira (plural *lire*) and euro	ITL/EUR
Ivory Coast	CFA franc	XAF
Jamaica	Jamaican dollar	JMD

NATION	CURRENCY	SWIFT CODE/ ABBREVIATION
Japan	yen	Y
Jersey	British pound	GBP
Jordan	Jordanian dinar	JOD
Kazakstan	tenge (plural *tenge*)	KZT
Kenya	Kenyan shilling	KES
Kiribati	Australian dollar	A$
Kuwait	Kuwaiti dinar	KWD
Kyrgyz Republic	som (plural *som*)	KGS
Laos	kip	LAK
Latvia	lats	LVL
Lebanon	Lebanese pound	LBP
Liberia	Liberian dollar and U.S. dollar	LRD/US$
Libya	Libyan dinar	LYD
Liechtenstein	Swiss franc	CHF
Lithuania	litas (plural *litai*)	LTL
Luxembourg	Luxembourg franc and euro	LUF/EUR
Macau	Macau yuan	MOP
Macedonia	denar	MKD
Madagascar	Malagasy franc	MGF
Malawi	kwacha (plural *kwacha*)	MWK
Malaysia	ringgit (plural *ringgit*)	MYR
Maldives	rufiyaa	MVR
Mali	CFA franc	MLF
Malta	Maltese lira (plural *lire*)	MTL
Marshall Islands	U.S. dollar	US$
Martinique	French franc	FRF
Mauritania	ouguiya	MRO
Mauritius	Mauritius rupee	MUR
Mexico	Mexican peso	MXN
Moldova	Moldovan leu	MDL
Monaco	French franc	FRF
Mongolia	togrog	MNT
Montserrat	East Caribbean dollar	XCD
Morocco	Moroccan dirham	MAD
Mozambique	metical	MZM

NATION	CURRENCY	SWIFT CODE/ ABBREVIATION
Myanmar	kyat (plural *kyat*)	MMK
Namibia	Namibia dollar	NAD
Nauru	Australian dollar	A$
Nepal	Nepalese rupee	NPR
Netherlands	Dutch guilder and euro	NLG/EUR
Netherlands Antilles	N.A. guilder	NLG
New Caledonia	franc	XPF
New Zealand	New Zealand dollar	NZ$
Nicaragua	cordoba	NIC
Niger	CFA franc	XOF
Nigeria	naira (plural *naira*)	NGN
North Korea	North Korean won (plural *North Korean won*)	KPW
Norway	krone (plural *kroner*)	NOK
Oman	Omani rial (plural *rial*)	OMR
Pakistan	Pakistan rupee	PKR
Palau	U.S. dollar	US$
Panama	balboa, U.S. dollar	PAB/US$
Papua New Guinea	kina	PGK
Paraguay	guarani	PYG
Peru	nuevo sol	PEN
Philippines	Philippine peso	PHP
Poland	zloty	PLZ
Portugal	escudo and euro	PTE
Puerto Rico	U.S. dollar	US$
Qatar	Qatari riyal	QAR
Reunion	French franc	FRF
Romania	leu (plural *lei*)	ROL
Russia	Russian ruble	RUB
St. Helena	pound	SHP
St. Kitts & St. Nevis	East Caribbean dollar	XCD
St. Lucia	East Caribbean dollar	XCD
St. Vincent & the Grenadines	East Caribbean dollar	XCD
San Marino	San Marino lira and euro	ITL/EUR
Sao Tome and Principe	dobra	STD

NATION	CURRENCY	SWIFT CODE/ ABBREVIATION
Saudi Arabia	riyal	SAR
Senegal	CFA franc	XAF
Seychelles	Seychelles rupee	SCR
Sierra Leone	leone	SLL
Singapore	Singapore dollar	S$
Slovakia	Slovak koruna (plural *koruna*)	SKK
Slovenia	tolar	SIT
Solomon Islands	Solomon Islands dollar	SBD
Somalia	Somali shilling	SOS
South Africa	rand (plural *rand*)	ZAR
South Korea	won (plural *won*)	KRW
Spain	peseta and euro	ESP/EUR
Sri Lanka	Sri Lanka rupee	LKR
Sudan	Sudanese dinar	SDP
Suriname	Surinam guilder	SRG
Swaziland	lilangeni	SZL
Sweden	krona (plural *kronor*)	SEK
Switzerland	Swiss franc	CHF
Syria	Syrian pound	SYP
Taiwan	New Taiwan dollar	NT$
Tajikistan	Tajik ruble	TJR
Tanzania	Tanzanian shilling	TZS
Thailand	baht (plural *baht*)	THB
Togo	CFA franc	XAF
Tonga	pa'anga	TOP
Trinidad and Tobago	Trinidad and Tobago dollar	TTD
Tunisia	Tunisian dinar	TND
Turkey	Turkish lira (plural *lira*)	TRL
Turkmenistan	manat (plural *manat*)	TMM
Turks & Cacos Islands	U.S. dollar	US$
Tuvalu	Australian dollar	A$
Uganda	Uganda shilling	UGX
Ukraine	hryvnia (plural *hryvnia*)	UAH
U.A.E.	U.A.E. dirham	AED
U.K.	pound sterling	GBP
U.S.	U.S. dollar	US$

NATION	CURRENCY	SWIFT CODE/ ABBREVIATION
Uruguay	Uruguayan peso	UYU
Uzebekistan	Uzbekistan som	UZS
Vanuatu	vatu	VUV
Vatican City	Italian lira	ITL
Venezuela	bolivar	VEB
Vietnam	dong (plural *dong*)	VND
Virgin Islands	U.S. dollar	US$
Western Samoa	tala	WST
Western Sahara	Moroccan dirham	MAD
Yemen	Yemeni rial	YER
Yugoslavia	Yugoslavian dinar	YUN
Zambia	kwacha (plural *kwacha*)	ZMK
Zimbabwe	Zimbabwe dollar	ZWD